D1569698

My City of Dreams

The last photograph taken of the Grünberg family together, Vienna, 1938. *(Left to right)* My father's mother Elka; my father Harry; his sister Mia; his father Leo; and brother Uri.

My City of Dreams

Lisa Gruenberg

TidePool Press
Cambridge, Massachusetts

Copyright © 2019 by Lisa Gruenberg
Published in the United States in 2019 by TidePool Press

All rights reserved.
No part of this book may be reproduced in any manner whatsoever without written permission.

TidePool Press
6 Maple Avenue, Cambridge, Massachusetts 02139
www.tidepoolpress.com

Printed in the United States

Library of Congress Cataloging-in-Publication Data

Gruenberg, Lisa 1955–
My City of Dreams
p.cm.
ISBN 978-0-9978482-8-1
1. Gruenberg, Lisa 2. Gruenberg—United States—Memoir
3. Holocaust—Vienna, Austria 4. Second Generation—Holocaust
5. World War II (1939-1945)—atrocities 6. Children of Holocaust Survivors—Vienna, Austria—Biography
I. Title.

2019939209

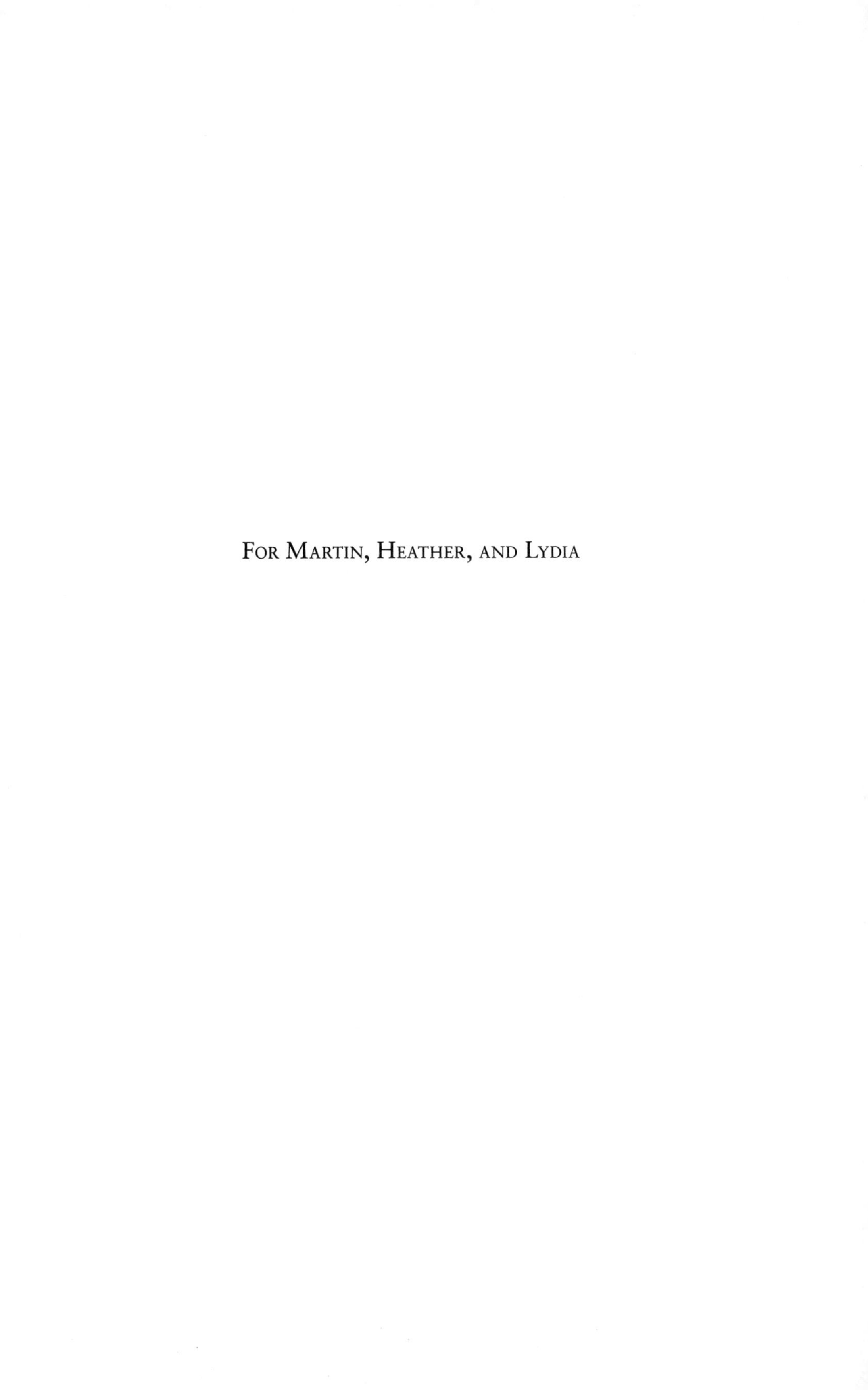

For Martin, Heather, and Lydia

All sorrows can be borne if you put them into a story.

Isak Dinesen

My City of Dreams

Leo Grünberg
Born May 3,1885, Kolomea

Elka (Elcia) Helwing*
Born Nov. 27, 1889, Kolomea

Married in Vienna 1920

Both were "relocated" with other relatives to Theresienstadt and died in the concentration camp in Minsk. Police records show that they left for Minsk May 27, 1942. Former caretaker of the house (Ferdinandstraße 31) says Theresienstadt or Buchenwald.

Children:

Harry (Chanoch)
Born Feb. 5, 1921, Vienna
Emigrated to England March 12, 1939.
Married Sept. 3, 1946 in Vancouver, Canada, to:

Eden Jane Wayles
Born May 27, 1921, Victoria

Uriel (Asher)
Born Jan. 18, 1923, Vienna
Emigrated to Palestine in Sep. 1938. Married Dec. 11,1952 to:

Sahava Greener
Born

Mia
Born Jan. 26, 1926, Vienna
Taken to Magdeburg in late 1941by Nazis. Fate not known.

One of my father's early family trees.

Introduction

In my late forties, the voice of my father's lost sister woke me from deep and dreamless sleep. I was compelled to write down her words. Mia is real to me, but she can only tell us what might have happened. I constructed her story from this nocturnal voice, as well as from family letters, careful historical research, my father's writing, and the wonderful tales he told me long ago.

A bit about Vienna: The center of the city is the First District, also known as the "inner city"—the Innere Stadt. It was once surrounded by walls, but in my father's time, the walls had been replaced by a broad avenue with a trolley line, called the Ringstrasse. The Second District, just northeast of the Innere Stadt and separated by the Danube Canal, was also called Leopoldstadt. This was traditionally the Jewish district. My father's maternal grandmother and most of the aunts and uncles on his mother's side lived there. My father grew up in the Ninth District, also known as Alsergrund. The Second through Ninth districts run clockwise around the Innere Stadt, so that the Ninth, First and Second, the tight circle of my father's childhood, all touched. My father's favorite cousin lived in the Thirteenth; the Vienna Woods spread farther west. The Prater amusement park with its giant Ferris wheel, the Riesenrad, was north and east. The Danube, "Donau" in German, flowed just beyond.

German nouns are capitalized. I maintain that where appropriate.

Names are often spelled differently in different family letters or even within my father's writing. I have chosen one spelling. For the most part, I quote my father's writing verbatim. The German quotes and translations are his own.

I have changed the chronology and the locations of some of my father's outbursts. I changed the names of most of my neighbors in Syracuse, and merged several of Niki's girlfriends into one, Andrea.

My own story is set down as I remember it.

PART I

Unraveling

Wien, Wien, nur Du allein wirst stets die Stadt meiner Träume sein!" Vienna, Vienna, only you will always be the city of my dreams!" In spite of the hardships my family experienced and the times when there was not enough money for food, I feel I had a very happy childhood. And most of all—I was in love with Vienna!

From the first and only chapter of my father's memoirs.

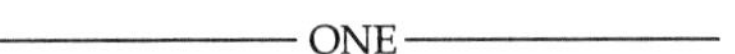

ONE

My eighty-one-year-old mother leaned back on the couch with her eyes closed, her hair permed in improbable brunette waves. The *New York Times* crossword puzzle, half-filled-in with ink, rose up and down with her breathing. Our younger daughter, thirteen-year-old Lydia, sprawled on the window seat, asleep yet again, one gangly leg over a pillow, the other trailing onto the floor. One of my husband Martin's sheepskin slippers was upside down in the center of the worn Tibetan rug. On the television screen an actor played *Clair de Lune* on the piano for his lover, and a brass lamp illuminated their faces.

"I made a lamp just like that at the technical school in Vienna." My eighty-two-year-old father's voice emerged from deep inside an easy chair. His thin wrist extended out of a too-large flannel shirt when he pointed at the TV screen. When he rested his arm again, his fingers began the classic pill-roll of Parkinson's.

"That's interesting," I said, not really listening.

Lydia's blond hair had fallen across her face. I pulled her grubby T-shirt down over her belly, lifted her leg off the floor, and tossed a multicolored throw over her. She didn't stir.

Diamond Ledge, our old cottage, sits on a hilltop rolled off the south edge of the Sandwich Range. Outside the front window snow still covered the ground. Fog floating above our pond

View from Diamond Ledge in winter.

obscured the view down to Squam, the glacial lake carved into the valley below us.

It was early spring of 2003. As often happened on our weekend trips to New Hampshire, Martin had had to run back to Boston for a meeting with some of his partners at his law firm. I was a gynecologist and had a part-time job in a Boston hospital. My full-time job was caregiver and family worrier. And there was a lot to worry about at that time. I hoped the Seder that evening would go well.

My parents had driven the entire seven hours from Syracuse in one day, my father behind the wheel. My mother was refusing to drive any distance by then; my father's Parkinson's was progressing. I realized it might be their last road trip.

And a few months earlier, Lydia had transformed from a joyful child into an anxious adolescent. First, she had terrifying nightmares about thugs breaking into our house and stabbing all of us to death. After a few weeks of that she became lethargic. She was sleeping more and more and was gaining weight, except her arms and legs remained delicate. I'd been running her in to the pediatrician's office frequently, saying, "This looks like an endocrine problem, don't you think?" Every time the doctors had replied, "Why don't you let us be the doctors, and you be the mommy? We've run all the tests. Maybe she's just depressed." That possibility had been raised a few times, and it always sounded like an indictment of our parenting, not a diagnosis. And because of my own history of depression, I felt doubly guilty.

I sat down next to my mother. Her newspaper slipped out of her hands onto the floor. I picked it up and put it on the scratched coffee table, strewn with unopened mail I'd brought up from our suburban home and a game of Scrabble my mother was winning. A family photo album from the thirties and forties lay open next to me.

"Who's looking at this?" I asked the room. No one answered.

I closed the book and shoved it on the shelf under the coffee table. A curled snapshot fluttered out onto the rug. Labeled on one serrated edge "Our First Meeting with Harry," the photo must have been taken in my grandparents' tiny rental in Vancouver on Christmas Eve, 1943. My parents, Eden Jane Wales and Harry Gruenberg, cram to one side of an upholstered couch. A Christmas tree looms behind them. My mother looks directly at the camera with an open smile. My father sits at an angle. He is surprisingly handsome compared to the old man seated near me, whose hair was still black with just a little silver, but whose nose had turned bulbous and cheeks jowled. My parents were both twenty-two years old in that picture. My father was in the engineering program at the University of British Columbia; my mother was finishing her nursing studies at a sanatorium in rural British Columbia and was home for the holidays. My mother's sister Phyllis and her future husband are beside them.

My father cleared his throat and crossed and uncrossed his spindly legs. I glanced at the movie on the VCR. I'd seen it before—*The Scent of Green Papaya*, a love story set in Vietnam mostly in the

OUR FIRST MEETING WITH HARRY

My father's first Christmas, 1943, with my mother's sister, Phyllis and my father's university roommate, Mel Julson, Vancouver, B.C.

fifties. In the final scene the woman is pregnant and sits serenely in her lover's garden in Saigon. A fighter jet flies far overhead, sounding like a distant scream. It is the only suggestion of the war that was about to tear that country apart.

When the credits ran I flipped off the set. Lydia was still asleep, my mother's mouth hung open, and my father's dark eyes were still fixed on the silent television. When I passed into the kitchen, our other daughter, sixteen-year-old Heather, didn't look up from the math homework arrayed across the dining table. She was wearing her Exeter crew sweatshirt, and her thick hair was tied back into a low ponytail. Her brows angled sharply upward, her profile was flat. I dumped potatoes into the sink and began peeling, looking out at a maple whose trunk had been half hollowed out by lightning. I was forty-eight, but in the window's dim reflection I looked like a dark older sister to my girls.

Like my father, Heather approached every question from a novel angle. She read everything: biology texts, historical novels, and sci-fi. She would plunge into deep thought and seem inaccessible for days. I'd see her go under; but I could never predict where she would surface again. She left for boarding school at Exeter, the same school Martin had attended, as a self-possessed teenager. When she came home to visit she seemed unsettled, but I sensed that I was the last person she wanted to talk to. I felt like I volleyed conversation over the growing canyon yawning between us, and that, more often than not, my words never reached her.

When she was in sixth grade, Heather had discovered my father's extensive genealogy research, written in the years after he retired from the engineering faculty at Syracuse University. He'd created almost a hundred family trees, tracing his family back from Vienna through Germany to a shtetl near Kolomea, in what is now Poland. He'd even traced my mother's family back several centuries from the north of England to Scotland. There were several pages of Austrian political history, and then he'd written something about most everyone, even relatives who died long before the war. His writing was cheerful and full of exclamation points, similar in tenor to the stories he had told me when I was a child, about growing up with his large extended family in wonderful Vienna. His lighthearted stories didn't match the carefully rendered trees, so many branches withered with phrases like "gassed at Auschwitz," or "died? Minsk?" His parents had a page each. His younger brother, Uri, barely had half a page. Their younger sister, who had disappeared into Germany in 1941 when she was fifteen years old, didn't even have a section of her own. A few of his large extended family and friends made it out of Europe, but many more "perished," a word that made them seem like fruits and vegetables forgotten in a drawer of the refrigerator. I'd only glanced at the cheap plastic binder when my father hefted a copy into my hands in 1994. I was busy with work then, and the girls were still small.

But Heather read the book from cover to cover and used it for a middle school project titled *My Champion*. My parents came out to our home in Wayland, Massachusetts, to watch her presentation. She wore my father's Burberry raincoat and his tweed cap. She narrated his solitary train journey out of Austria in 1939, at the age of eighteen. When he crossed the border from Germany to Belgium, he flushed his last *Pfennigs* down the toilet, after a soldier warned him it was illegal to leave the Reich with any German currency. With her cobalt eyes and taffy mane, Heather looked nothing like my father. At the end of her rendition of my father's escape from the Nazis, her teacher's eyes glittered with tears. My father looked pleased. Heather got an A.

I didn't hear my father join us in the kitchen until he spoke.

"I made a lamp like the one in the movie, as well as a metal paperweight with an Art Nouveau design."

I nodded at his faint reflection in the window.

"When the Brown Shirts came to our door they told us to leave. They took the lamp and the paperweight."

My mind struggled with my father's unemotional voice, the scene he was describing, and getting dinner ready. I replied with the first thing that popped into my head. "Were they polite?" I asked. My question hung in the air for a moment, giving me time to consider its absurdity.

An animal growl emanated from my father. It made me spin around to face him and I knocked a plate off the counter and it shattered on the floor. Heather started up from her work and looked down at the broken plate and then from me to my father.

The serene man we knew was gone. He looked terrified. "Were they polite? Were they polite? They were not polite." The quaver that usually held my father's voice captive had evaporated. "It was Kristallnacht."

Heat rushed to my face as he went on, speaking fast and loud. "They banged on our door, and when Mutti opened it they pushed her aside." It was as if he was in the middle of a scene that only he could see. "The local policeman was their leader, a man we saw almost every day. The rest were members of the fascist youth, wearing dark shirts and carrying clubs." My father moved out from behind the counter and stood next to me. He seemed to tower above me. His speech accelerated further. "They took our keys and pushed us out the door and we fled."

"Where did you go?" I shouted back at him even though we were just inches apart.

He didn't answer me, but stepped back, then mumbled and groaned. He spoke a stream of words in German. I couldn't understand him, although he said "Mutti" again. I tried to put my hand on him, but his arms windmilled. His eyes strained wide. He seemed to be looking through me to something far beyond. But just as suddenly, he focused on me and shrank back into his familiar, stooped form. His voice was quiet but steady.

"When we returned, the doors were open—the same with our Jewish neighbors, the Melzers and the Harbands. Everything was smashed and thrown across the rooms. What little we had of value had been taken, including my lamp, the paperweight, and a suitcase with clothes we were sending on to Uri in Palestine. A few marks my sister had hidden were also taken."

He held the counter as he staggered to the kitchen table. He struggled to drag a chair out and lowered himself into it. Then he flipped through Heather's math book. Heather looked at me. I indicated the text with a nod of my head. Heather slid her notebook in front of him.

He studied her solution then leafed through her textbook.

"How would you solve this one?" he asked, pointing at one of the challenge questions. He had told me that Heather e-mailed math problems to him from Exeter, and they corresponded back and forth, debating various solutions. I don't think they talked about any of their day-to-day activities or exchanged thoughts on anything other than math or physics.

He took a paper napkin, his stationery of choice when he wanted to explain something to me when I was Heather's age. Then he pulled a ballpoint pen out of his shirt pocket and clicked it three times. It circled over the page before alighting, and his unsteady numbers slanted down the page.

"Let's try another approach," he said. "Yours is good, I just want to show you a different way to come at it."

The broken plate crunched under my clogs when I walked to my father's side and put my hands on his shoulder. He reached up and patted me. I felt his familiar tremor.

My mother was reading the front page in the living room when I left them. Lydia had flipped onto her stomach and her arm hung down toward the floor.

"Did you hear that?" I asked my mother.

"Hear what?"

"Dad—did you hear him in there?"

"No." She folded the newspaper in half, then quarters.

"He was talking about Kristallnacht. Was he in Vienna on Kristallnacht?"

My mother thought for a minute. "What year was that?" she asked.

"I don't know, but did he ever talk to you about still being there?"

"He seems to be talking about the whole thing a lot now. Maybe it's that new medication he's on." She put the paper aside. "He used to sit across from me for hours and not say a word—forget about actually having a conversation. Then he went off to that room of his and closed the door. But now he's talking again. You can't get him to stop."

"But, Mom, this isn't Dad running on with one of his old stories. He was speaking German."

"Are you sure?"

"Of course I'm sure."

"What did he say—when he was speaking German?"

"I don't know. I think it was something about his mother and his sister. I don't know enough German to follow him, and he was talking pretty fast. Does he ever speak German with you?"

She picked up the paper again and unfolded it. "Never. Well, not since he tried to teach me when we were courting. All I know is that he gets started on one of those old stories and you just can't turn him off. And this stuff comes up at the most inappropriate times with the wrong people. No one needs to hear these things now. It has nothing to do with them."My mother started up on her puzzle again.

"What would be the appropriate time, Mom? Who are the right people?"

My mother sighed and didn't look up. "What's past is past. You can't do anything about it."

Lydia turned again but didn't wake up.

I went back to the kitchen. My father stooped over the dustpan, sweeping fragments of the plate into it with a whisk. Heather must have gone upstairs. The potatoes waited in the sink.

"Are you okay, Dad?"

"Sure, why not?"

I opened the cabinet under the sink and my father emptied the dustbin into the garbage. He cleared his throat and looked out the window.

"Let's hope the weather gets better tomorrow," he said.

I started peeling again. "When was Kristallnacht, Dad?" In the window's reflection my father's head barely came to my shoulder.

"1938, November."

"So you were still in Vienna then?"

"Yes, I wasn't able to leave until March of 1939—why do you ask?"

"Because you were just talking about it."

"I was?"

"You were."

My father unfolded a towel and pulled a plate out of the dishrack. "Yes, they came to the house and told us to leave. So, we left. Uri had already gone to Palestine. Fortunately, my father wasn't home. They arrested a lot of the men that day." My father swallowed.

"What else do you remember?" I asked.

"That's all I remember about that," he answered.

I wondered if that was true, or if he were somehow protecting me. He opened the silverware drawer and pulled out knives and forks.

"I'll set the table," he said, and turned his back.

Later that evening, Heather finished arranging the Seder plate on my favorite blue and white platter and brought it into the dining room. Martin, back from Boston, poured a French Bordeaux into a goblet next to each setting, his long arms reaching across the table. The embroidered *kippah* my father had brought for him had slipped sideways. His full head of black hair was dusted with gray at the temples.

Lydia stood up to ask the questions. Braces reined in her teeth; her hair was tangled in a rubber band.

"Different—this night—why is this night different from all the other nights?" Her eyes jumped around the page; I wondered if that was something she had always done, and I just hadn't noticed. My mother sat rod-straight atop a pillow, which brought her up to the same height as the rest of us; she snuck a piece of parsley off the Seder plate.

My mother had given up the Anglican church when she married my father. When my two older brothers and I were growing up she tried the Jewish holidays for a while. I have a vague recollection of stony matzo balls in salty broth. Later she told me, "Your father gave me no instruction, so I just gave up." We went back to the holidays she grew up with, although stripped of Jesus and the Holy Trinity. My father brought a tree home every December but sat in the far corner of the living room as we opened gifts wrapped in recycled paper from the prior year's revels.

Martin was raised a relaxed Catholic in Manhattan. When our daughters were small, he decided we needed some sort of weekend ritual and settled on the Unitarian Church. We both liked the minister and the music, but when Heather and Lydia had to be dragged out of bed, and nursery school responsibilities loomed for me, the girls and I dropped out. Martin continued for a while. After that, if someone asked us if we were religious, Martin answered, "We're lapsed Unitarians!"

Our Passover Seder was a holdover from those days, when I wanted something that would offset the Christmas season. I photocopied a coloring book Haggadah and covered it with construction paper. I always made twice as many matzo balls as I thought we could possibly consume, and they all disappeared by the end of the evening. The girls dragged bed pillows down to the dining room, so we could recline at the table. Heather and Lydia hid the *afikomen,* and then forgot about it. We would find the stale matzo months later, slid between books or under a chair.

My father read the answers to each question in Hebrew; under beetled brows his eyes tracked right to left. In a sing-song cadence, Martin made quick business of the plagues that befell the Egyptians, making the girls and my mother laugh. Heather got up to help me dole out the soup. Her matzo balls went into vegetable broth; she had given up meat when she was thirteen.

We slurped together. Candlelight illuminated the burl on the long, maple table. The woodstove glowed behind us. My father didn't seem to mind the butter in the matzo balls; he asked for seconds. Heather nudged Lydia, who was beginning to slump against her pillow, her lids closing.

"Wake up!" Heather said.

Lydia started. "I wasn't sleeping."

"You think?"

"I was just reclining."

After a chocolate desert, Heather stood up to close the door. "I think Elijah's been by already." She sipped out of the prophet's goblet.

Martin and I washed the dishes together after dinner.

"I need to head back down to Boston in the morning. Something else came up on a deal we're working on. You okay here?" he said.

"I'll drive down on Wednesday." I pulled a pan out of the drain to dry. "Listen, my dad had a sort of outburst today."

Martin submerged another pot into the enamel sink. "*Vhen* I *vas* young, it *vas vonderful!*" he said. He switched to my mother's clipped Canadian-British speech. "Oh, Harry, enough!"

I whacked Martin with a dish towel. "Quiet, they'll hear us." I tried not to laugh. "Anyway, their accents aren't that strong."

"*Vell, vhatever* you say."

"Seriously, they both have little accents. I can't even hear them."

Martin put a pot on the counter, I spoke to his back. "You're not really listening, you know."

"I heard you."

"Yeah? What did I say?"

Martin straightened up. "You said your father had some sort of—"

"Yes?"

"Episode."

"I think it was a flashback. He was speaking in German. He never speaks in German."

Martin turned back to the pot.

"It reminds me of what happened when they took that last trip to Vienna," I said.

My parents had taken the last of their many visits to Austria in 2000. My Uncle Uri had just died, and Uri's daughters were flying from Israel. They wanted my father to show them his childhood home. Neva and Maya invited me to join them. I considered making the trip, but I'd never wanted to go to Austria and couldn't fathom why my parents went as often as they did. Anyway, I was busy and didn't make the time.

After a week with my cousins in Vienna, my parents went on to Tyrol. On his first day out, my father looked up at the mountains, fell off a curb and broke his leg in three places. After surgery, he recuperated for three weeks on a ward with six other patients. My mother didn't call me until the day my father was discharged from the hospital, and only then because I was picking them up at the airport and they needed a wheelchair for my father. When my father came on the line, he rattled on in German with great animation and speed. Until then, I had only heard him speak German when we traveled in Europe, and then it came out in a halting fashion, as if it weren't his native tongue.

Although I was usually good at languages, German was so guttural and the structure so rigid I never got past the basics. "Dad, I can't follow you," I kept saying, the phone cradled against my shoulder while I unloaded groceries into the Sub-zero in our kitchen in Wayland. I was startled at the tenor and strength of his voice. He spoke a few slow sentences in English and then broke back into fluid German again. His German was melodious, as if it came from a part of his brain that was beyond the grasp of his Parkinson's.

"My father's voice had that same quality this afternoon," I said to Martin. "Like someone much younger."

"Okay." Martin handed the pot over to me.

I dried it and put it back on the stove.

"The dinner was good," Martin said.

"Maybe we should take Lydia to see a specialist?" I said.

"What kind?"

"I don't know—an endocrinologist or a psychiatrist?"

"We're kind of jumping around here." Martin appraised me with our daughters' wide-spaced eyes. The muscle in his right cheek twitched, the way it always did when he was considering what to say. "Maybe you need to wait for the bridges to come to you first, and then cross them?"

"Ouch."

"Come on," Martin pulled his hands out of the dishwater and gave me a hug.

"I'm worried," I said into his chest. Dishwater dripped down my back.

"What else is new?" he asked.

Correspondence

Dear Martin,

Most of the time, I don't see my depression as mood, or random firing across synapses. Rather, it is a blinding clarity of vision, where I see the void yawning below us, and the fragile construct of our lives balanced briefly and perilously above. When I'm happy, or at least when I'm not depressed, I don't hear or see the void knocking against the parquet below me, or see it shining a flashlight between the floorboards. But as soon as I swallow my dense stone, I'm aware the floorboards are ephemera, an illusion that in my day-to-day makes me feel as if I'm walking on solid ground. But there is no ground grounding us—just that vast emptiness. Should I walk toward the light?

Making love is a commitment to life, isn't it? How often is that supposed to happen now, anyway? You still seem to have desire, but is it necessarily for me, or is it for that girl I once was, the one you woke out of a dead sleep, tangled in the sheets on the mattress in your empty apartment? And my desire? It turns up at odd times now—when I'm washing the pots and pans or mulling over a graph in the *New England Journal*. By the time you get home, by the time we climb into opposite sides of our bed, morphed from a twin, an antique three quarters, a full, a queen and now a king, we both have to stretch out our arms if we want to touch. But we don't. Perhaps an argument lies between us like an opaque wall. We roll to face away from each other. I hear your breath deepen.

My dreams have all but disappeared; I guess that's the depression. But last night for some reason I had one. You were driving. We were in a red convertible with the top down. At first, we were in New Hampshire, driving by the chapel in Wonalancet. Then I smelled the fragrance of eucalyptus and we were on the winding roads up to Zfat, a place I traveled with my father and uncle long ago. We came around a hill and saw the Sea of Galilee shaped like a harp below us. You were distracted. Your lips were moving, yet I couldn't hear your voice.

The two wheels on my side veered off the road. Gravel hit the undercarriage and at the last minute you reined us back in. We glided through the narrow streets of Tiberius and passed the outdoor market. We joined a parade of cars driving single-file onto a rickety dock going out onto the lake. You looked across at the mountains of Syria and we slid into the water. You were still talking as the car filled. The water was warm.

"We're sinking," I said. "We should leave our things behind." You floated left and disappeared. I floated right and woke with my arms around you.

From my computer file labeled: "Letters to Write but Never Send," a therapeutic exercise.

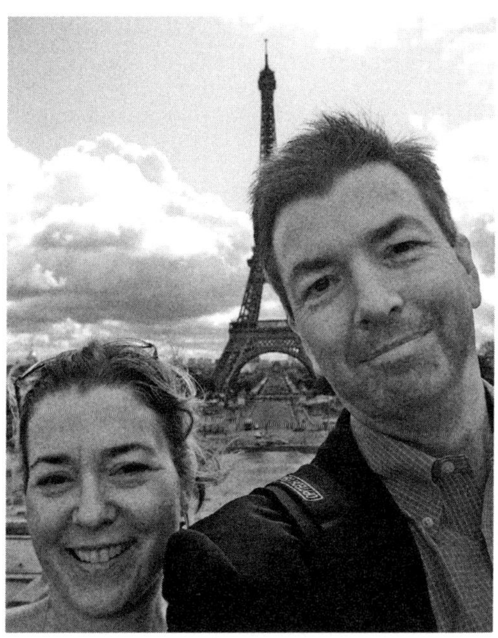

With Martin in Paris, c. 2005.

Early in the morning on Saturday, February 5, 1921, a momentous event occurred: I, Harry Grünberg, left the comforts of my mother's womb and for the first time saw the light of day. Undoubtedly my parents, Leo and Elka Grünberg, were pleased. Of course, I cannot really recall this moment. Nor can I remember anything from the first several months of my life, or even the first few years. So I have to rely on some physical evidence: my birth certificate, the first few photographs which survived, and the stories I have been told by my relatives. Of course, the evidence of these stories is always a bit suspect, since they get embellished as the years go by ... One thing is clear from these pictures: the face is the same on all of them ... For this and many other reasons, my relatives often told me that I was born an adult. I agree with that assessment to some extent. I was always very serious and I think considerate with my parents and others, but I also think there was always a little boy in me and that I retained this duality up to my present old age.

From my father's unfinished memoir.

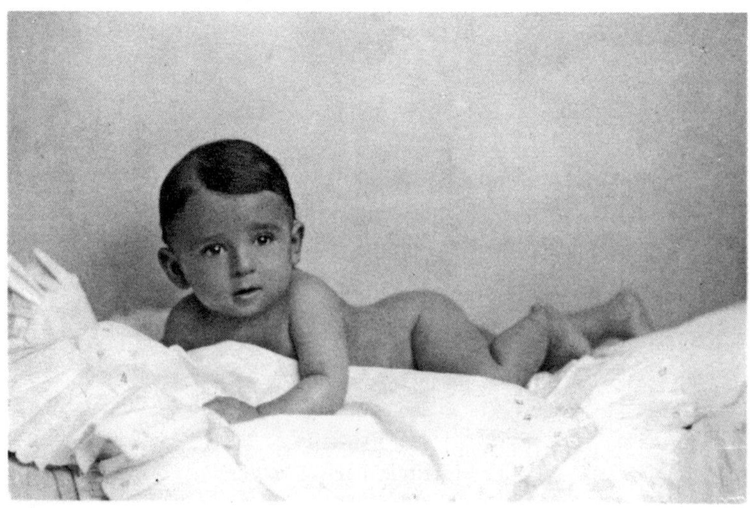

My father, 1921.

TWO

"YOUR FATHER'S OKAY," my mother said over the phone. "He was having stomach pains, but they're gone now. The hospital is releasing him tomorrow." It was five o'clock on a raw Friday afternoon at the end of the following October. It was as if she calculated when all the doctors would be unreachable before picking up her Princess phone to dial me in Wayland.

"Back up, Mom, what's going on?"

"He was having this terrible pain, but it went away."

"What's the diagnosis?"

"They didn't say."

"Why didn't you call me earlier?"

But I knew the answer and echoed it with her as she said it. "We didn't want to worry you."

"Mom. Worry me, okay?" I said, stacking the breakfast dishes in the sink. "Dad goes into the hospital, you call me. Hospital—phone call. Got it?"

She gave me my father's number and hung up.

My father answered after five rings, breathing as if he'd run the length of the hospital corridor to get to the phone.

"I'm fine," he panted.

"You don't sound fine."

"I'm okay," he gurgled. "They're sending me home in the morning."

He ended up on a respirator that evening. By the time my mother called to tell me, it was close to midnight.

"I've got to drive to Syracuse," I told Martin, who'd gotten home after Lydia had gone to bed.

The muscle in my husband's left cheek twitched. "Why not fly out in the morning?"

"It sounds bad," I said, throwing some t-shirts and underwear into my duffel. "I don't want to wait."

"Long drive," he said. "I'll go make some coffee."

"Call your mother for Lydia?"

"Why?"

"I told you. She has a fever again."

Lydia had seemed a little better over the summer, but when school started she had been sick with a fever every few weeks. She'd always been a good student, but now she didn't seem to be able to keep track of her assignments and was falling behind. Her pediatricians had run tests again but still couldn't find anything wrong. We'd hired a tutor.

Martin hugged me at the door to the garage.

"Keep an eye on Lydia," I said.

"I will."

"I mean really."

"I will."

Martin closed the door before I was in the driver's seat.

"I love you too," I said to the wheel.

I drove all night to Syracuse and arrived to a dawn veiled in haze. Cracks crisscrossed the concrete floors of the hospital garage, and I worried that the whole building might collapse under the added weight of our Audi. My mother was sitting in a plastic chair in the fluorescent-lit ICU waiting room. Her bones poked me when I hugged her. I could look down at the top of her head. She sported a black beret.

"It covers a small thinning spot," she told me, her voice muffled against my shoulder.

Neville, the younger of my two older brothers, came out of the restroom. His business suit was rumpled, as if he'd slept in the hospital.

He and his wife were having some problems; she had moved out. He pecked me on the cheek.

"Universal color number 22?" he indicated my hair.

"Thanks. You look great too."

Our oldest brother, David, arrived from Albany. His cappuccino skin glowed against his white shirt. He gave my mother an awkward hug and patted me on the back. My brothers fell into their usual repartee, but their jokes fell flat in the airless room.

It always surprised me how different the three of us looked—David with his dark coloring and his kinky hair clipped short; Neville with pale skin, freckles, blue eyes, and thinning, dust-colored curls; me with olive skin that darkened in the summer and straight brown hair that I'd started highlighting to camouflage the gray.

A young man in a crisp white coat arrived. "I'm the chief resident," he said. He had an accent, I thought maybe South American. We gathered around a fake wood table littered with empty Dunkin' Donut boxes and used Styrofoam cups.

"Your father's breathing was labored," the resident said. "I had no choice but to put a tube down and hook him up to the respirator. There were no instructions to do otherwise."

It surprised me that he thought we would have some sort of "Do Not Resuscitate" order for my father. Parkinson's Disease slowed his speech and his movements. He'd had myelofibrosis for years, a simmering condition that was destroying his bone marrow and had swollen his spleen to the size of a football. But overall, he seemed pretty good for his age.

As if reading my thoughts, the resident spoke directly to me. "We don't know what's going on," he said. "But your father's in really bad shape. There isn't much hope."

He stood up and held the swinging doors open for us. We washed our hands in the sink beyond the door. The air was dense with the sighs of respirators, the beeping of monitors, and the murmurs of the staff. My father was at the far end of an open ward, and it felt like I was looking at him through the wrong end of a telescope. His back arched to accept the breathing tube. His thin arms were limp at his sides. The respirator pumped his swollen abdomen up and down, occasionally exhaling with a mountainous sigh. I took in the steady beep of sinus rhythm and the blood pressure displayed on the monitor. There was almost no urine in the bag at the end of his bed. Without reading the chart I could see his heart was strong but his kidneys and lungs were failing.

One of my medical school professors once said, "We all walk a road through life, but as we age, the road gets narrower and narrower. We move out of a broad field onto a footpath up a mountain ridge. The air thins and the sides of the path fall into deep ravines on either side. There is no place to lie down, and it takes a very small blow to push us off the side and over the edge."

My mother stopped at my father's feet, as if unable to bring herself beyond his swollen stomach to look at his gaunt face. Neville and David stood opposite me. The curtain across from us was pushed aside, exposing the half-naked form of a big man with dusky skin and a three-day growth of beard. An endotracheal tube cut into his neck.

A nurse whose nametag greeted "Hi, my name is Maureen" bustled through and adjusted my father's IV. She didn't look at us. She didn't offer my tiny mother a seat.

"I'd like a hamburger, fries and a milkshake—no, make that a 'F-r-r-osty Maureen,'" Neville said under his breath. David cracked up. I didn't. My mother stared at the fluid dripping into the IV tubing.

I touched my father's shoulder and his eyelids fluttered open. He gagged, and his panicked eyes seemed to say, "Let me go in peace." Frosty Maureen rushed to inject a sedative and a disheveled resident in bloodstained scrubs pushed us away, dragging the curtain around my father's bed.

For the next ten days I made most of my visits alone. David had to get back to his law practice and Neville to his work as a commercial real estate agent, which he took up when he couldn't make a living as a graphic artist. I had just started what I thought at the time would be a one-year leave from my hospital practice. I wanted more time with Lydia, but I was also in and out of depression. I felt burned out with a practice filled with the worried well. My chairman had suggested, "Keep your toe in the door." So, I'd begun teaching first-year courses at Harvard Medical School, and seeing patients, mostly immigrants, in free evening clinics held in local churches and a synagogue. Although I was still busy, I was freer to take off when I needed to.

"You shouldn't spend so much time at the ICU," my mother said to me when I got up from breakfast a week into my father's hospitalization. Even though hospital rules about limiting visits to regimented hours had changed since my mother had trained as a nurse in the forties, my mother had not.

"You'll tire him out," she told me when I went out the door of the townhome they'd moved into in the nineties.

"I just sit there, Mom. You could come with."

"You bring me in tonight," she said, going back to clear the dishes.

I recognized some of the families in the waiting room. A short Asian man, who'd had abdominal surgery, had replaced the man across from my father. The South American resident had rotated off service, but still checked in now and then. Frosty Maureen had thawed; she pulled up a chair for me.

Remarkably, my father had learned to tolerate the choking feeling of the tube and stayed conscious during many of my visits. I rubbed his cracked feet and bony shoulders and talked about our life together and told him that I loved him. I reminded him how we used to take walks together around our neighborhood in Syracuse, chatting about science, and holding hands well into my teens. I didn't tell him I was low again. My father nodded when I asked him if he wanted to know what was going on with his care, because the doctors always directed their explanations to me, over my father's protuberant abdomen.

On this visit, when my father dozed off, I rolled the Naugahyde recliner in from the hallway, remembering my mother saying it was unlikely that any of the "inmates," as she called the patients on the ward, would ever have the strength to get out of bed. I opened a worn copy of *Pride and Prejudice* for ten minutes, then got up to stretch my arms over my head. My neck felt tight. I missed my daily walk or bike and my yoga class. I sat down in the chair and shifted to one side. I smoothed the blanket over my father's arm and ran my finger down his cheek.

The bond connecting me with my father was stronger than anything my older brothers said they felt. Sometimes I wondered if it was because he thought I resembled his sister. I saw that resemblance in the few family photographs my father had carried with him from Vienna to England to Canada, and into our tidy ranch house in Syracuse. It looked as if someone had Photoshopped my childhood face into those old pictures—my hair cut short like his sister's, my head angled to one side, my eyes squinting in that way that etched frown lines on my face. My father, as a boy, rested his hand on our shoulder. My Uncle Uri was to one side, the beginning of a smile playing on his lean, bespectacled face. My father and my grandmother, Elka, had the same dark eyes. Leo, my grandfather, looked like no one now living.

On the rare occasions my father said his sister's name out loud, he pronounced it "Maya," like Uri's daughter, my Israeli cousin.

"You remind me of Maya," he said as we walked around the neighborhood when I was around six. I remember being surprised, even at that age, as my father rarely brought his sister up if I didn't ask him about her first.

"She was intelligent. She had a good sense of humor," he said.

"She looked like me?" I asked.

My father hesitated. "Yes, except her hair had red highlights—and her eyes were very blue."

My father's tales of Vienna were lovely. When he spoke, the corners of his lips curled upward. I could never keep all his aunts and uncles straight because there were so many of them, and because everyone of that generation had two, three, even four names: a German name, a Polish name, a Hebrew name, and a nickname.

Pious Sarah holding my father (*left*) and his favorite cousin, Martin Grünberg, 1921.

And sometimes "aunts" were really second cousins by marriage, and "cousins" could be third cousins twice-removed.

I had heard about where he grew up so much I could picture it: my father's family apartment was a fourth-floor walk-up, a "cold water flat" in Vienna's Ninth District, known as Alsegrund, a few blocks from the university. My grandparents slept in one of the bedrooms; Leo's mother, my great-grandmother, Pious Sarah Grünberg, lived in the other. My father and Uri slept in the living room.

"Where did Maya sleep?" I asked when my father tucked me into bed when I was around seven.

He hesitated, looking up at a watercolor of two girls dressed in tutus whispering to each other. He cleared his throat. "She must have been in a drawer next to my parents," he finally answered.

He paused, then started again. "We shared a toilet and a water tap with the other apartments on our floor. We had to bring water in from the hall and heat it on the stove if we wanted a bath in the tub we set up in the kitchen. We walked to the public baths if we wanted a shower!"

My father wondered why his widowed grandmother settled in such cramped quarters with the least successful of her six children. And then, like always, he answered his own question. "Maybe she thought my father was her best son."

Once when I was home with a fever, my mother brought me chicken broth in bed for supper. Her wrist snapped when she shook down the thermometer. The back of her hand felt cool against my forehead.

"No school for you tomorrow," she said.

My father came in later with a tray and cleared my still-full bowl. He put the tray on my desk and sat on the edge of the bed.

"My father and all the Grünberg and Helwing uncles were veterans of World War I, what we called the 'Great War.' When the fighting ended they all moved west, to Vienna, Stuttgart, Chemnitz, and Berlin. They threw off the clothing and habits of the shtetl and became businessmen, clerks, and translators." Without coming up for air, he continued. "Your grandfather, Leib Grünberg, was called Lev, 'Heart' in Hebrew, but more often 'Leo' by his brothers and sisters. During World War I, he was wounded and imprisoned by the Russians. Because he grew up in the Pale, he knew many languages: Yiddish, German, Polish, and Russian among them. His captors put him to work in the camp office. Near the end of the war a document came across his desk. It was a release form for fifty wounded German soldiers to be sent home. My father changed the number to sixty and added his own name and the names of nine of his friends. He walked home to Kolomea, then helped his family pack up and move to Germany. He went on to Vienna. There, he married your grandmother, Elka Helwing, his childhood sweetheart."

My lids grew heavy. My father pulled the covers up to my neck. "My father worked on and off as a clerk in a bank and took in accounting work to supplement his tiny soldier's pension. I did whatever work I could to help out. I tutored classmates in math and science. I worked with my father to finish the bookkeeping he took in at night, adding great towers of numbers in my head. But, you know, despite our financial troubles, he was always in a good mood. He was the best listener—he read everything and could talk to you about anything. He loved life, and everyone adored him!"

The next morning, after my brothers had taken the bus and my mother had driven downtown to her job as a school nurse, I felt well enough to sit at the breakfast table with my father. My father bit into his pumpernickel toast and I moved my cornflakes around the bowl with my spoon. My father swallowed and started again. "My mother's younger brother, my Uncle Igo, was even less successful than my father. When I was five or six I opened the door and found him standing on the landing. His arm was raised as if he were about to knock. He wore a camel colored coat and a new bowler hat that was angled to one side. He winked at me. Despite his finances, Uncle Igo was always a dapper dresser! 'Hello, little Harryle!' He used the Yiddish diminutive for my name and patted me on the head. Pious Sarah—"

"Why was she called Pious Sarah?" I asked.

"My father's mother was very religious." My father quickly picked up the story again. "Uri, perched on Pious Sarah's lap, eyed his mother and Uncle Igo. Uri's blond curls fell onto his neck and with his pale blue eyes he looked like a fairy child. My mother took Igo's hand and led him into the bedroom. They looked out the windows and they turned back when I followed them. 'He looks like Papa, doesn't he? So serious!' Uncle Igo said and they both laughed. Then they shooed me out of the room."

In our kitchen in Syracuse, I imagined the soft slur of Polish consonants tickling my father's ears.

"When Uncle Igo left he took what was left of my mother's wedding silver wrapped in a linen towel," I imagined his mother went to wash the dishes in the sink, not meeting Pious Sarah's eyes.

My father *(far right)* with his family: *(left to right)* Uri, Elka, Mia, and Leo, 1930, in the garden of wealthy relatives outside of Vienna.

An alarm went off on the patient across the aisle, pulling me out of my reverie. Frosty Maureen rushed in and drew the curtain. My father's eyes opened for a few moments, then closed again. The respirator sighed. I tucked the covers under his chin and crawled back into the recliner and closed my eyes.

When I was eleven my father took me for a dip at Green Lakes State Park. My father had taught me to swim there, holding me up with one hand while I splashed about. When I got older, my brothers and I would spend hours throwing pebbles into the deeper water, diving down to retrieve them. We came to shore to eat the sandwiches our mother sent with us, sandwiches that crunched with the grit from our hands, even though we wiped them endlessly on T-shirts and towels.

"On the weekends," my father said as we laid out a blanket and towels, "my father would pile Uri and me on the tram and take us out to hike in the Vienna Woods, or to swim in the Alte Donau, the Old Danube, lakes north of the city. When we couldn't afford the tram we walked, hauling the picnic lunch my mother put together for us. The lakes were clear and cool and my father made a sling with his arms and Uri and I put our feet into his hands and he tossed us to the sky."

After we dried off and lay down in the sun my father went on. "In the summer I swam in the Danube with my favorite cousin, Martin Grünberg. We'd get picked up by the current and dragged into the center of the river."

I imagined the river was blue and I pictured my father and his cousin drifting in crystalline waters, watching his city glide by.

"I shouted to Martin," my father had gone on, "but the current was so strong he was already far behind me." As often happened in these stories, the other characters from my father's childhood would disappear. My father stopped struggling, lay on his back, and watched clouds drift overhead.

"I was dragged all the way down to the old Reich's Bridge. I saw the stone archways and I knew I would be shattered if I hit one of them, so I aimed between them. On the other side I was dragged down into a whirlpool." He turned onto his side and raised himself onto an elbow and smiled down at me, as if it were a wonderful memory.

"What happened then?" I asked, putting my arm on my forehead to shade my eyes.

"I don't remember," my father said. "I must have survived, right?" My father cleared his throat and propped himself onto both elbows. I did the same, and we stared out at a group of boys shoving water at each other. "When my brother Uri and I were old enough, my father splurged on the few *Schillings* it cost to buy standing room on the top balcony at the opera." My father unfolded some of his old stories so many times I could have recited them with him. "We climbed up and up the marble staircases, passing jeweled women in long gowns and men in evening dress. Once on the balcony we descended to the front, feeling as if one misstep would propel us over the railing into the laps of the wealthy patrons below. The lights dimmed and the overture began. We had to imagine the pageantry. At that steep angle, we could only see the singers' feet!"

"Did Maya go to the opera?" I asked. "Did she swim?"

My father hesitated, then cleared his throat and went on quickly. "Your Grandmother Elka married for love, not money. She was the oldest daughter of a shoe merchant. She was a little bit of an old maid when she married my father. Her legs were swollen and she couldn't walk very far. She was shy and never well. But she was always kind and generous to a fault."

My father was solicitous of his mother, running down to bring coal up from the basement, water from the tap in the hall, milk and bread from the grocers.

"Uri didn't help at all," my father said.

"And your sister?" I asked.

Again, the hesitation. "Well, Lisa would have been very small."

My father often substituted my name when he spoke of his sister. "Did you mean Maya?" I asked.

"What?" my father said.

"Maya was very small?"

My father didn't answer. He stared out at the blue green water in the distance where the lake plunged deep. He turned to me and his eyes seemed to focus again. "Our neighbors, the Harbands, had two children: Paul was about my brother's age and Susi was a bit younger than my sister. The Melzers also had two children, but I can't remember their names. The older child was a girl about my age; the boy was younger. The Melzers also had a dog, a big black monster about four times my size—"

"Why wasn't I named Maya?" I interrupted.

My father appeared disoriented, as if I'd derailed him.

"Why wasn't I named Maya?" I repeated.

My parents Eden and Harry Gruenberg with their three children: me, David, and Neville, Syracuse, NY, 1956.

"That's your cousin's name."

"But she was born after me, wasn't she?"

My father dug his white toes in the sand. He always wore socks, even with sandals, so his feet were ghostly.

"We were going to name you Anna Louisa, after Mom's mother. But at the last minute your mother decided she wanted a new name for you." He leaned over and swiped the sand off the top of his feet. He cleared his throat.

There was always a point where the stories didn't quite add up and I sensed something was missing. But even as I child I knew not to ask what happened to the people who populated his tales. It was as if I breathed in terrible knowledge from the air around me.

If I reach back to grab my earliest memory of my father, I see him bent over the vast oak desk in his basement office. I climb under his arm and make a place in his lap. He cringes when I throw my arms around his neck, the way he always would when I hugged him without warning. Then he relaxes again. The pens in his shirt pocket poke into my shoulder. I blow in his ear. He giggles. One hand moves in to hold me; the other keeps on writing long equations in elegant script.

I grab his face with both my hands and make him look at me. "Do you love me, Dad?"

"Of course."

"How do you know?"

"I just know."

My father puts down his pen and ponders the map of the world above his desk.

"What's your first memory, Dad?"

"I remember when my cousin Martin decided to cut off my hair. When my mother came in, I was sitting on a stool and the floor was covered with black curls."

My father gazes at the memory of his mother. I imagine a tear sliding down my grandmother's cheek and pooling in the dimple at the corner of her smile.

A monitor gave off another series of staccato beats. My father opened his eyes. I got out of the recliner and stood next to his bed. His finger nails, usually clipped short, were curled under like sea shells.

"How are you doing?" I asked, touching his hand.

My father blinked.

"Everything's okay with Mom. I'll bring her by later. I gave her some money and we'll go to the bank in the morning to get her a debit card."

My father waved as if trying to unscramble my words in the air between us. I rigged him up an alphabet on a piece of progress-note paper, and he spelled out: SHEHASACARDALREADYITS INTHEBANKFOLDERDESKLEFTDRAWER. A few minutes later, he closed his eyes again.

That was so like my parents. My mother was perfectly capable, but she let my father take care of most of the details of their life and all of the money matters. "Your father's the organized one," she'd say. "He is the genius, after all. I'm a bit of a dim bulb." Then she quoted from *Winnie-the-Pooh*, the book she always read us at bedtime when we were growing up: "There's just a bit of fluff between my ears!"

My father was the kind of person who rearranged your dishwasher to fit in a few more things. Detailed instructions in the event of his death were filed in a box in his closet, instructions he updated monthly. At the front of one of his drawers was a file labeled in his typewriter-like script: "THINGS REQUIRING ATTENTION." It was almost always empty.

For my parents, every day unfolded as similarly as possible to the one before. They rose early and ate their meager breakfast of cereal and coffee with skim milk in companionable silence. My father placed their morning pills in china saucers and the rest of the day's doses in plastic boxes, his shaking hands struggling with the child-safe lids. He counted out the capsules and secured them in day-of-the-week compartments. Then their morning doses went down, one by one, with sips of tepid water.

After breakfast, my mother dressed and went outside to work in the garden. My father carried dishes to the sink one at a time. Back and forth he went, using one hand to prop up his thin body on the table, on the counter, and back again. He scrubbed each dish with soap and scalding water before placing it in the dishwasher. He steadied himself against the walls to get back to his room. He put his outfit on the tray of his walker, socks and shoes on the bottom, underwear on top. He sat on the side of his bed to dress, leaving the struggle with socks and shoes for last. Once dressed he turned on the computer and looked at his bank accounts and investments, read his online financial journals, clicking the mouse, ignoring the long delay his Parkinson's inserted between each thought and action. After a few hours he moved back to the kitchen for his "elevenses," a slice of two-day-old cinnamon bun and a cup of tea. Once finished,

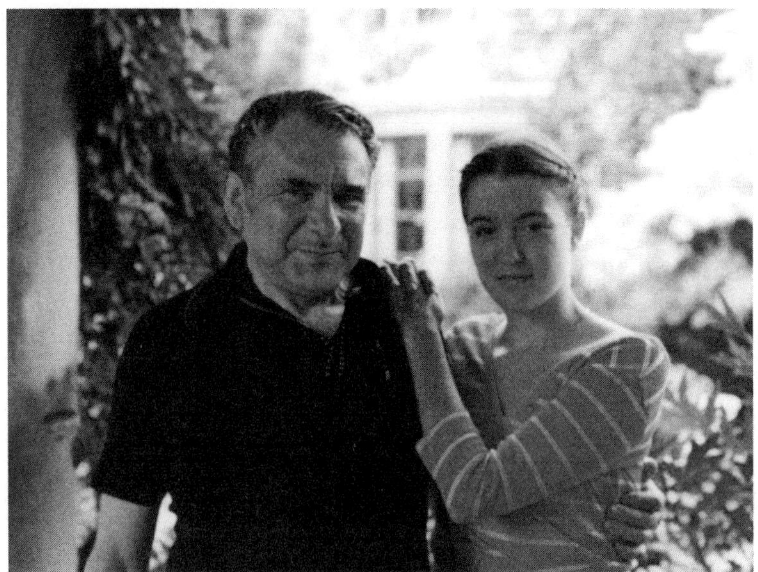

With my father, c. 1971.

he backed himself down the stairs into the garage, made his way, arm over arm, to the driver's side of his sparkling Toyota. He drove off, his gaze fixed and unblinking, his face barely visible over the dashboard, not responding to my mother's goodbye wave. He moved money from one bank to another, bought the milk and paper, and came home to a lunch of cottage cheese and fruit before stretching out, exhausted, for another slice of sleep, the portions getting longer and wider each day.

The respirator let out a long sigh and then began its steady rhythm again. My father's eyes stayed closed. I packed my things up and kissed him on the forehead. He didn't stir.

One week in the hospital turned into two. My mother came in with me more often. My father was conscious for shorter periods, but despite the odds against him, he emerged as the dark horse of the ICU. The South American resident and the surgeons persuaded us he should go to the operating room, thinking that perhaps a bowel obstruction was the root of the problem. They found a loop of intestine folded into an adhesion left from a hernia operation he'd forgotten he'd had in 1938. His lungs and kidneys recovered rapidly.

"It's good to have you back," I said in our first conversation without the tube.

His voice was still raspy. "You know, the nurses talked nonstop over me, as if I couldn't hear them. They have such terrible marital problems!" He told me about his first bath; he was so weak that the aides had to lift him into the tub. "It was ma-a-a-rvelous!" he said. I could almost hear his accent.

He told me he was writing his memoirs.

"Can I see what you're writing?" I asked.

"You can see the beginning," he said. "I'm still organizing it. It's not ready yet."

Once home again, my father lost all memory of his time on the unit. The blank filled with unease, and a recurring nightmare ripped into his slumber.

"I'm being buried alive." My father's eyes glittered in his hollow face. "I feel like my lungs are going to burst."

He gasped in dirt and gravel and flailed against the impossible weight of bones. He surfaced, coughing, into air soaked in the music of cicadas. The ground heaved and rotting corpses burst from the earth. Flesh hung off their skeletons like tattered cloth. Each caught my father's eye with empty sockets, then stumbled off and disappeared among the pines that lined the field. My mother called me after I returned to Boston, "Everyday he tells me about that dream. He has it over and over. He can't seem to get it out of his head."

It is on one of these sudden mornings, spring-filled and beaming, that I enter the basement of a large building in my small, suburban town. The entrance is marked "HOSPICE." I know the way well by now, past the kitchen and the nurse's station. His room is at the end of the hall, tucked into the corner of the building. My father's father sits in his wheelchair. His room retains nothing of the antiseptic flavor that permeates the hallway. Boxes line the walls, pictures of my family spring from every available surface, and various mismatched chairs have been planted wherever they fit around the brightly quilted bed. A computer and a television have somehow found their way into the mix and are pushed into the only remaining corner. My grandfather sits in his wheelchair in the middle of the room, and both my father and I turn to watch a toddler dancing across the screen into the arms of an old man, their bodies falling through time to the flowing rhythm of a melody that we all know well.

Heather writes about Martin's father for a school essay.
She describes watching home movies of herself as a child.

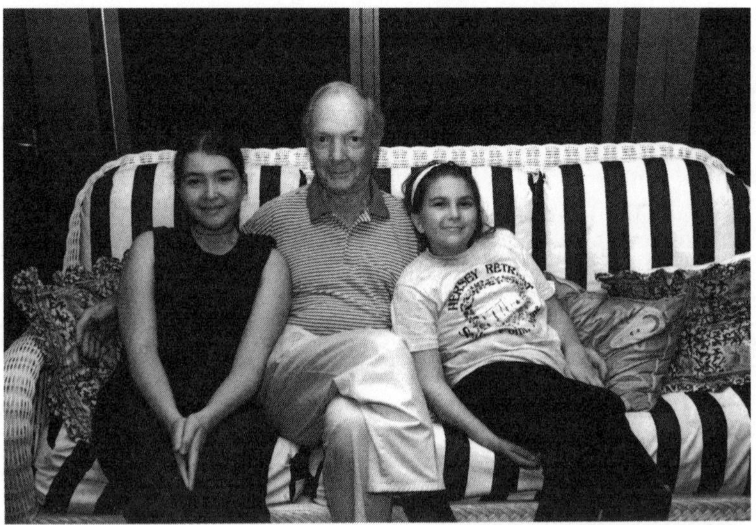

(Left to right) Heather, Martin's father Marty, and Lydia, c. 2000.

THREE

THE MONTH AFTER my father made this first trip to the ICU, my father-in-law, Marty, drove up from his home in North Carolina to New Hampshire for a visit. His second wife, Linda, had died after a long illness. Marty's back was bothering him, but he managed to hike up Red Hill. He treated himself with Linda's leftover painkillers, washed down with vodka. After he got back to Durham he collapsed. He was diagnosed with multiple myeloma, a malignancy of the bone marrow. In March of 2004, we flew him up, we thought to die. But we ended up working with a dedicated oncology team at Dana Farber, and Marty would live nearby us for another year and a half, biding his time while cancer finished digesting his bones.

I visited him regularly as he rotated between senior housing, the hospital and the nursing home. I ran him to the emergency room a few times a month, to treat infections and other complications of his illness. In retrospect, I regretted spending so much time with Marty and not with my own father. But Marty was in front of me and his suffering was extreme.

"We really don't have anything to say to each other anymore," Martin told me on the way down the hall to visit Marty at the independent-living apartment we'd found for him when he first arrived in Wayland. "I've heard all his stories. And I'm so angry with him most of the time."

I knocked and opened the door.

Lydia lay across Marty's unmade bed, reading a paperback. She'd taken to walking over after school. After a bout of pneumonia and new onset of asthma, she'd finally been diagnosed with a rarer form of hypothyroidism and another complicated endocrine disorder. She had started on treatment. She still wasn't herself and didn't like being alone, but she was sleeping less and wasn't getting the fevers any more.

Marty sat in his wheelchair reading the *Wall Street Journal*. He was dressed in boxer shorts, but he reached his hand out to us, as if he were still seated behind his cluttered desk back at CBS Sports, wearing a three-piece suit. His joints stood out like rosary beads on his emaciated limbs. Thick-lensed reading glasses magnified his eyes and two pair of forgotten distance glasses balanced on his forehead, giving him the appearance of a six-eyed bug.

"Hello, Darlings," he said. "I'm just catching up on bad news." The stubble on his chin scratched me when I leaned in for a kiss.

I sat next to Lydia. Martin settled into the only chair. Outside the window a redbud was just coming into bloom.

"He's been pretending he's dead again," Lydia said under her breath, without looking up from her book.

Marty and I chatted about this and that. He was trying to record bedtime stories for his grandchildren and his memoirs about working as a district attorney in Manhattan.

"How about recording some stuff about your second career as a social worker?" Martin said.

"I might well do that," Marty answered.

I started organizing the cassettes that littered the room. "Where's your med log?" I asked.

Marty waved toward the bureau. I tossed an empty bourbon bottle into the trash. His medication record was covered with chicken scratches, so I counted out the pills—fourteen OxyContin gone since last night.

As often happened, Marty about-faced from small talk to belligerence. "I can't find any clean shirts," he said, turning to Martin.

Martin's parents Stacy and Marty Carmichael, 1951.

"Goddamn it, someone's always taking my stuff."

Lydia put the paperback down and rolled off the bed to pack up her backpack. Martin went into the hall.

"Do you need something for pain, Marty?" I asked. Lydia and Martin had disappeared.

Marty looked sheepish. "I'm being an asshole, aren't I?"

"Yes," I answered, handing him a tablet with water.

The SUV idled under the portico and when I climbed into the passenger seat Martin was scrolling through his BlackBerry. He dropped it into the cup holder and put the car in gear. Lydia stuck in her earbuds. The bass notes of a pop song seemed to beat in time to the car wheels dropping into the cracks in the country road back to our neighborhood.

"I have to get to an appointment with David at four," I said. David Treadway was my longtime therapist.

Martin turned the car into the driveway, put it in park and shut off the engine. "How's that going?" he asked.

"OK."

My mood was getting worse; I was waking up drenched in sweat, my heart pounding. I wasn't able to fall asleep again. But I was functioning—I had to.

"Maybe it's menopause," Martin said.

"Maybe that's what started it," I said. "David thinks I'm having an existential crisis."

"Oh, brother." Martin picked up his BlackBerry and scrolled through.

I put my hand on his arm and he dragged his eyes off the screen. The muffled beat from the back seat continued.

"I'm taking Lydia to see someone up in Lexington tomorrow," I said. "A behavioral therapist David recommended."

"Isn't she better?"

"Physically, yes. Mentally less so."

"OK. Sounds good." He leaned over and gave me a peck on the cheek and reached back and pulled an earbud out of Lydia's ear. "Come on, Bidds," he said, using the nickname Heather had given her. "Mom's got to get going." I walked around to the driver's seat, and the two of them went into the house.

I backed down the long driveway into the street and drove to the main road. The trees were just beginning to green and a cardinal flashed in the woods and disappeared. I turned on the news and then quickly changed to the classical music station. But the Brahms trio made me too sad and I shut it off.

My depressions probably started in junior high when we went to Denmark for my father's sabbatical year at a university near Copenhagen. It came back in high school and then senior year at Williams College, making me postpone starting medical school. It returned after I had mono during a brief stint in graduate school. I was fine until my thirties, when I had an episode that went on for more than a year. I'd dutifully go to therapy and go through my lists of concerns. I tried medication—but didn't like the side effects, particularly the sense that I wasn't quite "myself."

In my early forties I found David Treadway, a psychologist who ran his practice out of his home one town over. David and I talked things through in his book-lined office. I'd sometimes hear his wife and two sons moving around the house. For some reason that comforted me. After nine months I began to feel better and we parted ways.

When I turned forty-six in 2001, I began having hot flashes that interrupted my sleep. I knew my mood was getting worse. "It will pass," I told myself, trying to ignore the telltale symptoms of another downturn. But I wasn't just deeply and viscerally sad; I was also gripped by fear—about everything. It felt like something terrible was going to happen or may have already happened. After 9/11 things only got worse. With my father's outbursts, the sadness felt like it filled my chest, making it difficult to breath. I started up with David again.

I turned into his driveway directly off of the main road. He'd built a high fence so the sound of cars rushing by was silenced. I parked and walked into the house—the door was always unlocked. The "waiting room" was at the back. The Treadways' corpulent tabby undraped itself from the back of the couch and twined around my legs. Right on the hour David opened the door with a coffee cup in his hand; the last client having exited out another door. He had a thin, kind face and smiled a greeting. He hustled back into the kitchen and microwaved his coffee.

"Want a cup?" he called.

"No thanks," I said, and settled in for another session.

Correspondence

My father's neighbor and childhood friend writes to Uri in Palestine, and describes the events of Kristallnacht. My father translated this letter and his comments are in parentheses:

LETTER FROM PAUL HARBAND (*the son of our neighbor in Vienna, about Uri's age, fifteen*) Written to Uri at Kibbutz Hashomer Haza'ir, Ein-Shemer.

Vienna, 27 November.1938

Dear Uri!

Your parents and therefore also we, received your last two letters and I am very surprised that you don't acknowledge the receipt of my letter. We are all glad that you are well and hope the same for your future. Now that I hear you are working so diligently, I am wondering what happened to your "staying in bed" routine? When I read about all the things you have learned, I imagine a machine gun toting "Ghafir" in a Jewish variety show with a great resemblance to you.

With us the routine is always the same and there is nothing new to report. We did not go on our journey as expected, but instead took up night quarters outside. *(The Harbands were thrown out of their apartment on Krystallnacht* [sic.] *as we were,)* The same applies to your parents. I am writing on a typewriter because I can get more onto one page. I heard from Harry that your former pen pal moved to California. Why have you not stayed in touch with her from Palestine? I received a letter yesterday from my pen pal and I hope I will soon be able to honor her with a personal visit.

Because of our forced absence from our apartment our poor fish starved to death. You cannot imagine how sorry we were. We sent the suitcase with your things in it to a wrong address and your parents have not much hope that it will ever come back. As you can see we still breath the fragrant air of the capital of the Ostmark. (*The Ostmark was established by Charles the Great, Charlemagne, late in the seventh century as a bulwark against invasions from the east. Hitler revived that name for Austria.*) According to you Ein-Shemer must be a fairly large settlement and I hope you find there what we all long for: a free and secure future.

Greetings and thick Bakies (*Comment: I have no idea what that word means.*)

From your friend, Paul Harband

Also the best wishes from little Mädi (*Paul's sister Susi?*) Mama and my father for your continued well-being.

Me, age 16.

FOUR

A MONTH LATER, I sat with Lydia in the office of her new behavioral therapist. I rushed through what had happened since our first meeting. "I feel like agitation has replaced her somnolence. She's really struggling to fall asleep at night and her nightmares have started up again. And she seems really flat, you know—no affect."

"Lydia? What do you think is going on?" Melody was young, probably in her thirties.

Lydia chewed on her thumbnail and stared out the window.

"Lisa, why don't you wait for us outside?"

I settled into an upholstered chair in the waiting room. I leafed through a copy of *Psychology Today*, then tossed it aside.

The summer I turned sixteen, 1971, I had my first serious bout of depression. I thought this sense that the color drained out of the world was something that came with growing older. My mother said I was "blue" and told me it would pass. My father was kind and my brothers took me out with their friends. The possibility of seeing a therapist never came up. I went to bed most nights hoping I wouldn't wake up the next day.

That September, I asked my father to take me to Yom Kippur services. I'd never been to temple, but he seemed pleased that I wanted to go. I had no idea if he had been since he left Vienna, or even if he went to synagogue as a child.

When we came out to the driveway, the neighbor's demented lab, Rumor, rushed across the street to greet us. I tried to pat her but she was spinning too fast. Her tail knocked my father with every turn. He recoiled. Rumor threw her front legs around my father's neck and planted a wet kiss on his lips.

"Aughhh," my father yelped.

I grabbed Rumor's collar and dragged her off. "Jeez, Dad, it's just a dog," I said, smoothing down my orange miniskirt. My father pulled an ironed handkerchief out of his pocket and wiped sweat off his forehead and Rumor's kiss off his lips. I straightened out his wide, patterned tie. My father always overreacted to dogs. Our family pet ownership never got past goldfish and guinea pigs.

On the drive over to the temple, we passed the sprawling campus of Syracuse University. "Where do you think you'll apply to college?" my father asked me when we passed the building that housed his office and lab. His brows curled against his black plastic glasses. He'd let his sideburns grow out.

"I dunno." I was irritated with his question.

"Do you still want to be a doctor?" my father asked.

I sighed and looked out the window. High school was boring and the social scene unfathomable. There had been outbreaks of violence. I'd once been punched in the head by a classmate in the hallway. I'd never told my parents. My father was tutoring me in calculus and physics so I could take the Regents exams and graduate a year early. We still took our walks together in the evenings, but more and more I felt like his advice was old fashioned and not very relevant.

"Well, whatever you do, it should be something you find exciting," he said.

How many times had I heard that? Life after graduation stretched out like a flat line to the horizon. "I think I want to take a few years off. Maybe I'll travel."

"Where?"

"Dunno."

"What about applying to Syracuse? We wouldn't have to pay tuition."

"Too many JAPs," I answered.

"What?"

"Too many JAPs," I said it quieter the second time, wondering if my father thought I was talking about Japanese students. Was it possible he had never heard that expression?

"What are you talking about?" He turned to me when we stopped at a light.

"Princesses, Dad—Jewish American—"

The light changed. My father drove in silence for a few more blocks. The synagogue rose like Egyptian pyramids on the hill behind the Christian Brothers Academy.

"I can't believe you could say that," he said at the next stoplight.

My father pulled into the packed parking lot. He slammed the door of the Volvo station wagon we brought home from our Fulbright year in Copenhagen. He pulled a yarmulke out of the pocket of his polyester jacket and placed it on his crown. I was relieved when he took my hand. He nodded hello to a few people I didn't recognize. The man at the door asked for tickets. With another sleight-of-hand, my father produced them from the other pocket of his jacket.

We sat near the back of the sanctuary. The room was dim, as if daylight reached us through some circuitous route. The cantor's voice rose out of nowhere with the unearthly strains of the *Kol Nidre*. The rabbi prayed and the congregation read along. My father's lips fluttered and he made a small bow forward at certain parts.

The rabbi began his sermon. His subject was the evils of mixed marriage and the dilution of faith. I wondered how many of the people in the temple knew that my mother wasn't Jewish.

At the end of the service, my father stood up and pushed his way out of the pew and disappeared. I was caught up in the crowd's winding current and drifted through the portal and out under the haze of the Milky Way. It was still warm—Indian summer. My father was already in the driver's seat when I reached him. We waited with the windows rolled down as the others jammed their way out of the exit.

"Well, that was weird." I said.

"Yes." He pulled the yarmulke off his head and smoothed it against his thigh.

A question popped into my head. "Tell me about your sister."

My father lifted his hands onto the steering wheel and leaned into it. He answered the way he always answered: She was smart. She had a good sense of humor. She was pretty. You remind me of her.

"What actually happened to your family?"

My father whispered to the wheel. "Martin's father, my father's youngest brother, Rudy, told me both my parents were likely gassed at Auschwitz."

"And Maya?"

My father looked bewildered. "My father wrote me in 1941 that she was taken to a camp in Magdeburg, a few hours from Berlin—I thought she was transferred to Theresienstadt later. But Uncle Rudy inquired at the police station in Vienna when he came back from Russia after the war. They had habitation records for everyone then. The police told him my sister and my parents were all deported to Minsk in 1942, and Uncle Rudy was told that from there they all went to Auschwitz. But Rudy sent me those records, and they showed Uri on the same train, and he had already left for Palestine in 1938, so I knew that wasn't right. And they said my sister departed Vienna a month before my parents. So I wonder if they made a mistake about my sister as well." My father paused and looked out the windshield. "If that's what happened, though, she would have been around sixteen when she was gassed. Your age."

My father's voice was flat. I don't remember if I responded.

He turned the key in the ignition. "She must have gone to Germany in 1941. That's what my father wrote me. So I don't know how she could have ended up in Vienna again in 1942." He shifted into gear and pulled out without looking at me. "She was already a young lady when I left. I worry about what happened to her."

Silence began to close a door between us, but after a few moments, my father continued."She developed early," he whispered, staring straight ahead. "I worry—" his voice trailed off. Then, even quieter, he said, "They say there were medical experiments in some of the camps." My father braked and put the car back into neutral. He looked at me then.

"But what if the police were wrong about her?" I asked, looking out the window to avoid his gaze. "What if she survived in Germany? What if she's still living someplace behind the Iron Curtain?"

My question held the door open between us for a moment longer.

"I hope she's not. I hope she's dead." The door slammed shut.

I still felt the reverberations in the waiting room of Lydia's therapist.

My father put the car back in gear, then pulled into the caravan making its way to the exit, and back home again.

Lydia came out of the office. She had a mild scoliosis that made one arm hang lower than the other. I stood up. I held myself back from saying, "Stand up straight!"

Melody peeked around the door. "Bring her back next week. Same time." She smiled, then closed the door.

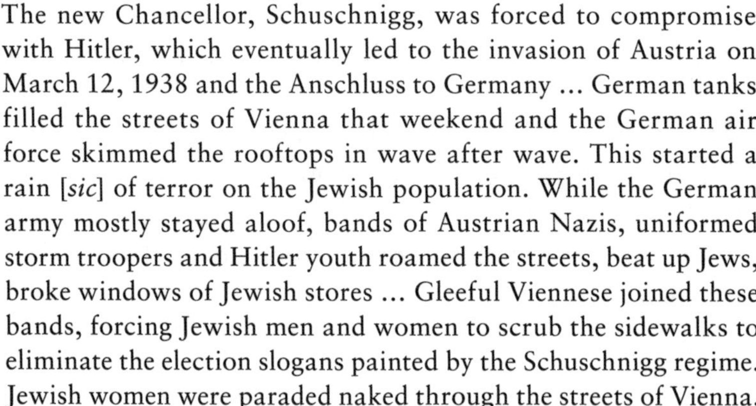

The new Chancellor, Schuschnigg, was forced to compromise with Hitler, which eventually led to the invasion of Austria on March 12, 1938 and the Anschluss to Germany ... German tanks filled the streets of Vienna that weekend and the German air force skimmed the rooftops in wave after wave. This started a rain [*sic*] of terror on the Jewish population. While the German army mostly stayed aloof, bands of Austrian Nazis, uniformed storm troopers and Hitler youth roamed the streets, beat up Jews, broke windows of Jewish stores ... Gleeful Viennese joined these bands, forcing Jewish men and women to scrub the sidewalks to eliminate the election slogans painted by the Schuschnigg regime. Jewish women were paraded naked through the streets of Vienna.

My father writes about the Anschluss.

FIVE

A FEW WEEKS LATER, in May 2004, it became clear Lydia had become the target of some of the more popular girls in her class. Two of them carpooled with us and they ignored Lydia when she climbed next to me in the front seat. With straight hair falling like silk around their faces—they both whispered to each other in the back seat. When I dropped them at their houses I turned to Lydia. "I should have said something, right?"

"Wrong," Lydia answered.

I was running into the nurse's office every few days to pick her up and bring her home, mostly for vague symptoms of feeling "unwell." On top of that, my father was back in the ICU after a massive gastrointestinal hemorrhage related to portal hypertension from his enlarged spleen, and Marty was back in the hospital with yet another infection. Heather was quiet on her few visits home, but I didn't have the bandwidth to figure out what was going on. Martin was traveling a lot. We argued about what he saw as my hypervigilance and what I saw as his willful blindness. There was a lot going on and I was dealing with it, but inside I alternated between sadness, panic, and numbness. I felt like I put one foot in front of the other without paying much attention to where I was going.

In mid-May I had a break from teaching and one of Martin's sisters was up to take care of Marty. I pulled Lydia out of school and went out to visit my parents. It was right after photographs of prisoner abuses at Iraq's Abu Ghraib prison were released.

A few days into the visit we all sat down for breakfast in front of the south-facing window. Tulips broke through the dirt in the front garden. My mother's used pantyhose restrained vines against the picket fence. Cotton crotches waited for leaves to cover their immodest display.

I hadn't seen my father since his hospitalization. His skin was washed of color and he'd lost a lot of weight. "I'm waking up in the middle of the night.," he said as he fiddled with the "Saturday" compartment of his day-of-the-week medicine holder; my mother reached across the table, took the dispenser from him, and handily opened it, dumping the contents into the china bowl next to his orange juice.

"I see a bright orb of light bouncing off the walls in the bedroom. I follow it into the living room. It lands on the mantel and then bounces off the window panes," my father said.

"I'm waking up at night, too," Lydia said. There was a hint of blush painted on her cheeks and mascara flaked off her already thick lashes.

"Are you frightened?" I asked my father.

"Not at all—it seems like a friendly spirit. Maybe it's my medication. But I can't get back to sleep after it visits."

He paused, as if collecting his thoughts. "I feel like there's something I've forgotten to do."

As soon as he said it, I felt the same thing. There was something I had forgotten to do. I thought about his file: "Things Requiring Attention."

"Such a gorgeous day," my mother said as she whacked the top off her soft-boiled egg.

My father rinsed down his pills. When his hands settled in his lap, the tremor took over. He stared out the window as if too exhausted to pick up his spoon.

"What a beautiful day!" he spoke suddenly.

I started. My father looked right at me. "A few days after Hitler marched into Vienna, it was a day just like this one." His voice was steady; he didn't clear his throat. "We needed to leave the flat to look for food, even though the streets were dangerous. My parents asked me to walk to the Second District to check on my grandmother, Omama Sabine, and my mother's younger sister, my Aunt Pepi. There was glass everywhere, and on doors and across storefronts was written 'JEW,' or 'DIRTY JEW.'"

I'd never heard my father mention his Aunt Pepi. He seldom mentioned his mother's mother, Sabine.

My mother stood up and muttered, "Here we go again." Even though her egg was only half-eaten, she grabbed the cardigan from the back of her chair, took Lydia's hand, and dragged her out of the kitchen. The front door clicked shut.

"I was seventeen," my father continued. "It was a beautiful day just like this one. A crowd gathered around something, and they were laughing and talking." My father's voice was modulated.

"Dad?"

He looked past my right shoulder as if he were speaking to someone right behind me.

"I walked to the edge of the crowd and then pushed my way to the inside of their circle. They were watching what appeared to be a pile of rags moving in the dirt." He told me a man lay on the ground. It was an Orthodox Jew with a long beard and forelocks, his dark clothes covered with dust, his face bloody from a beating. The man moaned and struggled to stand.

"The Jew begged for help," my father said. "A young woman, dressed in a blue suit, moved into the center of the circle. Wavy hair framed her lovely face. She grinned and winked at the crowd. She smiled down on the man with an expression of pity, and then reached down as if to help him up. He lifted his hand to hers. Turning again to the crowd, she circled her hips. She raised her skirt up over the tops of her stockings as she continued to gyrate, and then straddled the man who slumped back to the ground."

My father's eyes weren't old and watery; they were the clear eyes of an angry young man. I wanted to touch him across the table, but he

Viennese Jews forced to scrub election graffiti off the streets after the Anschluss.
Documentation Center of the Austrian Resistance (DÖW)

seemed very far away. He swallowed twice. "She urinated onto the man's face," he whispered.

My father looked down. "I saw the white lace of the woman's garter belt," he said. "I thought I saw the shadow of hair between her thighs."

I winced.

He looked directly at me again. "What kind of a thing is this for a young boy to see?"

It was a flashback; his speech was modulated and without the usual delays. But he didn't break into German and seemed more like himself. As before, though, once the story was finished, my father shrunk; the tremor in his hands returned. He turned back to his soggy Cheerios. A bit of milk dripped from his lower lip.

"Shall we go for a drive?" he asked.

I wiped the milk from his face with a paper napkin. He leaned against the table and pushed himself to his feet and waved me away when I got up to help.

"I can manage," he said.

After Lydia and my mother went to bed that evening, I asked my father about the scene he described. He seemed surprised that I knew about it. Once again, a flashback had emerged, he had forgotten about telling it to me, but had regained a chunk of memory. I wondered if he would go back to talking as if it had happened to someone else. I imagined the urine caught the sunlight and sparkled as it splashed against the Jew's upturned face. The crowd broke into applause. The woman laughed and they roared with her. Some of the men clapped each other on the back. The Jew coughed and then lay still.

"A policeman watched the whole thing and did nothing," my father said. His voice was steady. "What would have happened if I walked into that crowd to help the man?" But he turned away and ran up the avenue, toward the Danube Canal and his Grandmother Sabine and Aunt Pepi's house in the Second District. Passersby moved in slow motion. My father reined himself in to walk with them.

"I had to be careful," he said, his voice wavered again. "The Nazis changed the traffic rules after the Anschluss, and now the cars were driving on the right side of the street instead of the left."

I'd read through some of the history section of my father's genealogy book by then. Leaving aside everything that happened in Vienna during the months after the Anschluss—the beatings, the lootings, hundreds of Jews jumping out of windows because they couldn't bear the weight of their own lives—just this simple fact of a change in traffic rules, something I hadn't heard about until that day, added a tactile disruption to the lovely Vienna he'd constructed for me—swimming the Danube, going to the opera, visiting relatives. It was a city turned mad.

"Once in the courtyard of my grandmother's building, I took

the stairs three at a time." My father was speaking quickly again, as if the story itself propelled him. "I pounded on the door. It fell open. I heard my grandmother's reedy voice singing a Yiddish lullaby. The gilded mirrors in the salon were all smashed, breaking up reflections of books scattered on the floor. I followed the voice into my grandmother's bedroom. Pepi sat at the vanity, dressed in a slip, but didn't move to cover herself when I came in. A bruise in the shape of a hand marred her neck. Her dark hair was suddenly streaked with gray."

"How old was Pepi then?" I asked.

"I can't remember. Late thirties maybe? She was a spinster. She and one of my other uncles lived with my grandmother, who was widowed by then."

I imagined Sabine's tortoiseshell comb smoothing out Pepi's hair. She put a plump finger to her lips when she noticed my father. She led Pepi to bed and pulled down the coverlet. Pepi slipped between the sheets. Sabine moved away but Pepi moaned, then sat up, her eyes wide.

"Don't leave me," Pepi said. Sabine sat down on the bed.

My father continued the story: "I remember now, my grandmother had a mark on her cheek and her nose was swollen. I think I saw dried blood in one nostril. She asked me to make some tea. 'What happened to the maid?' I asked, and she answered that Theresa hadn't come since the Germans arrived. You see, Christians were no longer allowed to work for Jews after the Anschluss."

I imagined my father pumping water into a pot, lighting the stove, and putting the water on. Scraping a circle of mold off a rind of bread, he sliced it and spread it with marmalade. When the tea was ready, he loaded everything on a tray and carried it in. I imagined a grandfather clock in the hallway measuring empty seconds.

"My grandmother poured tea into a bone china cup and added a large spoonful of sugar and handed it to Pepi. That cup was almost translucent, it was so fine. Pepi took it with two hands but didn't bring it to her lips, her hands were shaking so hard. I went out on the balcony. It grew dim by the canal, and I could barely see the buildings of the Inner City across it." My father paused for just an instant. "An old Jew with a cane hobbled below, and a group of laughing boys chased him. 'Take off your disguise, old man! Take it off or we will have to help you!' they said."

I imagine the old man's breath was heavy and uneven. One of the youths grabbed his shoulder and spun him. Another took hold of his beard and shouted as he yanked on it, "Take off the disguise, old man!"

My father said, "He swung the Jew around by the beard. The cane flew against the side of the building and clattered to the feet of one of the bigger boys. He picked it up and swung it around to the back of the man's head. The sound as it hit the Jew's skull—I remember it seemed oddly muffled. The old man dropped to the ground. The boys looked up at the houses that lined the street. I thought maybe they saw me. I jumped back against the balcony doorway."

My father's fingers began to pill-roll again. His voice became more mechanical and barely louder than a whisper. "At midnight the streets were quiet again, and I got ready to leave. My grandmother threw her arms around my neck. I had to pry her fingers apart. I told her, 'I'll come back tomorrow, Omama.' Outside, the body of the old Jew was gone. I walked home along the dark canal." My father looked toward the dark window, then back at me. "I thought I heard someone coming up behind me. I broke into a run." My father suddenly stood up and walked tall and steady to the mantel and ran his hand along its surface. He turned around and looked beyond me. "When I turned off the Ringstrasse, I was sure I saw those boys walking toward me on the other side of the street. A young woman walked tall and straight in front of me. I came up beside her and pretended I was with her. I think she smiled at me—I think she took my hand."

I imagined my father ducking into an alley and making his way home.

Correspondence

American Red Cross

Syracuse and Onondaga County Chapter
636 South Warren Street
Syracuse, New York 13202
Phone: 315 425-1666
Fax: 315 425-1676

Saving Lives and Helping People Cope with Emergencies

August 18, 1997

Dear Mr. Gruenberg,

Please see attached copy of a letter to Mr. Mandell at the Holocaust and War Victims Tracing and Information Center at the Red Cross in Baltimore. I understand that this information is a little different in that the previous report regarding Leo (Leib) Grunberg was incorrect : all three sought persons were deported together to Minszk on 27 May ,1942

Also we have received the following response from the Austrian Red Cross Society:

> **Leib Grünberg, born May 3, 1885 in Kolomea, his wife Elka Grünberg, née Helwig, born November 25, 1889 in Kolomea, and their daughter Mia Grünberg, born January 26, 1926, in Vienna, were deported from their last address, A-1020 Vienna, Ferdinandstraße 31/16 to Minsk on May 27, 1942. Leib Grünberg and Elka Grünberg were declared dead by the Court for Civil Law in Vienna on May 29, 1959, under reference number 48T 1689/58-9 Nr. 3065/59 and 48T 1690/58-5 Nr. 3064/59, respectively.**

Should we receive any additional information , we will forward to you immediately.

I'm sorry none of this is new news to you

Sincerely,

Pat Androckitis

Pat Androckitis
Manager
Social Services

The War Victims Processing and Information Center answers my father's renewed inquiries, 1997.

SIX

A FEW WEEKS after my father told me about the woman urinating on the Jew, I decided to get my father's story down on tape. I read through the rest of his genealogy book, his notes and the few family letters he'd translated. He'd given me the first pages of the memoir he had started. I felt as if I were getting a handle on his extended family and a little bit of history. I didn't know then that this would be my father's last trip to our home in Wayland.

I set up the video camera on a tripod in the living room and sat on the couch.

"Come sit in the easy chair, Dad." I called out to the kitchen.

My father walked in, steadying himself on the Steinway and then the piano bench. His back was so bent that he had to angle his head up to look forward. That curve reminded me of Marty, whose cancer had collapsed his spine into that same pitiful C. My father picked up the pillow and tossed it to the floor. Steadying himself by wedging one bent knee against the chair, he pulled a handkerchief out of his pocket, unfolded it, and honked into it. He tried to fold it again but couldn't manage. He wadded it up and shoved it back in the pocket of his trousers. He lowered himself into the chair but couldn't control the drop at the end. The force of his fall made him bounce.

I turned on the camera. "Today I need to hear everything you remember, Dad. Everything."

Through the lens, my father's jaw grinded as if he were chewing a tiny piece of gum. "It's the history I want to get down," he said.

"I'm more interested in *your* history, Dad. And, who knows? This could be our last chance."

My father looked up at the camera, then began to speak as if he were reading from a script taken from his "Notes on Harry Gruenberg" written over ten years earlier.

"I started in *Gymnasium* to prepare for university, but then I decided to switch to a trade school, because places at the university were limited for Jews. My parents were really upset with me when I changed schools. But my cousin Martin was in trade school already, so I stuck to my guns—"

"Dad, can we start later? Maybe with the Anschluss?"

My father's face froze into the Parkinson's mask. He didn't blink. "If you like," he said.

"Why don't I read from your genealogy book and we take it from there?"

My father's head nodded, but I wasn't sure if he was assenting or if that was his Parkinson's nod.

"So, you wrote:"

> When the schools reopened again after the Anschluss, my Jewish classmates and I were allowed to continue until the end of the semester, but we were relegated to the last row with several empty rows between us and the rest of the class. I don't recall any serious incidents in school but there was no more fraternization. From the faculty, only Herr Haubner, the homeroom teacher, shook my hand and wished me good luck when he handed me my last report card. I will never forget the brave speech he made, pleading for tolerance and understanding. He said that as a devout Catholic he would find it difficult to accept the new order. He asked that the class be kind to those who felt like he did—

My father interrupted. "When Herr Haubner handed me my report card, there were tears in his eyes."

"What happened to him?"

"I tried looking him up when your mother and I first went back to Vienna in the early sixties, but he wasn't listed in the phone book. So, who knows? Rolled up with my grades was a note saying I wouldn't be allowed to continue in that school or in any other school in the German Reich since I was 'non-Aryan.' I passed everything with first class honors except for German. The teacher had asked us to write an essay about National Socialist feelings in films, a subject I couldn't very well write about!"

I read on:

> After being kicked out of school I joined the Blue-White, the Zionist youth group of the left-leaning *Hechalutz*, the Pioneer, and eventually the *Stadtkibbutz*, the town kibbutz. The kibbutz introduced us to communal living and was intended to prepare us for immigration to Palestine. We did odd jobs around town, mostly for wealthier Jews and Jews who were emigrating. We studied Hebrew, familiarized ourselves with the history of Palestine and celebrated Shabbat every Friday night. We danced the horah but looked down at such bourgeois rites as ballroom dancing! We had secret strategy meetings in the basement of the building next to Gestapo headquarters. It seemed the safest place to us at the time. I recall only one raid by storm troopers. They let all the girls go, but beat up some of the boys rather badly, especially a boy we called 'Borscht' because of his red hair.

I imagined a boy with hair the color of beet soup. "Were you hurt when your meeting was raided?" I asked.

"No, no." My father cleared his throat, which now seemed to signal when we were getting too close to an unpleasant memory. It was more like a bark.

"What was Borscht's real name?" I ask. "What happened to him?"

My father barked again. "I have no idea." His eyes seem to search for something beyond the lens. "I was too old to travel with Uri to Palestine in October, or on the Kindertransport with Uncle Igo's only son, Kurt Helwing, to England after Kristallnacht. It irked me that

Uri got to go to a kibbutz in Palestine just because he was younger. He didn't even care about the movement."

My father smiled when I recited the story about Kristallnacht, especially when I got to the part where I asked, "Were they polite?" I realized then what was strange about my father's face when telling me some of these stories. His lips were smiling but his eyes were not. I had been teaching anatomy, and I'd learned the nerves that make your eyes smile go through different circuits than the ones that just make the corners of your mouth turn up. That was why our eyes don't smile in photographs unless we hear something funny right before the picture is taken. So my father's upturned lips and sad eyes pointed to an internal disconnect.

My father didn't seem to remember having a flashback about that night, and he recited the tale again in the flat voice of a historian.

I tried again. "OK, so, in your own words, what happened in the few months between Kristallnacht and your departure in March 1939?'

"Not much. I just got ready to go."

In the book, he'd written:

> I finally managed to get a visa to England as an "agricultural trainee" through the efforts of the Zionist organization, which ran a preparatory training farm for emigration to Palestine near Maidstone in Kent. After running through several grueling bureaucratic hurdles, including a visit to Heinrich Himmler's "emigration office" and armed with a note from the German Wehrmacht certifying that I was a "full-blooded Jew" and was therefore not eligible to serve in the German army, I was finally able to get a train ticket to London.

"I had an offer from the technical university in Haifa, but I couldn't get a visa to go to Palestine. Then I got the visa to England. I was supposed to leave in January, I think—" But his departure had been delayed by his forgotten hernia surgery. So, in March of 1939, one year after the Anschluss and four months after Kristallnacht my eighteen-year-old father finally boarded a train out of Vienna.

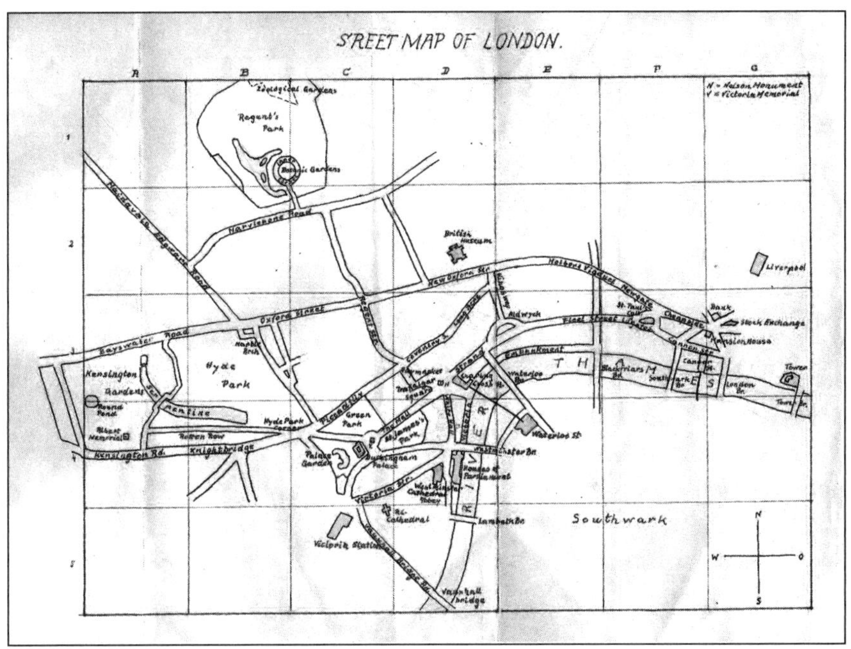

Map of London drawn by my father, from his English notebook, 1937.

"What did you say to your sister and your parents at the train station when you said goodbye?"

"I don't think we said much. I waved to them as the train pulled out of the station and that was pretty much it. There were a bunch of boys in my car from the Youth Aliyah—you know, the group that was training us to be pioneers in Palestine. We all sat together. I persuaded most of them to join me on the farm when we got to England."

My father began unfolding the story about the border crossing out of Germany in the same order I'd heard as a child. "'It is a crime punishable by death to leave the Reich with any currency,' the soldier announced," my father had said then. But here he deviated. "That soldier's eyes were two different colors, one blue and one green. I'd never seen that before."

"Are you sure?"

"His dog was straining on its leash, and when he got it to settle down he looked right at me. The sunlight came through the train window and I could see his eyes clearly."

"There was a dog?"

"Yes. A German shepherd. It had a—" my father put his hand up to his mouth, searching for the word.

I fumbled changing the tape. "A muzzle?"

"Yes."

"Are you sure it wasn't the dog that had two different eye colors, Dad?"

"That's not how I remember it." My father reached into his trouser pocket, pulled out his handkerchief, and ran it across his forehead. "I stuck my hands in my pockets to find my papers, and I found a single pfennig. I scrambled into the W.C. and threw my last coin down the toilet." My father clenched his hankie and dropped into the rut of prior renditions. I could finish the story myself from there: The train crossed into Belgium. My father and his friends tossed their caps in the air. They thumped each other on the back. They ran back and forth in the aisle, upsetting stolid burghers. They tugged open the windows and hung over the sills. "Hip, hip, hurrah," they cheered, as verdant fields rolled by.

My father's face froze again.

"Need to take a break for lunch?" I asked.

"Yes!" my mother called from the kitchen. "You're going to tire him out!"

After lunch we sat down again.

I started: "Alright, so you said that when you arrived in England the immigration officer in Dover suggested that you get rid of the umlaut in our name, using the poet 'Goethe' as an example." I opened his genealogy book.

> After about a month we were all moved to the David Eder Farm. We soon built several dormitories, a large kitchen and dining area which was also used for social functions and meetings. We

young pioneers came from a variety of backgrounds: refugees from Austria, Germany, Czechoslovakia, and Poland, and young Zionists from all parts of England and Ireland. Our regular general meetings were as chaotic as those run by the League of Nations. I sometimes had to act in the capacity of an interpreter, because many in the group did not speak much English at first. I was elected treasurer and accountant. I worked mostly in the fields. It was a healthy life. We had a fair social life: parties on Friday nights, hiking in the evenings and on weekends, the occasional bike trip to a movie house.

"And there were romances—" my father interrupted.

"Details?"

"Well, that was never my forte," my father smiled.

I handed my father the book and he read in his quiet, shaky voice:

We had some clandestine visits from emissaries of the Jewish Defense Forces in Palestine to teach us self-defense, the use of rifles, and army drill. I was always a lousy shot! I hitchhiked to London on several occasions to see some of my relatives: Rita and her sister Erna, and my cousin Cyril Grünberg when he first arrived from Germany.

At David Eder Farm, Kent, England, c. 1940.

My father looked up. "Cyril was the son of my father's oldest brother, Salo. They lived in Germany. Salo and Cyril were arrested and taken to Buchenwald early on. Salo died there. But someone bribed my cousin Cyril out in early '39. And Rita, we called her Rosy back in Vienna, and her sister Erna, were very, very distant cousins of mine. They found positions as domestics in London and got out in '38, before Kristallnacht. Rita was engaged to my mother's cousin, Ludwig Blaustein, when she was sixteen. Ludwig went to Dachau, but someone bribed him out, too. Rita and Ludwig were married in a British internment camp sometime in 1939, I think." My father bent over to read again:

> I was able to correspond with my parents and my sister directly until the war broke out. After that I managed to direct mail through my cousin Siegfried Grünberg in Holland. Of course, this stopped when Holland was overrun in May 1940.
>
> The disaster at Dunkirk early in May 1940 brought swift political changes in Britain. Churchill took over from Chamberlain as Prime Minister and issued his 'collar the lot' directive, which led to the internment of all aliens from Germany and Austria. The local alien officer arrived at the farm and asked me to get all the fellows on his list together. He then told us formally that we were under arrest, to pack a few things and climb into a waiting truck. A few days later we were taken to a suburb of Liverpool and then to the Isle of Man.
>
> The camps consisted of beachfront vacation hotels surrounded by barbed wires and machine gun posts. Some curious natives, including girls, would stroll by and there was some fraternization across the barbed wire fence. Occasionally we were allowed to go out to the beach under guard and under the watchful eyes of machine gunners on the rooftops. This idyll did not last very long. Within about a month all inmates were shipped to Canada or Australia.

Hearing my father recite his story in that expressionless voice took me back to sitting in front of the living room television after

My father at David Eder Farm. The caption from his scrapbook reads: "How can a pioneer call himself Harry?"

a particularly dull day at junior high. I suddenly sensed I was not alone. "Why don't you just sit down, Dad?" I asked, without taking my eyes off the set. *Hogan's Heroes* was a sitcom about a German POW camp run by an incompetent Nazi called Colonel Klink, with an even more incompetent sidekick, Sergeant Schultz.

My father sidled toward the couch in front of me, eyes fixed on the image of Colonel Klink. His posture forced his arms to hang in front of him, and his palms faced backwards with fingers curved, making his hands look like upside-down question marks. When his calves hit the cushions, he sat, and his arms collapsed behind him. Colonel Klink was, as usual, being outwitted by Hogan and his gang of allied POWs.

Sergeant Schultz's refrain, "I know *nussing, nussing,*" had become part of our family lingo. My father never belly-laughed, but a small "ha, ha, ha" escaped whenever Sergeant Schultz appeared, and a close-mouthed smile fixed on his profile when he wasn't laughing. On the screen, Hogan emptied dirt from his pant legs. It had been brought up from the tunnels they were digging, not for escape, but in order to run their operations in the surrounding towns.

It seems incongruous to me now that my father had actually enjoyed this show. But maybe he thought watching it was a way to connect with a daughter who was drifting into adulthood. At the time I was struggling to readjust after we came home from my father's Fulbright year in Denmark; I'd left at the end of sixth grade with lots of friends. It was okay to be a smart girl in elementary school, but it wasn't okay in junior high. I couldn't find my place. I watched a lot of television.

A commercial started. My father told me again about his transatlantic journey on the *Sobieski* at the end of the summer of 1940. "The ship had a Polish crew, but a British captain. Among the passengers was also a group of real German prisoners of war." In his notes my father wrote:

> We had no inkling where we were going, but we heard from the crew that a ship had been torpedoed and sunk the day before off the northern coast of Ireland. We sailed that evening after joining a large convoy including a battleship and several destroyers ... Apparently a German U-boat had been sighted and depth charges were dropped by our escorts. The sea was calm for the first three days but then a storm broke loose ... I believe it was during the storm that the *Sobieski* developed some engine trouble. We apparently fell behind the convoy during the fourth night and found ourselves in Newfoundland (in St. John's harbor) in the morning. By that time, we knew we were going to Canada.
>
> I think it took three more days to steam up the St. Lawrence River past picturesque villages to Quebec City. Here we were put on a train to Trois Rivières. We arrived on a hot sunny day and it seemed that the whole town was out to watch a long column of internees being marched from the train station to the stadium which was

> to be our home for a while. The crowd must have been amused seeing such a motley group: Jewish refugees of all ages, from teenagers to old men with long beards, professors from Oxford and Cambridge, leftist ex-members of the German Parliament, anti-Hitler priests and ministers, deserters from the German merchant marine, veterans from the Spanish Civil War who had fought on the Republican side, a German count, and an Austrian pretender to the Hapsburg crown. I found the local crowd just as interesting. I had never seen so many women with lipstick and rouge, nor had I seen men wearing slacks and hats in pastel shades.
>
> At the stadium a surprise was awaiting us: the German soldiers inside the barbed-wire compound greeted us with the singing of the *Horst-Wessel-Lied*, a foul Nazi song written in memory to a martyred Nazi punk. It contains a line which loosely translated says "when Jewish blood drips from our knives we feel twice as well."

The woman on the television screen scrubbed her kitchen floor. My father settled back in the couch, crossed his legs, and folded his hands in his lap. "We refugees were eventually separated from the German POWs. We were moved to camps built in Quebec and New Brunswick. We fabricated cardboard boxes and worked as lumbermen. I think the camp commanders made a tidy profit!

"When we were chopping down trees in Quebec, we were guarded by an elderly soldier. Sargeant Schultz reminds me a lot of Jacques; he had the same portly shape. Jacques leaned his gun against a tree and sat down during the long shifts. By the time the men got to work, he would doze off. We prisoners organized. While some chopped down trees, the others set up the camp school in a glen a few hundred yards away. There were quite a few professors among us, and even a rabbi, who taught us philosophy." My father would finish two years of university studies in that makeshift classroom.

The commercials ended. My father and I silently watched the screen. When the episode was over I got up to turn off the set. My father was no longer with me.

And back in Wayland in 2004, I was alone as well. The tape had run out again.

"Your father's gone to the bathroom," my mother called from the kitchen. "Are you almost done?"

"We're only up to 1941."

She sighed. I got up to stretch. My father's book was open, and I picked up where he had left off:

> I managed to restart my correspondence with my parents. Since Dunkirk I had sent letters via Uncle Arnold Grünberg in New York. Unfortunately, my uncle gave away the plot. Instead of just passing on the correspondence, he mentioned casually that he was enclosing my father's letters "from Vienna." The alert camp censor who was reading all the mail hauled me in and read me the Riot Act. Corresponding with the enemy was a serious offense. After that he directed me to send mail via the Red Cross as a Prisoner of War. Of course, this also became impossible after Pearl Harbor.

My father had told me that when it became known that Jewish refugees were imprisoned in Canada, voices were raised in the British and Canadian parliaments and some were released. He was unable to gain entry to the United States even though he had family there; he was told he was an "enemy alien." Then Canada agreed to release students whose university studies had been interrupted by the internment if they could find a sponsor in Canada. My father bent the truth a little and said he had started university in Vienna before he fled.

One of his mother's wealthier brothers, my father's Uncle Menio, had made it out to the free port of Shanghai with his wife in 1938, and two years later they were sponsored by the Jewish Community of Salt Lake City. When it was clear that my father wouldn't be able to join him in Utah, Menio arranged a sponsor in Vancouver and provided the necessary funds. My father wrote:

> I left the camp [in December 1941], received Canadian landing papers from an immigration officer and took the train to Montreal.

Uncle Menio had sent $500, but unfortunately the agency in Montreal which was entrusted with the arrangements used a good chunk of it to buy a first-class rail ticket to Vancouver and I was too dazed to object. It was too late to register for the university, so I got a job sweeping floors in a factory for twenty five cents an hour. I moved up to a machinist position in a foundry for twice the pay. I wrote Uncle Menio that I could take care of myself after that.

CAMP SCHOOL,
REFUGEE CAMP,
SHERBROOKE, P. QUE.

CERTIFICATE

This is to certify that Mr. HARRY GRUENBERG has enrolled with the Engineering Department of the Camp School on the 1st of July 1941 and has regularly attended lectures and tutorial classes up to this day on the following subjects:

Advanced Mathematics

Engineering Thermodynamics

Machine Design

Theory of Machines

Strength of Materials

Vector Analysis

Physics

Chemistry

Mr. Harry Gruenberg has proved his great interest by intensive work, and, in the last two months, he filled the place of a teacher in Strength of Materials showing great ability as for tutorial work.

For the Camp School Board

W Herrmann, B.A. Cambridge Certificate in Education. — W Loft Ph.D. — Emil Fackenheim, Rabbi

December 17th, 1941.

Diploma from the camp school in Sherbrooke, Quebec.

My father didn't seem bitter about those lost years. Punctuated by the occasional small laugh, the stories he told of his arrest, deportation, and long imprisonment became a detour from his otherwise uneventful life. I realized his narrations from my childhood, now captured on tape, were like packaged gifts I had never completely unwrapped.

My father came back from the kitchen. I adjusted the camera and turned it on.

"I talked my way into the third year of the engineering program at the University of British Columbia, based on a typed diploma and letters of recommendations from my professors at the camps. In 1943 my roommate, Mel Julson, invited me to my first Christmas dinner at the home of his fiancée, your mother's sister, Phyllis."

He ended that story with lines he often used.

"My fate was sealed. The rest is history!"

Correspondence

Dear Uri,

I have great news for you today. My permit for England has arrived. We will be in a large and beautiful farm in Kent. I have been told that there will be about 3000 chickens, also some horses, cows and sheep. We will also have our own truck so we can take the harvest to London. We will probably only stay a short time in England before we go on to Palestine.

How are things in Palestine? Write about it in detail ... Have you had mail from Kurtl? Please tell us where your Kibbutz is located, something about the surroundings, and the organization of the group. Is Cousin Erna near you? Perhaps you can visit her? Now I must finish because (1) there is no more room to write, (2) I spent a day chopping wood and taking it to the Stadtkibbutz and (3) I am a bit sleepy after observing the eclipse of the moon last night.

I hope to see you soon. Affectionate greetings and Chasak ve'amatz (strength and friendship).

Harry

My father translates a letter he wrote to Uri in 1939, right before his own departure for England. Like many letters, he asks about family dispersed after Germany annexed Austria. Kurtl is the Yiddish diminutive for his cousin, Kurt Helwing, the son of his mother's brother, Igo, who left for England on the Kindertransport right after Kristallnacht. Erna Aurbach was the daughter of his father's sister Anna, who lived in Germany. Erna left for Palestine in 1938 and joined the army, changing her name to Michal. Her parents and her sister, Henny, did not survive.

My grandfather Leo with my father and Uri, c. 1926.

SEVEN

I NEEDED TO STOP taping my father halfway through the afternoon. It was clear he was exhausted, and I realized it would take more than a weekend to get him to talk about the things he hadn't already written about, and even longer to get him to fill in all the holes in his old stories. No matter what I did that day, my father drifted back to one of the undetailed stories from his childhood, his time in Britain, or more often, his success after the war. When I tried to force him to give me more details about the Anschluss, Kristallnacht, or the months leading up to his departure for England in 1939, my father seemed to willfully ignore my questions. I noticed, then, that both in his notes and on tape, my father's family largely disappeared from his tales once the Germans marched into Vienna. From there on, he spun the yarn of a plucky hero making a solitary journey of luck and adventure.

Going through his writing in bed that evening, I realized my father also sidelined getting the news of his parents' deportation and probable death at the end of the war. For that matter, he didn't mention VE Day, the bombing of Hiroshima, or the emerging stories about the genocide. His writing was full of his new life: snow storms, friends, scholarships, his quest for U.S. citizenship, and his Fulbright.

"How's it going?" Martin asked, when he crawled in next to me. It was a warm night for spring, and we could hear the trees rustling through the screens.

"It's really slow. I can't get him to tell me much that's new."

"Do you think they want to come to visit my Dad tomorrow?" Marty had just had a procedure to try to straighten out his spine.

"Take Mom. I need to keep working with Dad."

Martin opened his novel and settled in.

I looked down at my father's writing. "Lydia's therapist thinks she needs to see a psychiatrist. She thinks she needs an antidepressant or maybe something for anxiety."

"She seems better to me," Martin said, looking at his book.

I reached over and put my hand over the page. "She's not. I made an appointment with someone at Children's. But it won't be for a few weeks."

"OK."

"So, we need to keep an eye on her."

Martin looked up. "OK. We will." He leaned over to kiss me on the cheek, closed my father's binder and put it on my nightstand. "I don't think this helps your mood, you know." He took my hand.

The next morning the sun shot through the east-facing windows. I rolled over; Martin's side of the bed was empty. A dove cooed. It felt like déjà vu, and my Uncle Uri was suddenly in my head.

When I was sixteen, my parents and I went to Nahariya, on the northern coast of Israel, for my cousin Neva's wedding. It was my third trip to Israel. On the day before the big event, morning sun shot between the slats of metal blinds into the cool bedroom. At exactly six, my Uncle Uri's plastic sandals slapped terrazzo tile on his way to the bathroom. I knew the routine, and wiggled out of my pajamas, plucked my micro-bikini off the floor, and tugged it on. Maya, a year younger than I, didn't stir in her cot. Her dark curls spread over her pillow. Neva, two years older, rolled over on hers. I pulled the coverlet over myself and dozed. Uri needed time to take his insulin and shave.

Doves cooed—the second knock. I pulled a T-shirt and a pair of Neville's cast-off running shorts over my suit and came out into the dark hallway. Uri wore a frayed but pressed dress shirt, buttoned to the top, over his swim trunks. He put his finger to his lips and led me

(Left to right) My cousin Neva, my Aunt Sahava, Neva's husband Moshe Glazer, and Uri, in Nahariya, 1973.

to the tiny kitchen. Breakfast was laid out on the narrow counter—a soft-boiled egg, instant coffee, a salad of tomatoes, radishes, onions, and cucumber, mixed with olive oil and lemon, salt and garlic.

I pulled up a stool and took a sip of bitter coffee, then doused it with sugar and milk. I liked that the "Nes" in "Nescafe" meant "miracle" in Hebrew and appreciated that my uncle would think to give me coffee for breakfast. Uri took the stool next to mine and pushed his glasses up his nose. He unfolded *Ha'aretz* and perused yesterday's news, blindly stabbing at his salad. His mustache twitched from side to side with each chew. His hair was already thinning and silver. Most people thought he was older than my father, who would keep his black curls well into his seventies.

When we finished breakfast, we stacked the dishes in the sink and left them for Aunt Sahava. "You never wash them well—don't bother," she always told us in her thick Polish accent. Uri picked up the beach bag he'd packed the night before and opened the door. He hit the timed switch in the hall to light the dim stairwell. We were blinded when we stepped out into the garden, where sun radiated off the concrete of the identical apartment building next door. We passed through the gate and one of the few wooden houses left in Nahariya. The rooster crowed, and his hens rushed after breadcrumbs scattered across the dust of the small yard. We crossed Herzl Street with its smell of eucalyptus, tar, and diesel exhaust, and passed into a quiet neighborhood of small apartment houses and villas. Bougainvillea wound along the walls of the Hotel Eden, where my parents were staying.

Uri conversed with me in the British English he learned under the occupation and kept fresh with novels and the BBC. It freed him up from the straightjacket of Modern Hebrew, with its limited verb tenses—past, present, and future. "And what kind of language has so many words for the spirit, but not one good word for 'subtlety'?" he asked me.

We passed the apartment Uri and Sahava had bought for Neva and her fiancé, using their inheritance from Uncle Menio combined with a substantial mortgage, a profligate act my father highly disapproved of, even though parents commonly bought their children homes in Israel.

"Explain again why your brothers didn't come with you for the wedding?" Uri asked me.

The answer that made sense when we left home, that the tickets were expensive, didn't make sense here, where family obligations were so strong. "They both had summer jobs," was the best I could come up with.

"I see," Uri said, even though he didn't.

The ruffled Mediterranean beckoned at the end of the road, but we passed through an archway, took a sharp right turn, and stopped at the high chain-link fence that surrounded Nahariya's town pool. The gate was secured with a chain and padlock. Inside, the lifeguard angled deck chairs toward the sun. His microscopic swimsuit made his muscular body immodest.

"*Boker tov!* Good morning! *Mar* Greenberg," the lifeguard said through the fence. My uncle was the administrator of the local hospital and was a bit of a celebrity in this northern Israeli town, whose predominant population was German and Austrian Jews washed ashore after the Holocaust. The lifeguard looked me over as if I might be edible, then turned back to his work, leaving the gate locked.

My uncle slung our beach bag over his shoulder and scrambled up the fence, using the padlock as a foothold. His skinny legs trembled as he almost impaled himself at the top. He dropped to the other side and arranged our towels on the chairs, unbuttoned his shirt, folded it, and took off his glasses. He stretched his arms overhead, then brought them down to his sides. Like my father, the same stoop, the same potbelly. He eased into the pool. My uncle once ran the mental hospital in Akko. Something he often said came to mind: "We're all a little *meshuga*, but not all of us have a certificate to prove it." Feeling a bit crazy myself, I climbed over the fence to join him.

After twenty minutes I hoisted myself out of the pool. Water dripped off me and steamed when it hit the concrete deck. Uri continued to cut through green water, his generous cheeks puffing out with each breath. His front teeth were enormous, and there was a gap between them that made him look like a slightly deranged chipmunk.

I clambered back over the locked gate and walked across the empty beach. The breakwater made a quiet bay and I swam out beyond it. I lay back and rolled in the waves, looking up at cloudless sky. It wouldn't rain all summer. After another ten minutes I swam back around the breakwater. Uri stood waiting for me on the beach. I reluctantly swam to shore and rinsed off at the outdoor shower.

"*Shalom, adonim*—goodbye, gentlemen," Uri said to the staff through the now-open gate of the pool. We walked back along the beach to the main street that ran along the dry drainage ditch of the Ga'aton River. Horse-drawn carriages loaded with fruits, vegetables, and milk clopped by.

"Tell me something about growing up in Vienna," I said.

"I don't remember much about it," Uri answered. After a few steps he added: "I suspect your father is a very boring lecturer. He could never tell a joke." I often asked Uri for details about Vienna and the family he left behind, but I sensed a wall around the subject. He never brought up his childhood himself, unless it was to regale me with some story about my father's excessive seriousness. He never mentioned a resemblance between his sister and me. I never heard him say her name out loud.

"*Guten Tag,* Herr Grünberg," the baker said over the counter. His wife pulled a loaf of fragrant rye off a pile, revealing a row of indigo digits on her forearm. The Arab fruit dealer next door sounded a guttural greeting to Uri and stared at me with green eyes. We picked through flawless oranges and grapefruit.

We wandered back along Herzl Street and into our building. Uri's neighbor, Gideon, swung open his door as we opened ours. "*Nu!*" his voice boomed out in Yiddish, "How is the future doctor?" A cone-shaped tumor the size of a golf ball rose from his forehead like a rhinoceros's horn; that tumor vanished by the end of the summer, leaving a circular scar. No one ever mentioned the tumor or its disappearance. It was as if that giant growth was just another member of the herd of elephants clumping through our lives in Nahariya. Like the rockets lobbed from Lebanon or the scores of missing relatives wiped out during the war, certain things were never brought up.

Gideon's wife clucked from the kitchen, "Close the door and stop bothering the neighbors."

The aroma of Sahava's cooking wrapped us in the fragrance of braised meat and mushrooms, chicken soup and *knedelach.* Three different cakes cooled on the dining table. I knew that after I sampled only two of the three at afternoon coffee hour, Sahava would say, "*Nu*, you don't like my cooking?"

Sahava sat in the living room with her coffee and sucked in the smoke from the Winstons we'd brought her from the duty-free. Her smile collapsed her face into wrinkles; her teeth were stained the color of cold tea.

Uri emptied the fruit into a bowl in front of her. He held out the loaf of rye.

"Mookie, Mookie, here is your bread."

"Bookie, Bookie—but where is the challah?" Sahava answered, "I said challah."

Uri turned to me in mock indignation: "Does your mother treat my brother this way?"

"*Betach*! Of course!" I answered with one of my few Hebrew words.

I leaned in to kiss Sahava. She put down the cigarette and reached up and held my face in her hands. I inhaled the smell of tobacco and thought of my mother, even though she had quit smoking years ago.

Sahava searched my face. "I can't understand why the boys think you are so pretty," she said.

I first went to Israel in 1966, during my father's Fulbright year. I spent several summers in Nahariya in my teens, went back again for six months after graduation from Williams College, and returned in my twenties for my first two years of medical school in Tel Aviv. Uri and Sahava's lives charmed me from the start: the early morning swim, the full dinner at noon, nap time, coffee hour, a light supper and evening television, then walking the town with Maya and Neva until late at night—deviations from routine were not well tolerated.

Aunt Sahava was descended from *vatikim,* the "old ones," Eastern European Jews who immigrated to Palestine at the end of the nineteenth and beginning of the twentieth centuries. "Your uncle was upset when I bought falafel from a street vendor on our first date," Sahava told me. "He couldn't get over that I would risk getting food poisoning. What a *Yekka*!" Yekka was Yiddish slang for a German Jew. The phrase implied fussiness and an excessive concern for rules and proper behavior.

Uri was a character, of course. He reveled in the local gossip. He sat on the balcony in an undershirt on Yom Kippur, reading the newspaper, waving at passersby dressed for synagogue. "Pray for me!" he would call out to them. When Sahava struggled to polish

Sahava and Uri on their wedding day, 1952.

her English with me, Uri would quip, "Your English is *Polish*ed enough!"

There were similarities to my father. They both had to restrain themselves from repacking your suitcase for you. They arrived at parties early, then stood outside until the precise moment they were due before they raised a hand to knock. But there were ways they were quite different. Uri was constantly seeing the irony of situations; my father often couldn't read that irony.

Used to home, where my mother always presented our disconnection from both sides of the family as a gift, the immediate intimacy of my Israeli family took some getting used to. And the term "family" applied to even the most remote cousins related only by marriage. They crowded me into their apartments and fed me four meals a day. Everyone spoke loudly and emphatically. Once I learned some Hebrew, I realized they weren't angry with me; it was just the way the language sounded. And they all assumed I was dead if I didn't call every few days to check in.

My relatives enjoyed sharing my little snafus with each other, like when I mixed up the salt with the sugar the one time Sahava let me bring her afternoon coffee. That was when I was in my teens, but my cousins still bring it up on the rare occasions we get together now.

Although they liked my mother, I think my Israeli family couldn't understand how my father could marry a Gentile after everything that happened. When I came back to start medical school in 1978, they predicted I would fall in love with a Sabra, convert to Judaism and make *Aliyah,* "go up," and immigrate to Israel. I well might have. But I fell in love with Martin on a visit home, and that ended that. I went home to finish medical school in Albany. I didn't return again until 1994, when Sahava was near death from emphysema.

"Sahava and I were in perfect health until the day I retired," Uri told me during my last visit with him in the late nineties, "She went downhill fast, and my legs started acting up." Nerve damage from diabetes forced Uri to walk with a cane. He couldn't manage in the apartment after Sahava died, even with his daughters' help, so he moved to the nursing home that replaced the old Hotel Eden. He sat alone in his sparsely furnished room most of the day.

I eyed the dining room on our way out for lunch in town. The staff was setting up equipment for a small band: a keyboard, drums, amplifiers, and mikes.

"Will we go to the concert later?" I asked.

"I prefer to read and not be bothered by all these old people," he answered.

Uri ignored the ramp to the sidewalk and the wheelchairs parked just outside the front door. He struggled down the stairway, his gait was like a marionette's, as if invisible strings jerked him up by the knees and elbows. It took us an hour to walk the six blocks to sit in his favorite café, the Penguin.

Uri pulled out a starched handkerchief and wiped his brow. We ordered our schnitzels from a harried waiter. The owner came out with our meals and fussed over Uri.

"Herr Grünberg, so good to see you again!" he said.

In the middle of our coffees, a handsome, white-haired gentleman stood up at a crowded table across the room. He strode over to us and shook Uri's hand. He looked me in the eye when he took mine.

"Is it your niece from America, Uri?" The accent was Viennese.

My uncle didn't answer.

"How is your father?" the man asked me.

"He's very well, thanks."

"Your uncle and I both live at the Hotel Eden. We grew up in the same neighborhood."

Uri looked out the window.

"Well, I guess I will get back to my dinner," the man said. "So good to see you both." He went back to join his friends.

"He seems like such a nice man, Uri. Why don't you talk to him?" I whispered.

Uri snorted and answered loudly. "This man asks me to look over his bank statements for him every month." He took a slurp of his coffee. "He's completely blind."

I pictured my uncle relaxing enough to work out an arrangement with the blind man. Uri would look through the blind man's bank statements and read from *Ha'aretz*. The Viennese would help Uri into a wheelchair, and then push him to the Penguin while Uri directed him. They would eat their schnitzels and have a coffee and Uri would describe all the pretty girls passing by.

It hit me full force, my uncle's pride and his inability to overcome his own isolating behavior. I kept my thoughts to myself.

Uri died in his sleep in 1999. Soon after, my father, my brothers, and I went back to Israel for the wedding of Neva's daughter, Galit. My mother stayed home.

"It's too hot there," she said.

The catered event was held in a giant hall near Akko. Most of my father's generation were gone. I wondered what Uri would have thought when Galit and her groom marched under the chuppa to the theme from *The Lion King*. I can only think he would have been proud.

A few days after the wedding, Neva and Maya took us to Nahariya's cemetery. Tombstones were packed together like apartment buildings crowding the beaches of Tel Aviv. Odd to think of Uri lying under bleaching sun, lulled to sleep by the murmurs of the orthodox rabbis he so disdained, and forever dreaming to the song of the Mediterranean beyond. I recalled walking the beach with my cousins when we were teenagers, our skin toasted brown and our hair glittered by the end of those long summers. Now the Nahariya beaches were strewn with garbage, and the water was so polluted you risked a rash just wading into it. We finally found Uri, wedged between Aunt Sahava on one side and a stranger on the other. It was tight quarters for my uncle, who disliked closeness with people he didn't love. Pebbles cast shadows on the other graves. I bent to pick up a stone and handed it to my father. His hand shook when he put it on Uri's empty marker.

He spoke. "Uri summed up his decision to leave the kibbutz by saying he sent his one good shirt to the laundry to be washed and ironed on Monday; on Tuesday someone else's wrinkled shirt would be folded at the end of his bed." My cousins and I laughed the way we always laughed when Uri said that line. Maya had a Helwing face, her blue eyes set deep above full cheeks. Neva's long face reminded me of Sahava's.

My father didn't laugh.

"He was only fifteen when he got to the kibbutz, Dad. He was all alone."

"Still—" My father seemed to stop himself. He had always spoken about Uri as if he were the spoiled younger son of doting parents, as if he hadn't suffered at all. On the tapes he had told me: "He left before Kristallnacht. Relatives were sent to Dachau; many were beaten up. We had no money, no food. But Uri wrote home asking for clothes and money and international postage stamps." But my father hadn't talked about what it was like to say goodbye to a brother he might never see again, or what they said to each other at the train station, when Uri left for Palestine.

"Do you remember saying goodbye to my father?" Maya asked.

He paused as if his mind were searching behind many closed doors to find an answer. "He nagged me to give him the heavy World War I army coat that Uncle Menio left me when he sailed for the free port of Shanghai. There would be no need for such a heavy coat in Palestine, but your father wanted it anyway."

"The boat trip will be cold and I will be all alone," I imagined Uri saying.

"We were on the platform together," my father said. "I think we shook hands."

"Were your parents and sister there?" I asked.

"Yes," my father looked down at Uri's grave. "Well, they must have been. I can't really remember."

I imagined Uri wearing his first pair of long pants and looking old compared to the other boys. One of the chaperones from the Jewish Community checked Uri off a list and gave him a label to hang around his neck with his name and his destinations: Trieste, Haifa, and Ha'shomer. As soon as the chaperone moved on, I imagined Uri pulling the label off, shoving it in his pocket, and pushing his glasses up his nose.

I'd just seen a documentary about Jewish children sent away on the Kindertransports. Children of all shapes and sizes jammed a train station. The little ones clung to their parents and let out a wail as they were pushed into the arms of strangers. They gripped their mother's clothes in their fists, and the chaperones pried them loose and dragged them to the train.

I imagined mothers screaming on the platform in Vienna. I imagined one father pushing past Uri and jumping onboard the train. A moment later he threw himself back on the platform with his son in his arms. He fell to his knees with the impact but managed to keep his son upright. The wife ran to them. She wiped the tears off her son's face and covered him with kisses. The father pulled himself to his feet and hugged them both. He tugged the label from around the child's neck and threw it to the ground.

I imagined Uri climbing onto the train with the older children. He hung out the window and was still complaining about the coat as his train groaned away from the station. Those standing on the platform would have kept their arms by their sides; they'd been warned not to wave goodbye. Jews weren't allowed to raise their arms in the *Sieg Heil,* and the Jewish Community didn't want anyone arrested for confusing a last farewell with the Nazi salute.

My father, standing next to Uri's grave, looked out to sea, "I threw the coat up and Uri caught it." I envisioned my seventeen-year-old father running alongside the train, tearing at the buttons of the coat as Uri accelerated.

"But my father didn't get the coat," Maya said. "He told us you kept it."

My father's face remained impassive. "That's not how I remember it," he said.

Perhaps my father was still dressed in the coat when he left the train station. Was he wearing it four months later when he left Vienna and when he crossed the English Channel? I wondered if it warded off the damp cold on the Zionist farm in England. Did he have it when he was arrested in the early summer of 1940, and finger its rough cloth as he was carried over the Irish Sea to the British internment camp on the Isle of Man? And did he pull it around himself when he looked up at the stars from the deck of the *Sobieski* at the end of that summer?

My father and Uri didn't write each other for years after the war ended, and only started up when Sahava and my mother insisted they should. They first saw each other again in 1963 across the crowded reception hall at Tel Aviv's Lod Airport. My mother told

My last visit with Uri, Nahariya, 1998.

me that she and my father had walked together out of customs, but then my father dropped his bags and cried out. He ran into the arms of a middle-aged man. They embraced fiercely and for a long time, and they made sounds that didn't seem human, but no tears came down their cheeks. My father and his brother were not alone that day.

Many embraced like lost children, now found.

My thoughts were interrupted by the sound of a car starting up in the driveway. From the window I could see Martin behind the wheel and my mother next to him. Martin honked the horn and Lydia came out, one arm in her coat and earbuds in. I waved, but she didn't look up. I pulled on sweat pants and a T-shirt and headed for the stairs. I felt weary, despite having slept through the night. In the empty kitchen, I poured myself a half cup of coffee out of the dregs at the bottom of the French press. In the living room, my father sat in front of the camera. I settled down across from him.

"Dad, I've been wondering. How come it took so long for you and Uri to get back together after the war?"

"Well, I couldn't travel for a while. Remember, I didn't get my US citizenship until the sixties. And we didn't really have the money."

"What about writing to each other?"

"Uri wasn't much of a correspondent."

I thought of all the letters I had received from my uncle over the years; he always answered mine immediately.

"Why did it take so long for you to start writing each other again?"

"I'm not sure it was all that long. I mean, we would have lost touch at some point."

But why? I wondered. There was no reason they couldn't have written each other directly once my father was released from the camps. Palestine was administered by the British until 1948. Uri was at the kibbutz until the late forties.

My father cleared his throat.

I'll ask him later—I thought to myself. If I push today, it's going to be about his sister. I sensed she was the emptiness at the center of this abandoned landscape.

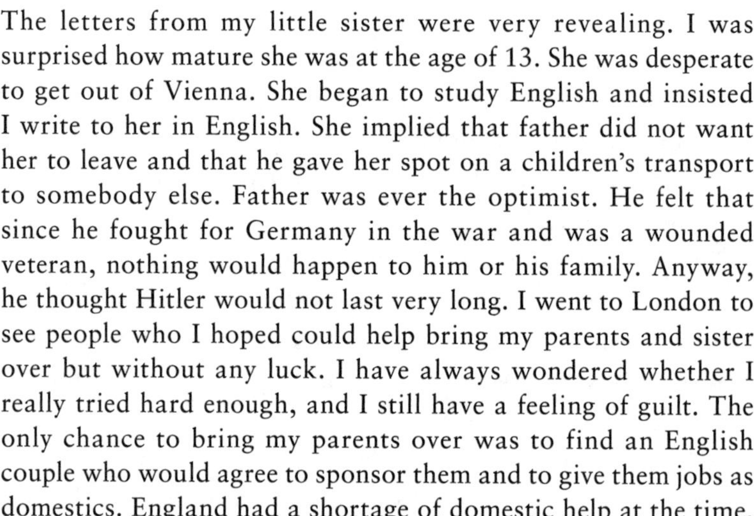

The letters from my little sister were very revealing. I was surprised how mature she was at the age of 13. She was desperate to get out of Vienna. She began to study English and insisted I write to her in English. She implied that father did not want her to leave and that he gave her spot on a children's transport to somebody else. Father was ever the optimist. He felt that since he fought for Germany in the war and was a wounded veteran, nothing would happen to him or his family. Anyway, he thought Hitler would not last very long. I went to London to see people who I hoped could help bring my parents and sister over but without any luck. I have always wondered whether I really tried hard enough, and I still have a feeling of guilt. The only chance to bring my parents over was to find an English couple who would agree to sponsor them and to give them jobs as domestics. England had a shortage of domestic help at the time.

From my father's "Notes on Harry Gruenberg."

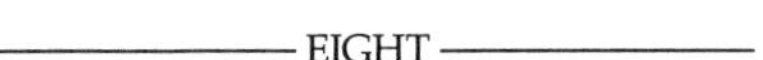

EIGHT

My father slipped back to the time before the war as soon as I started filming that morning. "When I was twelve, I read a book about astronomy and decided to build a telescope. I talked about it with my physics teacher, who was also the director of the Urania star observatory. I set to work, constructing it from an old water pipe, a broken mirror, and some Zeiss lenses I bought from Martin's father, my Uncle Rudy. It took me a long time to save the money for those lenses. I hoarded any coins that could be spared by my family. I used to take it out to Cousin Martin's house, to get away from the lights of the city. His family lived on the edge of the Vienna Woods. Their apartment was in an old hunting lodge that once belonged to the royal family, and they had a huge garden behind their building. We could see the rings around Saturn with that telescope!"

My mind wandered, but then I thought: Maybe it wouldn't hurt to let him cover happier territory for a while. He went through his childhood again, talking about a summer camp on the Danube that the city ran for poor children, his love of drawing and science, and the free art classes Vienna supported for a few years. Then he jumped to another story about his time on the David Eder Farm in England. I checked my watch. It was approaching noon. After my father finished up another old story about his time at the camp in New Brunswick, I said, "Let's talk about your sister."

Summer camp on the Danube. My father is in the back row (*third from left*). Uri is in the second row (*first from left*) and their cousin, Martin Grünberg, is in the front row (*first from left*).

My father winced. "I can't understand why my parents didn't send my sister out on the Kindertransport before things got really bad. But my father was forever the optimist."

That phrase was one I had heard over and over growing up. I wondered if "optimist" changed meaning for him when translating from German to English; he said it as if the word were tinged by foolishness—or something worse. "Tell me something about your sister. Maya would have been thirteen when you left Austria, right?"

I thought maybe he didn't hear me, but then he began to respond as he always did: "She had intense blue eyes. She was clever. She had a sense of humor." Another pause. "She was tall. Her hair had a reddish tint. She was a good student. She was lovely." My father coughed. "I think I need a break," he said.

I turned off the camera reluctantly. We threw together a couple of sandwiches and went out on the screened porch. Bees hummed in the giant rhododendron bushes that surrounded us on three sides and a lawnmower whined in the distance. We finished our lunch in silence.

As I got up and began clearing the dishes my father said, "I'm writing about all this stuff I've discovered since I finished the genealogy book."

Auskunft ohne Gewähr!

Der (Die) Gesuchte

Name: Elsa Grünberg

erscheint .... gemeldet

zuletzt 2. Ferdinandstraße 31 I/III/16 am 24. 5. 42 nach Minsk abgemeldet.

gel.

12. JAN. 1946

Wird vom Zentralmeldungsamt ausgefüllt.

Gebühr RM —·50 bezahlt.

Der Polizeipräsident in Wien
Zentralmeldungsamt
I. A.

The police record for Elka Grünberg obtained by my father's Uncle Rudy in 1946.

"Mom told me you were working on something. Can I see what you've written so far?"

"You saw the first pages of my memoir. The rest isn't ready yet."

"When will it be ready?" Both my father and Marty acted as if they still had all the time in the world. I was sometimes lulled into believing it was true.

He took a sip of water.

"Make sure you leave it someplace safe, Dad," I said.

He didn't answer.

"Have you had a chance to translate the letters from your family for me?"

"Some of them," he said. "And I wrote a synopsis of Simel Blaustein's letters to his son Willy, my mother's cousin. I can show you all those."

My father cleared his throat. "You know, the Austrians finally released the deportation lists from 1941 and '42."

I put the plates back on the table and sat down.

"My sister was listed on the same transport to Minsk with my parents, on May 27, 1942, not the one in April, as written in the habitation records that Uncle Rudy sent me after the war."

"I think maybe you told me that when you and Mom came back from Vienna this last time."

"I still don't understand how she ended up with my parents on that train. Your grandfather wrote me she was sent to Magdeburg the year before, so how did she end up back in Vienna?" My father took his napkin and wiped a mustard stain off the table. "And my Uncle Rudy thought they were all gassed at Auschwitz. But Minsk is nowhere near Auschwitz."

I was ashamed of what passed through my mind— what difference did any of this make now? Maybe his family was together at the end, maybe not. Maybe they died at Auschwitz, maybe not. I looked through the French doors at the video camera waiting for us in the living room, but then I looked inward. Why was I putting my father through all this if it really didn't matter to me? I felt the hint of a migraine lurking behind my left eye.

"That transport didn't even go to one of the camps," my father whispered, his eyes directed past my shoulder. "It turns out those passengers were dropped in a forest outside of Minsk. Then they were marched someplace and forced to dig a ditch."

I instinctively covered my ears and closed my eyes.

"The Germans didn't have enough bullets, so a few were shot in, some were pushed in, and the rest climbed in and lay down. The few who survived jumped in at the last moment and somehow dug themselves out later."

I have no recollection of what happened immediately after my father told me that. Did I try to comfort him, did I cry, or did I just clear the dishes?

Once we started recording again, my father went back to his question. "Your grandfather wrote that Lisa was taken to a camp in Magdeburg in 1941. So how could she have been on that deportation on May 27th, a year later?"

I didn't point out he'd substituted my name for his sister's. The tape ejected. I fumbled with a fresh one.

"*Mee-ya* was already a young lady when I left in 1939."

I felt a jolt like an electric current. "Dad, who is Mee-ya?"

My father looked surprised. "Mia—my sister, Mia."

"Dad, you've always pronounced it 'Maya.'"

"That's your cousin's name."

All these years, and my father had never said his sister's real name out loud. I put down the tape cartridge and went to his side, sat on the armrest, and put my arms around him. He recoiled the same way he did when I was a child.

"May 27," I said, standing up again. "That's Mom's birthday." I took my seat on the couch.

My father's face took on that distant look. "She was a lot like you at that age—in manner I mean. But she developed young. I worry about what might have happened to her."

"Dad, maybe you could tell me some story about Maya—Mia—as a child, something simple from when she was small. You never really tell me anything about her, other than she was a lot like me. How was she like me?"

My father's small smile evaporated. His lips moved, but nothing came out. He looked down. He looked up. His face froze. Our eyes blurred with tears.

"I simply can't remember," he said. "I can't remember anything about her."

(Left to right) Uri, Lotte Hofmann (a school friend), Mia, my father, 1938.

Correspondence

Dear Dad—

I love and admire you, but the you of you is largely cut out, your three dimensions cut to one. Left intact, you are the brilliant, shy hero of a sad saga. Plucked apart, you are a boy deprived of your essential self. Part of your mind fled and disappeared. (forever?)

Telling your story—the Anschluss, Kristallnacht, your aunt humiliated, your grandmother beaten, your family in cattle cars. Your feelings gone, buried, lost?

Tears start—a wall—don't go there. Rushing on to tell of the happy days in England, your success in university—

STOP.

Stop and tell me where you were and are.

Menio sent the money to your parents to leave and join them in Shanghai and then the U.S. They never did. You say Mia was given a place in a Kindertransport to go to England. You say your father gave her spot away.

Where is your rage, your despair?

You are guilty—but of what?

I love you, but where are you?

From my "Letters to Write but Never Send," a therapeutic exercise, 2004.

After I left in 1939, my parents were moved, first to a house on Boltzmannstrasse, and later to Ferdinandstrasse 31 in the Second District (Leopoldstadt). According to the Vienna police, my parents and my sister were taken to the concentration camp in Minsk on 27 May 1942. This conflicts with an earlier letter from my father, who said that Mia had been taken to Magdeburg, Germany.

From my father's "Notes for Leo and Elka Grünberg" written in 1994.

NINE

"It's like all my feelings have sharp edges. Everything hurts," I said into the cell phone.

"Are you alone up there?" David Treadway asked.

"Yes. I needed to get away after taping my dad. And Lydia isn't better. Marty is worse. Martin keeps telling me I shouldn't feel this way when we have it so good. Sometimes he looks at me as if he knows something is up, and he looks terrified."

I sat on a boulder and looked down at the soggy leaves that carpeted the woods below our fields on Diamond Ledge. Nineteenth-century graves erupted out of the long grass, the names on the stones worn to nothing.

"But you're ok?"

"I'm not suicidal, if that's what you mean. These thoughts keep popping into my head—like 'what would happen if I turned the car into oncoming traffic.' But I'm not going to do it. It just feels like there's a short circuit in my head, like my brain is feeding me images and thoughts. Maybe this time I'm really going crazy."

"You're overloaded, and I think there's nothing you can do about it except ride it out."

"It's like all these people are prying me open and disordering my thinking. I feel as though I've lost my edges, and my father's ghosts are rushing in."

"You should write that down, it's good." David was a writer.

"Give me a break."

"No, seriously—write it all down. It will help."

"You think? I'm trying. I'm still not sleeping, and ever since I taped my father I'm waking up with fragments that feel like memory. But it's not my memory. I'm compelled to write it down. But it isn't cathartic. It makes me feel worse." I looked up through the branches of a swamp maple. "I'm sad and scared all at the same time."

"Lisa, you keep thinking if you organize this or rectify that, that somehow you're going to find a formula for living life correctly, like the whole messy business is just going to fall into place."

"Years of therapy, and now you're telling me this?"

I thought I heard him suppress a chuckle. "In a way you are mourning your father, even though he's still alive. Maybe you are mourning his family in a way he wasn't able to. And you're thinking about these people whose civilized neighbors turned against them. Of course it's frightening. And then there's everything else—your father-in-law, your kids."

"So you think I'll get back to normal?"

"Who knows what normal is. I think you're strong, and for now you need to feel these feelings. And you know you can call me any time."

"I know."

"And you're ok?"

"I'm ok. I'll come in next week."

I closed the phone and looked down at my boots. The leaves by my feet faded as the sun went behind Sandwich Dome.

That night, I started awake, my heart knocking against my ribs. I fumbled for my glasses, threw back the bedclothes, and felt my way out to my desk. Sitting down, I flipped on the lamp. The house creaked as if someone were walking upstairs. I was used to this. Martin and I always joked about Diamond Ledge still being inhabited by the ghosts of the people who built it in 1928, a doctor from Concord, his wife and daughter, who summered here.

I looked out the window and my middle-aged reflection looked back. I picked up a framed photograph. My young father held me as a baby. Behind it was another he had given me after he returned from that last trip to Vienna. "Your cousins had this framed for me," he had told me. "It's a Passover celebration with our neighbors—the Harbands." He pointed out Mr. and Mrs. Harband, his parents, and Uri. "Mrs. Harband was brought up Catholic, but she kept a strict kosher household. Still, there was never animosity around religion at their Passover celebrations. Both sets of in-laws came, and Christian or Jewish, everyone just got along."

In the photograph my father couldn't have been more than thirteen. Uri, though younger, was taller. Mia, probably around age ten, circled her arm around another little girl. My father had peered at them. "That must be Paul Harband's younger sister, Susi," he said. He used to tell me about Susi. He had described her as adorable but also as a chatterbox and bit of a "pill," one of my mother's favorite terms.

Passover with the Harbands. My father and Uri are in the back row (*second and fifth from left*). Elka is standing on the far right. Mia is probably at the end of the table (*left*). Possibly Susi is next to her.

I put down the photograph and opened a drawer, looking for a pad of paper. I found a three-year-old *Boston Globe*, its edges torn. I pulled it onto my lap and took off my glasses. "12 suspects eyed in hijackings; grim search for victims goes on." Rescue workers snaked through rubble in a photograph that took up half of the page. "Fears rise of a body count in the tens of thousands," the caption read. I dropped the paper into recycling. I dug into the drawer again and found the *New York Times* wedding pages from the Sunday before 9/11. I must have saved that, too. I flipped through the pictures of smiling couples. Something fell into my lap—my wristwatch, its hands frozen at 8:54.

I'd ridden my bike to work on 9/11. I'd been running late, so I was pleasantly surprised to see the time when I left the locker room to head up to my office for my nine o'clock patient—8:54. After I came out of the exam room, the time on my watch was unchanged. The second plane had hit by the time it occurred to me the battery had gone dead. Few patients showed up the rest of the day, but the hospital wanted staff to stay on just in case there were other attacks. Martin went home to be with the girls. I finally reached my parents; the circuits had been busy all day. They both seemed oddly unperturbed.

"Are you alright?" I had asked my father.

"Sure. Why do you ask?"

I wondered if the TV images of people leaping out of the buildings might have somehow triggered the release of some of my father's suppressed memories. I put the watch on the desk to take back to Boston. I threw the rest of the newspapers into the recycling bin. I found the pad of paper, pulled off my glasses, and stared at the empty page.

"Failure sits at the center of love," I wrote with a dull pencil. I squinted at my blurred reflection and saw myself as a teenager.

I crossed out "failure." I scratched in "emptiness."

"Emptiness sits at the center of love." I tore the paper off the pad, crumpled it up, and threw it on top of the newspapers.

"I'm unravelling," I wrote. I crossed this out and started yet again.

"What happens to the souls of people who are there, and then, suddenly *not there?*" The planes careened into the towers and people counted the minutes until death. "What does it feel like to see your own end approaching, to see it so clearly that you call your family to say goodbye, then take the hand of a stranger and jump?"

I looked up at the photograph of the Seder at the Harbands' home. My father's young face in the back row, Mia smiling at one end of the table.

"My name is Mia." My voice surprised me; my pencil kept moving.

My name is Mia Grünberg. Born in Vienna on January 26, 1926, I will vanish soon after my fifteenth birthday. Daughter of Leo and Elka, beloved sister of Harry and Uriel, some think I was taken to a camp in Magdeburg, then on to Theresienstadt, where I was a prostitute, first for the Germans, and later, when I lost my bloom, for the *kapos.* Some say I survived the war as a nameless catatonic, records of my journey hidden behind the Iron Curtain. Perhaps you inhale me when you creep by the crematoria at Auschwitz or maybe the stealthy current of the Danube carried me away after I flew through the arches of the old Reich's Bridge. Perhaps, as your father feared, I followed our parents into a mass grave and was swallowed whole.

I have lived on, first as a tiny hole in Harry's heart, leaking blood into some nameless place. Walled up inside his chest, I am bursting to come out. I appear to him at odd times: standing next to you at family Christmas celebrations, wandering past David's bookshelves, peering out from Neville's watercolors, and watching from your mother's blue eyes.

I am buried under the weight of forgotten stories, but when Harry digs and sifts through the past, I catch a glimpse of moonlight and spill upward to fill his sleepless nights with sorrow. Memories sweep him along; he shrieks and wails in their telling. You gather his stories together, like a child picking up stones washed up in the wake of a flood.

Harry's Hebrew name is Henoch, after his grandfather; that means "Educated One." Uriel is from the Bible; it means "Light of God." His Hebrew name was Asher, "a Happy Blessing." My Hebrew name is Miriam, after Moses's sister, who kept her brother safe.

Mia.

There is power in a name that remains unspoken.

Harry had an English name and escaped to England. Uri had a Hebrew name and went to Palestine. I had a proper German name and stayed behind, *to be torn from earth, from memory.*

My reflection faded as the sky behind Red Hill began to glow. I put my glasses back on and pulled the newspapers out of recycling and put them back into the desk with the pad of paper. I placed the watch on top and closed the drawer.

Did my father really love me, or did I just inhabit a void Mia's loss cut into his heart? Maybe his love for me was really a love for things left behind—richer for that reason, but also less real. I tried to remember if he ever told me he loved me without my saying it first.

Growing up in Mia's place, did I steal her memory from him?

The velocity of light is probably the most fundamental physical constant. A knowledge of its exact value is of great importance because many other physical constants are derivable from or related to it.

From my father's doctoral thesis, California Institute of Technology, 1949.

My father's graduation from California Institute of Technology, 1949.

TEN

IN THE LATE FALL of 2004, fourteen-year-old Lydia carried her bag up the narrow stairway at Diamond Ledge without being asked; by the time I unloaded the groceries and turned up the heat she called me from the living room. She was dressed in her parka, carrying bright flannel blankets and a flashlight. She handed me one of Martin's old coats and smiled at me with newly-straightened teeth.

"We're going out to look at the stars," she said.

There was no moon and we couldn't see the lake below us. Lydia spread one blanket on the slope and we lay back together. We threw the rest around us and she slipped her arm under my shoulders and turned off the flashlight.

She'd had a rough summer and was started on antidepressants. At first, we thought she was getting better, but a few weeks in, over breakfast, she had told me, "I feel like I've been smoothed out on the outside, but underneath I'm having thoughts."

"What kind of thoughts?"

"Like out of control kinds of thoughts."

"I think you need to give it some time." I had reached over and smoothed her hair off her face.

A week later she sliced herself on the arm with a paper cutter.

"Why would you do that," I had asked.

"It made me feel better," she answered.

The psychiatrist couldn't fit her in right away. "What do we do now?" I asked her over the phone.

"Kids sometimes react to antidepressants this way. Take her off the medication for now. We'll have to get her in again soon. In the meantime, if she's suicidal you know the drill. Bring her to the emergency room."

But within a week Lydia was suddenly herself. It was as if a switch had been flipped, changing her world from black and white back to color. She even grew another inch.

"Maybe her thyroid meds finally kicked in," her psychiatrist said when we finally got in to see her. "It's so difficult to understand the wiring of the adolescent brain."

She started high school that September and within a month had dropped the tutor and the therapy. I was able to shift my focus to other things. I had been leaving her with Martin and visiting my father a little more regularly. My mother thought he was depressed but it was hard to tell. The Parkinson's had frozen his face further; he had trouble moving around the house and was having mysterious back pains that they thought might have something to do with stress fractures because of malnutrition in childhood. And just weeks earlier, my father-in-law Marty's femur had snapped. Radiation silenced his pain but left him bedridden. He accepted hospice. He could no longer tolerate alcohol and relished our visits. We each began to make our peace with him.

One day Heather had come down from Exeter for a visit. She still wasn't telling me much, but I sensed that whatever had been troubling her wasn't troubling her as much anymore. I felt a twinge of guilt for not being more connected with her, but it was a relief to see her just a little sunnier. We went to visit Marty, and he asked her to play her cello for him. In concert performances Heather wrapped herself around her instrument and seemed to go into a trance. But in Marty's sunny bedroom, she tuned for many minutes and finally played the most difficult passage of a piercing piece. She stopped every few notes to apologize and returned to the beginning again.

"Can you play something simple straight through?" I asked.

Heather looked at me with irritation but started a folk song. Just as the notes began to sing, she stopped and went back to the beginning again.

Marty shouted, "What if this is the last time I get to hear you play? I can't hear the mistakes, so just play it through, goddamn it. Every time you stop like that, it hurts. And it could be so beautiful."

So she did; and it was.

Back on Diamond Ledge, Lydia cradled me onto her chest. "What are you thinking about Mom?"

"I don't know. Everything that's been going on, I guess."

We both looked up at the stars.

"It's scary to think the universe is so big, and we are so small," Lydia said. "On the other hand, maybe it's kind of comforting to know that we are just two people on a small planet among many small planets." I had the uncanny sense that my daughter was now taking care of me.

The dark outlines of trees emerged around us. Stars glowed through their branches, lighting them up like they were strung with Christmas lights.

"There, a shooting star." Lydia pointed.

And then I saw one, but it was gone by the time I raised my hand. Why is it that all the stars don't race across the sky? The earth is spinning so fast, it seems like their movement should create one big blur above us.

I'm sure my father must have explained that to me once.

Correspondence

Vienna, 16 October.1938

Dear Uri Punzi!

Your letters are very interesting. I hope that I will soon get a certificate. Then I will also go to Palestine. Such a ship journey must be really classy!

I went to *sicha* [discussion group] My guide [*madricha*] is Irma Körper. Perhaps you know her? She is terribly nice. We sang, danced the Horah and played. Now I must ask you many questions. Does the kibbutz consist of one house or a number of houses? Are there gardens and fields? Approximately how many people are in the kibbutz? What are their ages? Where do you work? Did the immunization hurt? Do you have friends? What are their names? And now, finish!

Many, many *Bussi* [kisses] from your little Punzi.

Letter from Mia to Uri, one of the few letters my father translated. His additions are in brackets. "Big Punzi" and "Little Punzi" were their nicknames for each other. My father couldn't remember what the names meant.

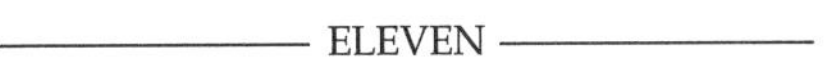

ELEVEN

"Perfect Child Syndrome." The bald psychiatrist sitting across the table said as he folded his hands atop a coffee-stained copy of my workshop submission.

The others smiled and nodded their heads.

"What?" I said. This was April of 2005, and I was attending a conference at Harvard Medical School for doctors who wanted to be writers.

"Perfect Child Syndrome," echoed the psychiatrist with horn-rimmed glasses. My group had a lot of psychiatrists. "The parent has a big loss and the child spends her life trying to replace something that's missing."

"It's a common root of depression among children of survivors." The bald psychiatrist said.

The young internist in the ruffled dress tapped the pages of my submission together, clipped it with a paper clip, and handed it back to me. "And your father has survivor's guilt," she said.

I'd hoped to get helpful feedback on my writing, but it seemed my father and I were going to receive a diagnosis instead. "My father never uses the word 'survivor' when he describes himself," I said. In my head I thought—it's not like he was taken in a cattle car or found starving outside the gates of Auschwitz, *Work will make you free.* "Anyway," I went on, "They've done studies to show that children of survivors are no more prone to depression than anyone else." My voice went up an octave. "In fact, they say children of survivors often have greater resilience."

I wasn't that depressed any more. Although I still wasn't dreaming, my insomnia was better. Even the anxiety had improved. Writing had become a compulsion in the months after my father finally said his sister's name out loud. I sometimes felt inspired, as if I were mystically channeling my father and Mia, yet mostly the writing left me despondent and drained. I had stopped after only a few months. But the winter after Lydia's remarkable recovery I started again. I bought some fancy notebooks, lined up pens, and sat down at my desk to write my family story, perhaps from Mia's point of view. I'd only taken one English class in college, and I'd never been a writer; my prose flattened as soon as it hit the page. I collected my nighttime scribbling from months earlier, typed it up, and sent it in to the MFA program at Lesley University in Cambridge. I was accepted and would start the program that summer.

The bald psychiatrist hesitated, as if he were thinking of an argument. "I've lectured about traumatic memory and PTSD," he finally said, looking around the table. "Where terror is involved, memory is no longer channeled through the frontal cortex to be packaged into a rational, chronological narrative. Rather, only the most vivid memories related to what the mind focused on for survival become etched on primitive brain structures." He pulled off his reading glasses and slipped them in his tweed jacket and looked at me. "That's why your father's traumatic memories can't be reconstructed to 'make sense.' Pushing for details will be fruitless, because no memory was actually ever recorded. Most victims replay those 'sound bites' over and over. Your father managed to submerge them for most of his life. That's how he survived." He added his comments to my pile. "And your father *is* a survivor. He has survivor's guilt."

As I walked out of the meeting those words rung in my head. My father survived. He felt guilty. But those two words, "survivor's guilt," cannot begin to convey the emotions I think he endured—those feelings do not have names in any language. He couldn't find words to describe his own suffering, so for a very long time, I think he set it aside. And small tragedies shrink in the shadow of big ones. Among "real survivors" who had lived through the camps, his misfortunes were hardly worth mentioning. And next to my father's losses, mine seemed completely unworthy of concern.

He had told me that others went to great lengths to find positions in Britain for family members left behind. Some of his friends on the farm went as far as knocking on the door of a Rothschild mansion in London, begging for sponsorship and an affidavit for a relative or friend. If my father had been bolder, would his family have lived?

A few weeks before the writing workshop, I had told my father that I was writing about his family. He didn't ask to read anything that I had written. I asked him, "Can I read what you have?"

"I'm trying to get it all down—then I'll show you." His expressionless face was unreadable to me.

I didn't tell him that I was reconstructing and reimagining Mia's story. Perhaps I was afraid I was telling a story that didn't "actually happen." But I think I also knew that if I probed too deeply, I might discover there was actually some basis for my father's guilt—that deep inside him was buried a memory of some terrible omission on his part. If I managed to unlock that knowledge, I wasn't sure either of us could bear it.

Leaving home was a shock, but I did not realize it until much later. In fact, I realized much later that the experience left me without feelings except anger for many years to come.

From my father's "Notes on Harry Gruenberg"

Auskunft ohne Gewähr!

Der (Die) Gesuchte

Name: Harry Grünberg

zuletzt 9., Alserstraße 12/2/3/22

erscheint 16.3.39 nach ~~gemeldet~~

England abgemeldet.

3.1.46

Z

Gebühr RM —·50 bezahlt.

Der Polizeipräsident in Wien

Zentralmeldungsamt

Wird vom Zentralmeldungsamt ausgefüllt.

Police record obtained by my father's uncle Rudy when he returned to Vienna in 1946, documenting my father's departure for England.

TWELVE

My father's death in August 2005 should not have been a surprise. Yet it was. He turned onto the main road on his way to the bank and didn't see the other automobile driving fast. The cars hit head on; both were totaled. Fortunately, the other driver wasn't injured, and my father climbed out of his car, only slightly dazed. After a short conversation, the police drove my father home. That evening, his neck was bothering him, so my mother took him to the emergency room. The doctors overlooked the small vein seeping blood into his brain. My parents drove home again, my father behind the wheel of my mother's car.

My parents sounded shaken over the phone. I would have gone to visit, but my father-in-law Marty was near death. He had lost interest in food and had to be reminded to eat. The hospice staff told us not to give him anything unless he asked for it, but we'd all had trouble following their orders.

Toward the end, Marty's speech was full of oddities, probably the result of small strokes or tumors that had metastasized to his brain. Between bites of "cowboy ice cream," his new name for rocky road, he told me, "You are a piece of a peaceful dream."

"About what?"

"A medicine dream—dreams are dreamish are dreams." Marty spread his fingers wide. He turned his head sideways so the ice cream wouldn't go down his windpipe.

"It seems the cancer is acing me," he said after he swallowed.

"Are you in pain today?"

"The pain is aimless." He looked me in the eye. "Fragile," he said.

"Fragile?"

"Handle with care."

I gave him another spoonful of ice cream. He turned toward the wall. "Dreams are just a waste of rhyme," he said. He died the next day with his four children around him.

A few days later, my mother called me from a hospital pay phone. "Your father woke up with this terrible headache. I told him to go lie down. When I went in to check on him he was breathing funny and I couldn't wake him up. I called an ambulance. They're going to operate."

Martin drove me out to Syracuse, trimming the normal driving time by almost an hour. We met my brothers and mother at the hospital. The surgeon came out to tell us there was no hope; a subdural bleed had pushed my father's brain aside. We made the decision to let him go, and he never woke up again.

My mother didn't cry those first weeks. She walked from room to room, entering each with purpose, but then forgot the reason she was there. "My days are full of footsteps leading nowhere," she told me. She washed the sheets and remade the bed. She laundered my father's clothes and put them away. She reined in her scrawling script and wrote a final note in his medical journal. She closed it up and wedged it at the back of the top shelf of his closet.

A few months later, when I took another trip out to Syracuse to check on her, we spent an afternoon going through my father's things. I found a worn manila envelope stuffed to the back of a drawer. I eased a stack of onionskin papers onto the desk. When I held each up to the light, I could see the mirror writing cramped onto the other side of each page. "*Lieber* Harry!" they all started.

"Dad never did finish translating his letters for me," I said.

My mother didn't answer. She pulled something off my father's bookshelf and sat on the bed.

"Do you remember when Dad bought me a last-minute ticket to come home for Christmas when I was in my second year of medical school?"

"I remember you came home."

"He called me at Uri's." We didn't talk on the phone much in those days; it was expensive. "He told me he'd been reading his sister's letters and that he missed me terribly. He'd changed his mind about the ticket being too costly. It was weird because I was feeling really homesick at the time. So, I flew home the next day. I arrived in Syracuse in the middle of a snowstorm and no one was there to meet me. I had a moment when I thought I might have dreamt his phone call, but then he turned up."

My mother didn't look up from the scrapbook she was going through. I leafed through the old letters. "I had no idea there were so many."

My mother glanced up for a moment. "There do seem to be a lot," she said.

I left the letters and picked up a nineteenth-century mathematics book and leafed through it.

"Dad got this off one of the carts from the Jewish Community. When rich Jews fled they donated their libraries, and kids loaded up carts and went out into the city to sell them, to raise money. Dad said he took a couple of books off the cart and took them home. I think he felt a little guilty about not selling them."

My mother didn't look up from a scrapbook she was going through.

I rifled through a file cabinet and found a wooden box whose sides were stenciled with flowers. It looked like something made in a high school carpentry shop. I lifted the lid. On top were his two embroidered yarmulkes. In a worn leather case with a broken clasp was a set of drawing pencils carved to sharp points, and a compass burnished black. Underneath was a childish clay bust of a woman. When I set her on the desk her head angled so she seemed to look up at me. Below that were five lenses wrapped in crumbling tissue paper. I unwrapped and lined them up, then held the largest up to the lamp. Time had clouded it.

"Mom, are these the lenses from the telescope Dad made as a boy?"

My mother looked up. "I couldn't say," she answered.

"May I take this stuff?"

"Take whatever you want."

"What's that you're looking at?"

"My mother's scrapbook," she answered.

"Why is Nan's book with Dad's stuff?"

Instead of an answer, my mother held out a few papers that had been folded into the scrapbook. Nan's even writing traced her genealogy back to thirteenth-century Scotland. I sat next to my mother and she leaned into me like one of my daughters. We pulled locks of baby hair out of wax paper packets taped to the first page of Nan's book. Phyllis's was dark; my mother's fair.

"Phyllis was always the better sister," my mother said. She carefully tucked the locks back into their envelopes and turned the page. Programs from my mother's piano recitals, news clippings of graduations, births, weddings, and deaths—everything was out of order, as if Nan had slapped the book together some dreary afternoon after she moved in with us in Syracuse in 1962.

Further on, a gaunt Aunt Phyllis sits on the edge of our couch, holding my two-year-old self on her lap.

"Phyllis came to Syracuse?"

"She and Mel came out for a visit without the children. She was very ill by then."

We turned a leaf and Phyllis looked out from her university graduation picture. Abundant hair surrounded her pale face; her lips parted in a half smile. Below were identical columns of newsprint, as if the person who put the book together had two and didn't want to waste one, or as if the news were so awful she needed both notices to wrap her mind around it. Each column began with Phyllis and Mel's wedding announcement. But the church wedding ran into Phyllis's death notice from 1957, when Phyllis had just turned forty-one. The

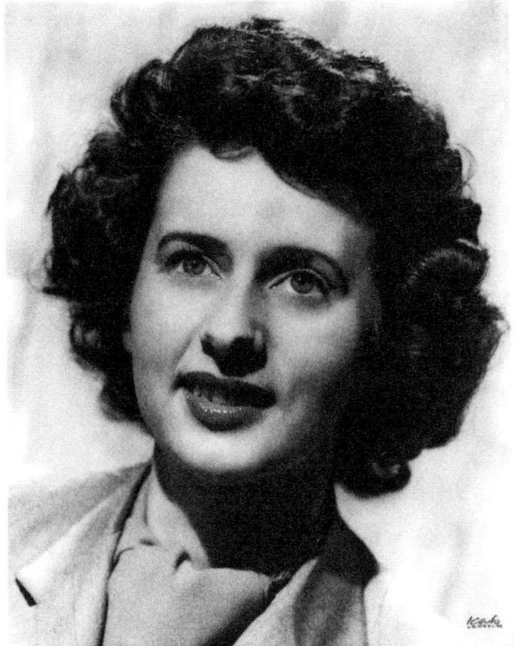

My mother's sister Phyllis, c. 1937.

word before "illness" was blocked out with blue ink. Was the word "brief" or "long?" The notice didn't mention the cause of death, metastatic breast cancer.

"Nan wouldn't sit in the main part of the church at Phyllis's funeral," my mother said. "She sat in an anteroom. She didn't want people to see her cry."

"You were there?" I asked.

"Yes."

"I never knew that."

"I flew out when the end seemed near. When I came home you were hiding under the kitchen table. I finally had to crawl under there to get you."

I tried to remember that scene but couldn't. "Did your father come to the funeral?"

"I saw him later, at the back of the church. He didn't sit with us." My mother's father abandoned Nan and his daughters a few times when my mother was growing up. After Phyllis died he moved back to England with a neighbor. He outlived Nan by almost a decade. Of course, I didn't know about any of that as a child.

My mother flipped through the last pages of the scrapbook. My parents' courthouse wedding announcement from 1946 floated like an island in the middle of its own page.

"My father was furious that I would marry a Jew. We had to have the reception at a neighbor's house. And Nan was so unhappy we didn't get married in the church after all the arrangements had been made. But after your father saw a neighbor's christening, he just couldn't go through with it."

"You always tell that story, Mom. But the war had ended, and Uncle Rudy wrote to Dad that he had traced Dad's parents and he thought they were gassed at Auschwitz, and thought his sister was gassed as well. Don't you think it's more likely that Dad didn't want to get married in a church after he'd just received that news?"

My mother looked out the window. "Yes, I suppose it might. Your father was pretty upset."

"So you remember how he reacted when he got the news?"

"Not exactly, no. I think he closed himself up in his room at the university." My mother turned the page. "But I also have a memory of finding him sobbing on his bed. Was that the same day? I don't know."

In the center of death notices for soldiers from World War II was an envelope labeled "Harry Gruenberg Family." On the back of each passport portrait of my grandparents, written in faded pencil, was their address in the Ninth District: 12 Alserstrasse. My father's dark eyes look out from Elka's face.

"It's interesting Nan had their photographs in here," I said.

"Nan adored your father," my mother said. I tried to remember if I knew that. Nan had been so reserved.

"Where is Dad's sister?" I asked.

Page from my grandmother's scrapbook with an envelope containing photographs of my father's parents, Leo and Elka Grünberg.

"I don't know."

"Did you put this scrapbook together, Mom?"

"I don't remember."

I took the scrapbook back from her. "I'll put this with your stuff." A loose paper slipped out of it onto the nylon rug. I picked it up.

August 12, 2001

A POEM

KADDISH

For my parents and my sister
On May 27, 1942 a train left Vienna
For the death camp in Minsk.
The cattle cars enshrined 1000 Jews.
My parents and my sister were among them.

The train rambled through the steppes of Poland
toward the blood bath in the forests of Minsk.
The cries went up to heaven
but men and God remained silent

I handed the paper to my mother. "Did you know Dad wrote poetry?" She read it through but didn't answer my question. Instead she said, "It doesn't make any sense. Maya wasn't with his parents at the end—and his parents were gassed at Auschwitz."

I didn't know what to say. Maybe my father had never told my mother that their train went to Minsk. Maybe he never corrected her pronunciation of Mia's name—or maybe she hadn't listened when he had. I didn't point out to her that May 27, 1942, was her twenty-first birthday, and after they were married, my father would be thinking of his family every year as he celebrated her special day. I put the poem with the letters.

My mother pulled a loose thread at the hem of her shirt. "Right before we were married, your father told me he was only marrying me so he could put what had happened behind him and move on with his life."

"That's horrible, Mom. Are you sure?"

"I'm sure. But when I asked him about it after David was born, he denied ever saying it. He denied ever thinking it." She stood up, went to the doorway, and then said some lines from *Winnie-the-Pooh*, changing her voice for each character the way she had done when she read bedtime stories to me.

In her deep Eeyore voice, she said: "There's no point in being boggy and sad."

In a voice like gravel, Pooh added: "It's time for a little something."

When I joined my mother in the kitchen, she was pouring sherry into cut-crystal glasses. She opened a box of crackers that David had made me buy so she would have something to offer friends who visited after the memorial lunch we'd arranged. She had saved the crackers in the pantry, the visitors had come, but when she had offered to feed them, they told her she shouldn't trouble herself. She took their word for it. So the crackers were fresh. But as she pulled the cheddar cheese out of the refrigerator, I noticed one side was crusted with mold.

"I'm sure it's just fine, just a little penicillin." She trimmed the green off with a dull knife and cut the cheese into pieces and arranged it in a circle on a china plate. She put the plate and the glasses on a tray and carried everything into the living room.

"Waste not, want not," she said, just like she used to say when serving us limp lettuce and stale bread when we were growing up.

Pictures of the grandchildren crowded the surfaces of the Danish Modern furniture my parents had purchased after my father's Fulbright year. I suspected the photographs rotated depending on who was visiting, so Heather and Lydia were prominent. I tried not to think about the fact that under each item that decorated that room—the twin African carved elephants, the pieces of majolica, the glass bowls—was a small piece of masking tape with "Neville" or "David" or "Lisa" written on it. I suppose it started innocently enough, when David said he wanted the elephants. Neville picked them up later, and, seeing the labels, went ahead and put his name on a few items, and my mother must have continued until everything was assigned.

"It's nice to be able to talk without all those interruptions, without all your Hangers-On," my mother said.

"My what?"

"Well, you know—" My mother took a sip of her sherry.

"I like to think of them as my loved ones, Mom."

"Well, if you're going to be sentimental—"

The sherry tasted like rubber. My mother put a piece of cheese on a cracker. She raised it to her lips, took a bite, and chewed it with her mouth tightly closed, just the way she had taught us when we were children. "What if you were invited for dinner with the Queen?" she used to say. In the sixties, she had changed it to, "What if you were invited for dinner with President and Mrs. Kennedy?" That line always made my brothers giggle hysterically; Neville would have milk dripping out of his nose. I watched her finish her mouthful and place the rest back on the plate. Maybe she was right. Maybe I was wasteful when I threw out the outdated food at home.

But as I reached for a piece of cheese she said, "I wouldn't eat that if I were you. It's a little off." Her eyes were filling up. I turned away. I thought of Nan saying, "stiff upper lip." My mother wouldn't want me to see her cry.

When my mother lay down for a nap, I drove the short distance to Green Lakes State Park. The center of the sky was washed blue, with gray clouds watercolored on the horizon. November light slanted onto barren trees. I started out along the man-made beach that crescented one end of the bigger lake. Bright leaves carpeted the raked shoreline.

The lakes are really just two large ponds set next to each other. There is no place on their periphery where you can't see the other side. They are distinguished by their startling shade of blue-green. I left the beach and passed under pines to circle the big lake. I walked in the same direction that my family took, beginning with the old-growth forest, which my mother called the Hundred Acre Wood, and ending at Dead Man's Point.

When I was eighteen and Neville was twenty, we had a conversation with my mother about funerals, and, in particular, her funeral. "It would be nice if people just got together and talked about me," she had said. "Then one of you could read the last chapter of *Winnie-the-Pooh.*" She wanted her ashes spread here, in her Hundred Acre Wood, like the place that Christopher Robin and Winnie-the-Pooh came to say their last goodbye.

Neville said, "Damn, that's where I'll be scattered, and I can't believe we'll be together in the same place for all eternity!" Was my father there for that discussion? He might have been, but I imagine our laughter startled him out of some reverie.

Along the path, trees leaned over the clear deep water, their roots exposed and straining, barely gripping the earth. Below the lake's surface, trees that had released the shore had flipped upside down, their roots branching up, the bottomless depths of the lake like a new sky.

"Green Lakes were carved out by glaciers as they withdrew at the end of the Ice Age," my father once told me. "The lakes are meromictic. The old trees and steep banks assure that the slightest breeze never breaks the water. The lakes are so deep and so still that the water on top never mixes with the water below. The lower level is denser because of chemistry and temperature. A layer of plankton is trapped between, giving the lakes their color."

When my father could still manage this walk he was bent forward and his feet barely cleared the ground. I slowed my gait to match his shortening stride and tried to place myself in a way to steady him, to catch him if he fell back or stumbled forward.

I sat on a worn park bench at the edge of the water. Far below me, I imagined ancient trees that had let go of the shore—preserved but forever lost from view. Someone told me when I was a child that the lakes were bottomless. I liked thinking about what that meant, the same way I was fascinated when my father tried to explain infinity.

"Think of the biggest number you can," he said. "Then, just add one." A leaf floated down through submerged branches and disappeared.

As had happened often during the last few months I suddenly realized my father was dead. Each time I remembered, I couldn't grasp that it was true. His quavering voice pierced me when I called home. He continued to tell me, in no uncertain terms, "Please leave a message after the beep." A heap of his shoes yawned outside my mother's bedroom, waiting to be taken to Goodwill. He ambushed my email inbox with posthumous messages—really from my mother, who couldn't figure out how to get her own account.

My father had arranged his own cremation. There was no urn, no funeral, no sitting shiva. The twelve-year-old son of the funeral home director delivered the "cremains" to my mother's door. They were in a plastic container, a little bigger than a shoebox. She signed the receipt and took them inside.

"I was surprised by how heavy he was," she told me over the phone.

Over the next week that small box must have weighed on my mother. When I called from Boston to check in on her before the memorial lunch, I asked, "Has Neville been by to visit?" My middle brother was hot and cold with my parents, so there were sometimes long pauses between visits, even though they lived fifteen minutes away from each other.

"No, he hasn't," my mother said. But after a pause, "Oh yes, he has. We went to Green Lakes and did it—you know—we took care of it, and then we went out for breakfast."

"Took care of what?" I was digging dirt out from under my nails.

"Well, Neville came over and we took care of your father—the ashes. He picked me up at six in the morning and we took your father to the Hundred Acre Wood." She said it was a lovely morning. Neville put my father off the path, far enough not to be visible, under one of the old trees where it is cool and dark, but where you could still see waves reflecting on the trunks.

"I kept watch," my mother rushed on. Maybe she knew I was crying at the end of the line. "It's probably illegal to spread ashes in a state park, or whatever it was Neville did. I'm sorry I didn't wait for you and David. Are you hurt? I couldn't bear having them in the house. Maybe I should have saved some for you, but once the box was opened I was afraid the ashes would get all over the place. And, how could I divide it up? With a spoon—plastic bags?"

My father was buried or scattered somewhere nearby. I hadn't thought about that when I walked across the beach, but when I came into the woods he was on my mind as soon as I saw those old trees. I pulled out my cell phone and looked up "Nev."

Neville didn't pick up, so I left a message. "Listen, I'm at Green Lakes. I want to see where you put the ashes. Call me back."

I knew he would call me back later, saying, "You called?" He wouldn't acknowledge listening to my message. So I would need to decide whether to ask again or let it go. But why should I care where the ashes were? What did it matter if they were scattered or buried?

My middle brother and I had grown apart in adulthood, but in my early memories, Neville's pale face is always close. He splashes tepid water during our weekly bath and grimaces at me over the metallic taste of cod liver oil. He is the small Zorro jumping around my room when I am stuck in bed with the mumps one Halloween. In family albums we bend over a book as he teaches me to read and we squint up at our father from the shallows of Lake Ontario.

In a later scene Neville and I huddle under faded bedspreads on a worn couch, watching *Sea Hunt* on the black and white television in the basement. Our father calls from the top of the stairs. "Turn it off! It's a beautiful day!"

"Okay!" we say.

We keep watching.

During a commercial, we pull our shirts up over our heads like wet suits and drag our socks halfway off for flippers. Neville checks our father's old watch, hanging from his skinny wrist. We slither into icy linoleum waters.

Once under the surface, our world turns from shades of gray to color. Sea plants roil with the current. Neville's eyes open wide as a toothy shark sidles out from behind the furnace. He pulls out a rubber dagger and signals for me to surface. I burst out of turquoise waters and leap onto a chair. The fin of the giant fish cuts nearby and heads back toward my father's workshop. My brother throws himself onto the stairway, runs to the top, and flips the lights off, leaving me stranded on my chair island in the dark. I hear him giggle as his footfalls pound overhead, and I imagine wet footprints across the kitchen floor and droplets of seawater on the dining room carpet falling from his hair as he runs.

I stood up from the park bench and bent to run a hand along the surface of the lake water, breaking up the reflection of the trees. I dried my hand on my jacket and went back to the path, which forked at the far end of the big lake. I decided not to add the walk around the smaller lake. It was a short circuit, but on my last visit I had been so lost in thought that I had missed the turn back. I ended up circling and circling, only realizing my error when the nature signs repeated themselves the third time. When I came home after that walk, my mother had said, "You're just like Phyllis. Always late; always trying to fit in one more thing; always coming home with some lame excuse." It had jarred me. My mother hardly ever mentioned Phyllis, and she certainly never compared me to her.

I stooped to pick up a stone and shot it out into the water. It skipped across the surface and then dropped.

Skip, skip, skip. I hold Harry's hand, his other hand holds the coalscuttle, my other hand touches the smooth railing above my head. Hop, hop, hop 'round and 'round to the very top of the worn stone stairs.

"Hold me up, Harry!" Harry picks me up and I lean over the banister, light from the courtyard blue on the floors.

There is Mutti in the doorway, her face warm—skip, skip,

The Grünberg family: *(left to right)* my father, Mia, Elka, Uri, c. 1931.

skip—Harry and I singing *The Blue Danube* at the top of our lungs. Harry feeds coal into the monstrous *Kachelofen* while I hang out the window, looking down on the rump of Josef's old horse that lives in the courtyard.

Paul and Susi come in from the street. Paul's dark forelocks stick out in front of his ears, his yarmulke sits at an angle off the top of tight curls. Susi's yellow hair catches the light. Their shadows are fat against the cobblestones. "Paul, Susi, *Gut yom tov*! We are off to Grandmother Sabine's for Rosh Hashanah!" Mutti gently pulls down the grimy window.

I skip back across the room, blowing a kiss to Papa sitting with his newspaper in the one good chair. I skip into my parent's bedroom to look out at the other courtyard. Pious Sarah naps on the bed. Her wig is folded on the nightstand. I skip back again. Uri leans against his hand at the kitchen table doing his homework. His spectacles are set askew. He lets out a little cough. "Fat Punzi!" I call to him, but he doesn't look up. Harry says Uri is lazy. He doesn't help Mutti with the chores.

Harry smiles at me. Mutti and Harry's dark eyes are like echoes. Papa and Uri have ice-blue eyes, like mine.

"Mia, go outside," Mutti says, "you are making me dizzy!"

Out in the hallway, Paul and Susi are just topping the last step. When Paul opens the door to his flat, you smell his mother's holiday cooking. Mutti says Frau Harband is more Jewish than the Jews! She is a *shiksa*, but of course you shouldn't say that word out loud. I think it means "worm" in Yiddish. Harry says it isn't a very nice thing to say.

I take Susi's hands and we spin in the hallway. We ricochet off the lavatory door, pulling away from the water tap. Susi's ringlets fly behind her. You hear the Melzers' Doberman barking inside their flat. Tiny growls when you get close to him, but really, he is just a big baby. If you bop him on the nose he runs for cover.

We fall against the fourth door and—bang!—we are laughing on the floor. The door opens and one of the sharp-faced Fräuleins scowls at us, then shuts the door again. "Juden," she mutters.

Susi and I freeze for a moment, then we start giggling again.

The two Fräuleins live with the fat priest. Once, when the door was left ajar, we saw their kitchen, filled with dirty dishes and food that looked days old. The smell was something awful. From the back room, the Fräuleins argued. Harry said they were speaking Italian. Sometimes you hear the most terrible shrieking and knocking from behind their door, but when you see them in the streets, the women walk together arm in arm, un-bruised and serene, *and the priest walks behind them, looking neither right nor left.*

As I reached Dead Man's Point, the ridge above the Hundred Acre Wood glowed orange and then faded. The moon rose and the water turned the dark green of a 7-Up bottle. I walked out onto the ledge, hugging myself against the cold. A branch floated just offshore and the inky water trapped behind it looked like it was breathing.

One summer day my father and I stood on this shelf of white rock and stared down at this underwater cliff made of the skeletons of microscopic lake life. If I ignored the crowded beach on the right and the rest of the shoreline on the left, I could imagine we were by the Aegean about to dive among bright fish and exotic plants. We peered down into water that was a blue-green so glorious I have never seen it since, and so clear the chalky rock gleamed as it disappeared into the depths.

"I want to jump in right here and see what's down there," I told my father. He laughed.

I felt the weight of his hand on my shoulder. Then, it was gone.

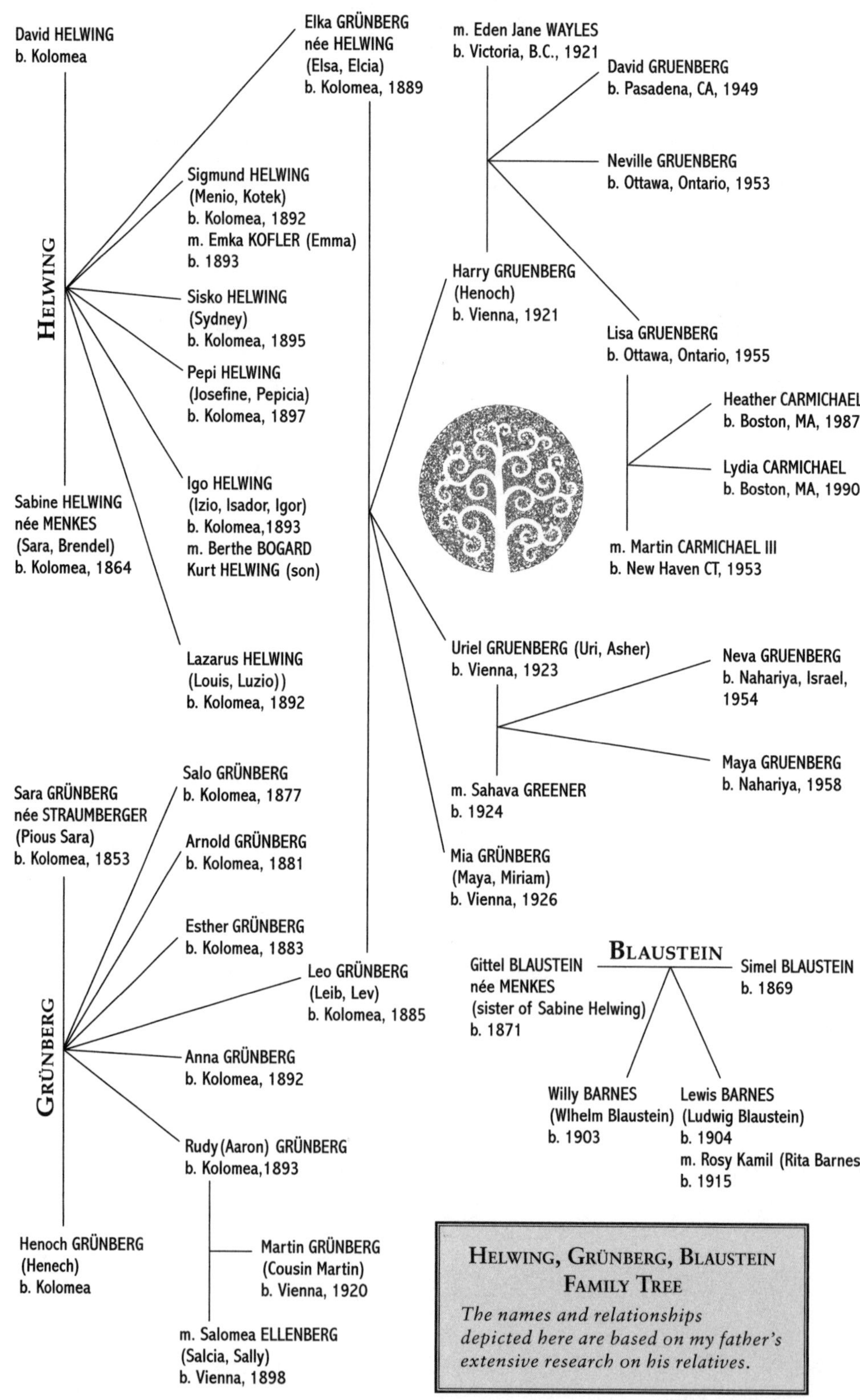
HELWING
David HELWING
b. Kolomea
Sabine HELWING
née MENKES
(Sara, Brendel)
b. Kolomea, 1864
Elka GRÜNBERG
née HELWING
(Elsa, Elcia)
b. Kolomea, 1889
Sigmund HELWING
(Menio, Kotek)
b. Kolomea, 1892
m. Emka KOFLER (Emma)
b. 1893
Sisko HELWING
(Sydney)
b. Kolomea, 1895
Pepi HELWING
(Josefine, Pepicia)
b. Kolomea, 1897
Igo HELWING
(Izio, Isador, Igor)
b. Kolomea,1893
m. Berthe BOGARD
Kurt HELWING (son)
Lazarus HELWING
(Louis, Luzio))
b. Kolomea, 1892
m. Eden Jane WAYLES
b. Victoria, B.C., 1921
Harry GRUENBERG
(Henoch)
b. Vienna, 1921
David GRUENBERG
b. Pasadena, CA, 1949
Neville GRUENBERG
b. Ottawa, Ontario, 1953
Lisa GRUENBERG
b. Ottawa, Ontario, 1955
Heather CARMICHAEL
b. Boston, MA, 1987
Lydia CARMICHAEL
b. Boston, MA, 1990
m. Martin CARMICHAEL III
b. New Haven CT, 1953
Uriel GRUENBERG (Uri, Asher)
b. Vienna, 1923
m. Sahava GREENER
b. 1924
Neva GRUENBERG
b. Nahariya, Israel,
1954
Maya GRUENBERG
b. Nahariya, 1958
Mia GRÜNBERG
(Maya, Miriam)
b. Vienna, 1926
GRÜNBERG
Sara GRÜNBERG
née STRAUMBERGER
(Pious Sara)
b. Kolomea, 1853
Henoch GRÜNBERG
(Henech)
b. Kolomea
Salo GRÜNBERG
b. Kolomea, 1877
Arnold GRÜNBERG
b. Kolomea, 1881
Esther GRÜNBERG
b. Kolomea, 1883
Leo GRÜNBERG
(Leib, Lev)
b. Kolomea, 1885
Anna GRÜNBERG
b. Kolomea, 1892
Rudy (Aaron) GRÜNBERG
b. Kolomea,1893
Martin GRÜNBERG
(Cousin Martin)
b. Vienna, 1920
m. Salomea ELLENBERG
(Salcia, Sally)
b. Vienna, 1898
BLAUSTEIN
Gittel BLAUSTEIN
née MENKES
(sister of Sabine Helwing)
b. 1871
Simel BLAUSTEIN
b. 1869
Willy BARNES
(Wlhelm Blaustein)
b. 1903
Lewis BARNES
(Ludwig Blaustein)
b. 1904
m. Rosy Kamil (Rita Barnes)
b. 1915

HELWING, GRÜNBERG, BLAUSTEIN FAMILY TREE

The names and relationships depicted here are based on my father's extensive research on his relatives.

PART II

Illumination

Correspondence

Vienna, 9 May.1939

Dear Harry!

I really liked your letter, my dear Harry! That's the way to do it—write eight whole pages! I guess that is acknowledgment for all my patience!

In your letter, you write that you have prepared a moral sermon for me, but you've forgotten to include it in your letter! If you have an American accent when you say, for example, "r," then so do I! Don't even dare to laugh. My English pronunciation is terrific!!!!!!!! Harry, I didn't know that you were so splendid. I'm really looking forward to the English book! When we are both in Palestine, I'll give you your six pence back. Is the dictionary English to German or German to English? I hope to get my certificate by mid-May. Once I get it, I'll be able to travel immediately.

Now I really don't know anything more to say! Therefore I'll only send you 'many kisses.'

Your Mia

Vienna, 21 June.1939

Dear Harry!

I'm really angry about all the mistakes that I made in my last letter. But I don't think that I was really in a good mood that day ...And now listen and be amazed: I'm learning English (private lessons, alone!). And my tutor says that my pronunciation is excellent. I'm using the book "How to speak correct English" for advanced adults. I bet that really surprises you, doesn't it? I emphasize—not colloquial English! Today in the Jewish newspaper, I read that the new schedule is out and that there are certificates for many young people and students. I hope I'm next ...

Lots and lots of kisses, Mia

Now all our hopes of bringing Kotek's [Menio's] relatives from Vienna and Shanghai, for whom we sent affidavits ... to the States were void. It was another terrific blow! We knew that brother Igo with Berthe were taken to a concentration camp in Poland. We even exchanged several letters and managed to send money to them every month. We hoped that the affidavits will redeem them! Sister Josephine [Pepi] passed away in Vienna. My mother-in-law [Sabine Helwing] was sent to an extermination camp, and the same happened to Elsa [Elka] and her husband. Mia was separated from the parents and placed in some labor-camp in Magdeburg, Germany, and we never succeeded in tracing her.

From my father's aunt Emka Helwing's unpublished memoir
My Neighbors and I.

My father's aunt and uncle, Berthe and Igo Helwing.

THIRTEEN

ON A VISIT to Syracuse the winter after my father's death, my mother went to bed after our second round of Scrabble. I'd won both games.

"I'm just not myself," she said.

When the line of light under her bedroom door went out I walked into my father's office, sat on his Eames knockoff, and unlocked his Mac—she had given me his password. I scrolled through his files to see if I could find anything new.

He had left me only the first part of his memoir. Perhaps he couldn't bear to put the painful chapters down, but I wondered if there might be something waiting for me in one of the out-dated floppy discs I couldn't open or in a place I hadn't thought to look. I was writing steadily now, and my writing mixed with mourning for this man I had loved but never fully understood.

I had located two family memoirs. One was sent to me by John Greenslate, the stepson of my father's cousin Cyril Grünberg. The other was in the archives at the University of Utah. Titled *My Neighbors and I*, it was written in the fifties by my father's Aunt Emka Helwing, my father's uncle Menio's wife. Emka lost her entire family in the Holocaust, was eventually institutionalized for severe depression and likely committed suicide in the early sixties.

I closed my father's files, clicked Safari and typed in his name as I had done many times before. I discovered a new listing. He'd

My father's Uncle Menio (or possibly Lazarus) Helwing is in the back row. Second row: *(left to right)* my father's Aunt Emka, my father's maternal grandmother Sabine Helwing, Elka, Mia. Front row: *(left to right)* my father's cousin Kurt Helwing, Igo and Berthe's son; my father, Uri. The handwriting is Aunt Emka's. Kotek was her nickname for her husband, my father's Uncle Menio.

helped fund the indexing of Kolomea's vital records, in memory of his parents, just a few months before he had died. I rolled back from my father's desk. The computer screen signaled it was after 1:00 a.m. It wasn't unusual in the year after his death to find myself following up leads and losing all sense of time. It wasn't insomnia or a sign of depression but more the thrill of the chase and the pleasure of discovering something new.

I turned the computer off and sat in the dark. It would be nice to get a run in before breakfast and I didn't want to be groggy in the morning. My visits had become less frequent and my mother complained if she felt I wasn't entirely present. I was still seeing patients in a free clinic and had taken up more hours teaching. Martin and I were spending more time together in New Hampshire. Even though Heather had started college that past September and Lydia was busy with friends, art, and music, I was finding it difficult to get out to Syracuse more than once every couple of months.

Guiltily, I turned on the desk lamp—just a little more, I thought, pulling open a lower desk draw. I found a heavy envelope postmarked the same week as my father's death stuffed into the front. Inside was a thick stash of birth and marriage records from the nineteenth century, all written in Polish. There were several Helwings and Grünbergs listed. I wondered if my mother put it there after my last visit.

I added the records to the papers I was taking home, mostly printouts of dozens of email exchanges between my father and people he'd connected with through services like JewishGen and Allgenerations, organizations that helped people looking for relatives lost during the war. For example:

> Dear Harry,
>
> My ancestors were very poor. My grandfather, who died in 1928, was in the horse and cattle business. I guess he was a Galitzianer horse thief. He worked as a peddler when he came to America, working on the Lower East Side. My father, thank God, became a success. Perhaps we can find some other things in common. I did discover that my father's name was Grünberg according to the immigration documents. Stay in touch.
>
> Joe

All the energy he put into researching these distant relatives puzzled me. Why hadn't he thrown that energy into tracing Mia? And if he wasn't completely convinced she had died with his parents, why didn't he search for her after the Berlin Wall came down? I got up to stretch, adding the printouts and records from the desk to the growing pile on the daybed that I would take home.

Going through closets and files, it had become clear that my father was the final repository for everything that had anything to do with our family. I found the original birth and marriage certificates for Cyril's father, Leo's eldest brother, Salo, along with Salo's 1938 death notice from Buchenwald, which doesn't list a cause of death, but states the time of his passing was "19 hours, 0 minutes." There was the army discharge of a relative by marriage, many medals from the First and Second World Wars, and boxes and boxes of unlabeled photographs that must have been forwarded to him as each surviving relative had died. Among these were several pictures of a distant cousin as a toddler, dressed, incongruously, as Kaiser Wilhelm II, complete with full helmet and sword.

Then there were several hundred photocopied letters in addition to the originals to my father. I had worked with a few translators up to this point, starting with the original letters to my father from his parents and Mia. The translators had to be interested enough

My grandfather Leo *(left)* with his older brothers Arnold and Salo.

to learn the names and nicknames of his very large family circle and had to imagine a two-way exchange from one-sided conversations. The letters were out of order, sometimes barely legible and written in a German that is no longer spoken. German was not the first language for anyone in my grandparent's generation, so they interspersed Yiddish, Polish, Hebrew, and words from the lost language that families use only with each other. Neighbors, friends, and go-betweens (relatives in England, Holland, and later, in New York) scribbled messages in the margins of the letters, adding to the confusion. Historical events were mentioned indirectly, if at all.

In addition, the letters were written in code to get by the censors. If someone was taken to a concentration camp, relatives wrote he was "on vacation" or "still on vacation." Others would say they were on "hachshara," the Hebrew term for a training program to become a farmer or a laborer in preparation for going on to Palestine. Still others used "sanatorium" as their code for the camps. One of my translators, an Austrian young man who worked at the United States Holocaust Memorial Museum, surmised that the references about "going to Uncle Samuel" meant the writer was speaking about traveling to "Uncle Sam," that is, the United States. But, in fact, the meaning was more ominous. That was code for being "sent east," as a branch of my father's family included a Samuel who lived in Lodz.

I had contacted one of my father's friends from graduate school at Caltech, who had recently moved into senior housing in another Boston suburb. He agreed to translate some of the letters. Werner Buchholtz was born in Berlin and was sent to high school in London with his younger brother. As we spoke about his experiences, I realized he was interned when he was barely sixteen. He was shipped over to Canada on the *Sobieski* with my father and followed him to the POW camps. Neither of them remembered they had been imprisoned together.

Werner described arriving in Quebec. He told me they were greeted in Trois-Rivières by soldiers with bayonets. Some of the Quebecois hurled anti-Semitic taunts and spit on them as they were herded toward the stadium. Their mail was limited and what came through was heavily censored. In his lightly accented voice, his internment, deportation and imprisonment were infused with a desperate quality that was absent from my father's narratives. Probably because of his age, he was released earlier and allowed to join relatives in the United States, but he was not reunited with his brother for many years. His parents did not survive.

In Werner's translations of the Vienna letters there were multiple references to "going to the dentist" and "paying the dentist." My grandparents were seeing the dentist very often. I wondered if they had been assaulted, as so many Jews had after the Anschluss. It was Martin who suggested that the "dentists" were Nazi bureaucrats, and this might be a reference to going through the hurdles necessary to obtain an exit visa, getting money "extracted" with each visit.

The letters to Uri began in November 1938, right after Kristallnacht. The letters to my father began in March 1939, when he arrived in England. The letters were dated weekly, and for a while they were numbered. For the most part, they were very repetitive, as if his family's lives held little variety, or as if there was a lot they couldn't write down in a letter. My Grandfather Leo wrote first, then my Grandmother Elka. Sometimes Mia added a short note at the end. Other times she wrote a longer letter in the middle. Her letters were full of underlines and exclamation points. She complained often that life was boring and that my father and Uri didn't write enough.

According to the letters, my father's neighbors, the Melzers, had two sons, not a son and a daughter, as my father wrote and remembered. Mr. Melzer was taken away to Dachau on Kristallnacht and later returned. Mrs. Melzer wrote several notes to my father in the margins of his family letters. She asks him to visit her older son, another Kurt, in England. Later letters suggest my father did visit him; it seems odd he didn't remember. Their younger son, Hans, was still in Vienna with his mother when the letters ended.

Although my father recalled Paul Harband was more Uri's friend, he was actually much closer to my father's age. Paul's father was taken away early on. The letters mention several times that he was "still traveling." Mrs. Harband and Paul sailed to San Francisco in 1939. Susi Harband adds a "hello" at the bottom of a letter to Uri, but she doesn't leave with Paul and her mother. What was her fate? Blond and blue eyed, was she left behind with a Christian relative? Was she sent back to Poland with Mrs. Harband's family? Could she still be alive?

The family letters stopped abruptly in January 1941. The Red Cross letters my father mentioned were nowhere to be found. The letter from Leo to my father, telling him about Mia being taken to Magdeburg, was missing. Did my father's memory fail him on this point, or did he hide the later letters, or destroy them?

I glimpsed inconsistencies in my father's stories, and wide gaps in my own memory and understanding. I knew certain things but couldn't remember how I knew them, and sometimes stories my father must have told me in his last years would pop into my head as if out of nowhere. I tried to realign my childhood experience of my father's narrative and the reality I was coming to understand, and struggled to stitch his few outbursts, his writing, the letters, my memories and his old stories into a coherent pattern of events.

And there were so many questions. Some of his father's family fled to the United States from Germany in the mid-thirties, but others were left behind, deported, and then driven back and forth over shifting borders until they vanished. His parents, Mia, Pepi, Sabine, Igo and Berthe, his uncles Lazarus and Sisko Helwing—all received money from Elka's brother, Menio, to travel to the free port of Shanghai. Lazarus and Sisko and his wife followed Menio in 1939. What kept the rest of them from fleeing? Menio then arranged visas to the United States and sent money for tickets. Why didn't they escape then? In her letters, Mia seemed anxious to leave and seemed to have had several opportunities to do so. Did those all fall through, or did my grandfather's hesitation doom her?

The digital clock made a click at 2:00 a.m. I put the papers and photographs in cardboard boxes, turned off the light, went upstairs to the guestroom and peeled off my contacts in front of the bathroom mirror. There were shadows under my eyes. I threw cold water on my face and put my glasses on. In the bedroom, I lay back and stared up at the pattern the light from a streetlamp made on the ceiling. I couldn't close my eyes.

I had replayed the first videos I made of my father after he died, but I couldn't get through them. He spoke too slowly, repeated himself too many times, and rambled endlessly about topics that didn't interest me, or facts I could get from history books. Of the few revelations that came out during that weekend of filming, many fell into the gaps when I was changing tapes or when we broke for a meal. I never went back to push him for more.

I regretted that I hadn't had the letters translated earlier so I could know what questions needed to be asked when he was still alive to answer them. And watching the tapes, I didn't just regret lost opportunity. I missed my father. Not the old man in front of me, but the young man I never knew, who smiled shyly at me from the photographs on my writing desk.

I turned onto my stomach.

My father's lighthearted tales were now cast in the shadow of imminent catastrophe, and even the sentimental stories from my own childhood were now imbued with a sense that things were off and could go way off. My past was merging with my father's and Mia's, but I was left with fragments floating in a landscape lit by a setting sun. I would need to pick up each piece and turn the dark side to the light, then set each down in a different place in order to illuminate what was left behind. I would need to bring back what was missing with my own voice.

I slept well for what was left of that night and woke to the sounds of my mother making breakfast. I threw on a shirt and jeans and went downstairs. She was just putting out the eggs.

"Sleep well?" She slipped my hair behind one ear. "It looks better up," she added.

I ignored the comment and answered the question. "Yes." I sat down as she added a piece of toast to my plate. I scraped off the burnt edges and buttered it.

"Why do you think Dad didn't take us to Vienna when we were living in Denmark?" I asked her.

"He wanted to go on his own."

"He went on his own?"

"Yes. I didn't want to go again. Remember, you and I had that nice trip to Norway. Neville was being such a pill we left him with a friend. Your father had a terrible row with his Uncle Rudy."

"About?"

"What else? Communism. Capitalism."

My mother sat down across from me. "I read part of your manuscript. It was at David's house."

"And?"

"It's very sad."

"Yes."

My mother took a mouthful of eggs. She wasn't eating much, and I'd noticed she'd lost weight since my last visit. "I'm wondering if you might change something."

I thought maybe she had taken offense at the part about her and Neville getting rid of my father's ashes.

"You mention I have a bald spot," she said. "It's really just a 'small thinning spot.' Would you change that?"

"Sure, Mom. No problem."

"And some of what you write about me—I don't know."

"I'm just writing the way I saw it, Mom."

"Still—" She took her plate and dumped the uneaten food down the disposal. She turned to me as she rinsed. "Take all that stuff of your father's with you," she said. "Or just get rid of it. It makes me sad to have it around the house."

At some time during those four years my teachers discovered my talent for sketching and drawing. They suggested to my parents that they enroll me in an art class run by the City of Vienna ... Occasionally we had visits by the famous Austrian painter, Oskar Kokoschka. I learned later that he had strong antifascist leanings, but his visits were strictly for teaching, encouragement and criticism.

My father writes about the city-run art school in the 1930s; Oskar Kokoschka was later deemed a degenerate by the Nazis and fled to Czechoslovakia and then to England.

My father, c. 1936.

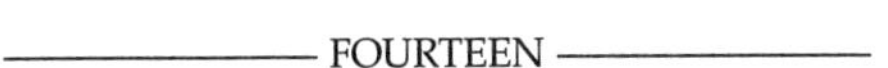

FOURTEEN

TOWARD THE END of Syracuse's long winters, impromptu games of kick-the-can, hide-and-seek, and kickball began on our street, stretching out into crisp evenings until the cold and then the mosquitos brought us in. Neighborhood children of all ages and sizes, innumerable Fitzgeralds and Francinis, my brothers and I, all played into the night, pausing frequently for arguments over rules and technicalities. We centered the games in the street, stopping for the rare car bringing a neighbor home. Most of us were scruffy; the arms of the Fitzgerald kids were always covered with mysterious scabs.

"You're out, Skinny Minnie!" Jimmy Francini yelled when I tried to run from the folded-up jacket of second base to the flat rock at third. This was a Friday night in July when I'd just turned six.

I sat down on a stump in the high grass of the Fitzgerald's property. The shingles of their old farm house were stained a color that was probably once green. Oversized lilacs in spring, mock orange in summer, the blooms of their haphazard bushes sent their fragrance out to us while we played. Crabgrass and dandelions screeched to a halt at the edge of our property, held back by the unnatural perfection of my father's lawn.

I wiped off some gravel that had imbedded in my knees. Every summer I turned brown and my protruding knees even browner. I wasn't growing. "Failure to Thrive," our pediatrician said to my parents in

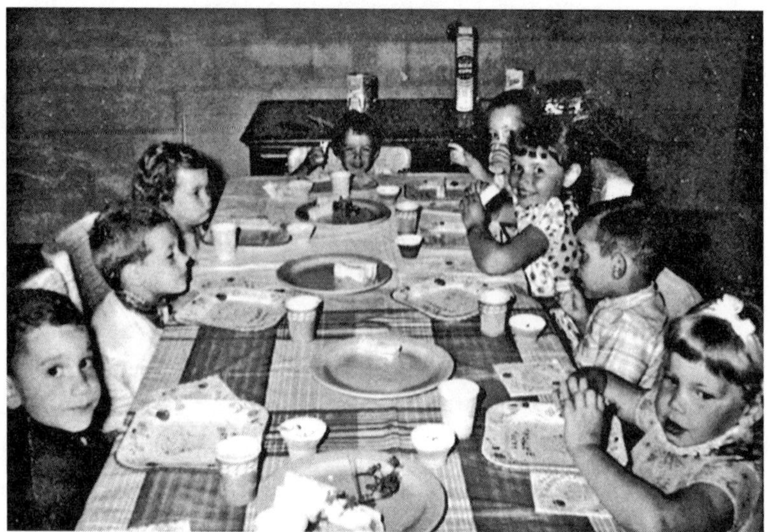

The street gang on my birthday, before I started growing.
I am at the end of the table.

his sing-songy accent whenever I stepped on the scale. Dr. Hartenstein was from my father's old neighborhood in Vienna and would sometimes speak German, even though my father only answered in English.

"You need to get her to eat," Dr. Hartenstein had told my mother, who would make me stay at the table long after my brothers had wolfed down their food. I would spend an hour or so rearranging the meat and vegetables on my plate, until my mother returned and threw them in the trash with a sigh.

"Children in Africa—"

"Is that where you grew up, Mom?"

I also had an "orthopedic problem," some defect in my hips. I wore a brace at night when I was very small, but my feet continued to twist inward. Dr. Hartenstein decided the antidote would be shoes with metal soles whose sides came up over my ankles. The big shoes embarrassed me; so did the endless teasing about being short, pigeon-toed, and scrawny.

Not everyone teased me. Barbara Wallace sat next to me on the stump. She was a year older, a head taller and always kind. An only child, she lived in the split-level a few doors down. That evening, above her pressed Peter Pan collar, her cheeks had a blush like a barely ripened peach. She bent over to pick up my shoes and helped me put them back on. I had taken them off so I could run faster during neighborhood games.

After the game my brothers and I ended up at the Fitzgeralds', as we often did on the weekends. A particular scent hit you as soon as you opened their door, a combination of fried food, mothballs, cigarette smoke, and old house, together with the stench of dog and cat urine from their constantly replenished supply of strays. Dishes piled in the sink and there were holes in the linoleum. Mrs. Fitzgerald sat at the kitchen table with her cigarette, a library book, and her bourbon; a tired smile greeted us whenever we passed through to make snacks or listen to rock 'n' roll on the radio.

We threw ourselves on the assortment of faded chairs and broken sofas arranged around the black-and-white television set in the living room. Many of us ended up on the threadbare rug. Mr. Fitzgerald watched with us from the recliner, a cigarette burning in one hand, a can of Bud in the other. Casey, one of the younger Fitzgeralds, whined about not being able to find a seat. Mr. Fitzgerald leaped from his chair, grabbed Casey, and wordlessly carried him outside. Through the window we watched him toss his son into one of the long series of plastic pools that appeared in their yard when the weather turned warm. A few minutes later they both came back. Mr. Fitzgerald sat back in his recliner. Casey, wrapped in a towel, squeezed in by his side. We watched TV and ate Jiffy Pop. I wandered home around nine and climbed under clean sheets with feet black from running.

Mutti chops potatoes and cabbage at one end of the kitchen table when the three of us come in from the street. Her dark hair is pulled back and she smiles, puts her knife down, and wipes her hands on her apron. Paul Harband sits at the other end of the table and looks up from his homework. His pale legs look like a stork's growing out from his short pants. Has he grown since we saw him just last week? His yarmulke is gone and his forelocks are shorn; his Papa decided it would be safer if he didn't stand out. Uri cuffs him on the head and picks up his school satchel and sits at the table. Harry goes to the desk in the bedroom we all started sharing after Pious Sarah died.

Papa, his hair like straw in the light streaming through our window, puts his newspaper to one side so I can climb into his lap, then picks it up again, and circles me with his arms. It isn't easy for me to fit anymore.

Susi opens the door. She's fresh from city art classes, wearing one of Paul's cast-off shirts with the sleeves rolled up. A blue-black smudge sits under her left eye. There is probably more paint on her than on her canvas. Even her blond curls have bits of green and blue flecked through them.

"I thought you were here," she says to Paul.

"Would you like some tea, darling?" Mutti asks. She stops her chopping and moves back to the stove. Her ankles are swollen below her calico skirt.

Susi slides into the last chair at the kitchen table, and Mutti makes up a cup of tea whitened with warmed milk and sweet with the last of the sugar. She puts her hand on Susi's shoulder and sets the tea in front of her. Susi lowers her lips to the rim, then tips the cup so the liquid pours into her mouth. She puts the cup down with a clang and the tiniest drop of tea slides onto the blue saucer.

"How was Herr Kokoschka, today?" Papa asks.

"*Gut,*" she answers.

"Did he bring his Alma Mahler doll with him today?"

"What nonsense is this?" Mutti asks.

"They say Frau Mahler cast him out, and that he had a life-size model made of her so she will always be at his side. They say he brings her along to the opera so he won't be lonely." We all laugh, imagining this scene.

I used to love playing with Susi, but now the year between nine and ten seems like an insurmountable gap. I slip out of Papa's lap and go into the bedroom and sit on Uri's unmade bed. Harry bends over a heavy volume and the light from the lamp he built in metal shop casts warm light over his papers. Homework is stacked to one side, with pictures of spheres and columns labeled with graceful numbers and letters. His paperweight sits on top. Shaped like a miniature Egyptian pyramid, the sides are tooled with vines and the surfaces shine from the polishing Harry gives it every day. The bust he carved when he was in the city art classes sits on the nightstand next to his neatly made bed. Her head angles up as if she is studying him.

It will take a few moments for Harry to notice me. Unlike Uri, who always seems aware of what is going on around him, Harry seems to inhabit some distant place. We are all smart; that's what everyone says. But Harry is something beyond that. He just sees the world differently.

Susi stands by Uri and watches him doing his lessons. Uri chews on the end of his pencil as he stares at a column of numbers. His schoolbooks sprawl around him. Peeping from under the table are papers that he crumbled and then flattened out again.

Susi comes to the door of the bedroom. The color rises to Harry's face but he doesn't look up. She edges closer. A small star of yellow paint stands out on her pink cheek.

"I have a new tooth, Harry, see?" She lifts up her lip and leans in to show him. Harry looks up with a sigh.

"Very interesting," he finally says. He stares at Susi for a moment, then looks back down at his work. He looks up again, as if one of the thoughts he was trying to tie down were floating off the page and is now about to disappear out the window.

"I'm really very busy," he says.

Susi ponders Harry. "Are you *aufgeklärt?*" she asks him.

The color rushes to Harry's cheeks again, leaving bright circles. He looks back to Susi.

"Are you enlightened?" she asks again. "Do you know where babies come from?"

He looks at her as if she were a giant bug, as if perhaps he should squash her before she continues. Through the door, Uri and Paul look up.

"The woman opens her legs." Susi moves her feet apart. "She opens her legs and the man," with this she spreads her arms wide, "the man takes a giant needle and puts it inside of her and squirts the baby in."

With that, Uri and Paul laugh so hard they almost fall off their chairs. Paul comes into the bedroom and takes Susi by the hand.

"Susi dear," he giggles. "*I think I hear mother calling.*"

Summer days stretched and receded. Neville propelled me down a sunny hallway at Percy Hughes for my first day of grade school. I gripped the lunch my father packed in one hand and a sharpened pencil in the other. Past the first-grade doorway wooden desks stood in formation. Neville shoved me inside and mumbled goodbye. I slithered into the chair next to Lucy Fitzgerald and admired the way her mother had set her long hair into sausage ringlets. I sported a pixie cut, a slightly longer version of my brother's crew-cuts, all created by my father's home barber set.

I traced the grooved initials on the wooden surface of my desk and rolled my fingers around the edges, sinking my nails into the soft give of old gum. I opened the lid and placed the lunch inside. The school bell made me jump. Towering over us in black stilettos, our unsmiling teacher commanded, "Everyone stand!"

We faced the limp flag next to the picture windows running along one side of the room. A regiment of maples filtered green light. Mrs. Bixby told us to place our hands on our hearts and we echoed the pledge. I stumbled over the words "indivisible" and "allegiance." It felt like an incantation from a new country, especially the words, "under God." We started our lessons with the alphabet. Relief

My father and David, c. 1954.

flooded me—school was just about displaying what you had already learned at home.

Midmorning a different bell clamored. Between a hoot and a siren, it went on and on.

"This is just a drill," Mrs. Bixby said. "When you hear this warning bell, you must duck and cover."

I thought about ducks quacking and smiled uncertainly.

"It's no laughing matter," said Mrs. Bixby. "If the Soviets drop the atom bomb, you better know what to do."

She slipped off her high heels, folded down on all fours, and crawled under the first desk. She rolled into a tight ball and covered her head. I moved around my desk to get a better look. Lucy sniffled.

The other kids dropped onto their hands and knees. I looked down on the striped dress Nan made me. The pocket held a nickel for milk. Frilly socks slumped around my ankles and my knees reminded me of unscrubbed potatoes; I searched them for eyes. My brand-new dress shoes, the Mary Janes I begged my mother to let me wear that morning, reflected a dull sheen.

I imitated the others and dropped to all fours and crawled under the desk and put my arms over my head. Lucy Fitzgerald's shoulders shook as she tried to suppress her sobs. I thought about one of my nightmares, a black-and-white recreation of World War II bombers flying overhead, dropping bombs like birds dropping turds onto drab Syracuse streets. The siren whined, and the camera panned down from the murky sky and my dream changed to color. I was standing next to our front door, now the turquoise of the Caribbean Sea.

The flowerbeds flowed in front of me with an entire season in full bloom, spring tulips next to Autumn sedum. I heard the grind of gears as a tank came into view. I froze into silence. Metallic green with the Nazi insignia, the tank continued down the street as if its occupants didn't realize I was human. But I knew it was there for me, and the tiny relief I felt as it passed was replaced by gut-wrenching terror as it stopped and the gun turned and pointed toward me.

When the lunch bell finally rang we climbed out from under our desks. Mrs. Bixby had us line up in pairs. Lucy's hand was sweaty.

The older part of the school housed the "handicapped" students, and we would have to walk through it to get to the cafeteria. I had seen the children unloaded from special buses to come into their own entry that morning. The flashes of light off their wheelchairs and their misshapen forms were bright in my mind. Some of the children were so tall that they looked like teachers from a distance. Unlike the neighborhood kids in the schools' new wing, some of the disabled kids had skin shades ranging from cinnamon to deep black.

David's friends at junior high did the "spaz" walk when he told them he went to Percy Hughes. They turned their legs in and moaned and stuttered; they held their arms pulled in and rigid and rolled their faces up to the sky. When David had complained about it at the

With David and Neville, c. 1960.

dinner table, my father said, “Those handicapped kids are people, just like you. You should say something when your friends make fun of those kids.”

“Right,” David said under his breath.

We followed Mrs. Bixby past the empty second- and third-grade classrooms. She turned to see if we were all still with her. Her lips moved as she added us up, her long second and third fingers extended as she counted up fourteen pairs of children. She plunged down the granite stairs into the catacomb of the original building. Our footsteps echoed back from high ceilings and then a sound like the tuning of a massive orchestra swelled. The darkness mixed with the astringent smell of chlorine as we passed the door to the therapeutic pool.

The pool smell receded and was replaced by something with a sweet tang, a smell I came to associate with the disabled kids, although I never identified its source. The tuning orchestra hummed louder as we entered the serving area of the cafeteria. Mrs. Bixby indicated the trays with a nod of her head. She pointed, "Hot lunch here," indicating a tall, metal counter, with a tray rail that stood at my eye level.

"Drinks there!" She pointed further on.

"Pay there!" She waved her arm toward the woman dressed in a pink waitress uniform sitting at the register. The woman's girth hiked her skirt onto thick thighs, exposing the top of support hose and the fasteners on her girdle. From under yellow hair constrained by a brown hairnet, her empty eyes looked through us.

"Then go through the door at the end." Mrs. Bixby pointed to the mouth of the dining room roaring beyond.

She made an abrupt about-face. Her tartan skirt twirled away from her legs. Her heels clicked down the hall.

Lucy let go of my hand and moved with the other kids to buy a drink and potato chips. I stood rooted to the floor as the others were swallowed, one by one, into the room beyond.

A tall boy wearing sunglasses remained next to the high counter. His skin was a delicate pink and looked like it was dusted with sugar, like the Turkish delight my father was always sampling at candy stores, searching for the tastes of his childhood. My father would spit the candy out, "*Ach*, nothing like from home." The boy wore black pants, a black button-down shirt with long sleeves—black belt, black shoes, black sunglasses. All that black contrasted with the pale pink of his skin and his snowy, kinky hair.

I uprooted my feet and walked toward the drink section, keeping my eye on the boy. The cafeteria worker slammed a plate onto the high counter and the boy picked it up and raised it to his nose, then lowered it onto his tray. As he slid toward the end of the counter, yellow-brown lava poured out of a mountain of mashed potatoes and spilled into the terrain of the puck-shaped fried meat and the gray-green beans. The boy reached down into the cooler. As he angled in, I saw the pink iris of his eye rolling in and out of view under albino eyelashes. I jumped when he asked, "chocolate or regular?" holding two cartons of milk out to me.

I grabbed the chocolate out of his dusty hand and threw my nickel into the air over the lady in pink, who shot her arm up and caught it. I dashed through the wall of noise into the high-ceilinged dining hall.

Lucy sat at a table in the center of the room. Barbara Wallace, a second grader now, carved dimples in her face when she smiled up at me. "Those are Negroes," she explained when I sat and looked across the room. She shook a few Fritos into my hand. "My mother says you have to be really careful about washing your hands when you're around these kids." I had no idea how far it was to the restrooms and wasn't about to go back into the hallway alone.

I wrestled with the carton of chocolate milk until Barbara showed me how to punch the straw into the perforated hole on one side. Crisp, store-bought paper bags and lunch boxes scattered across the table. I looked down at my plastic bag labeled "pumpernickel." My father must have pulled it from the stack my mother kept in the drawer by the sink.

"Bring the bag home, we can reuse it," my mother instructed me before I left that morning.

I lay my lunch out on the table. My sandwich was wrapped in waxed paper, pleated together at the top. When I opened it, a scrap of paper flittered up and onto the floor. I lifted the hunk of brown bread to see a thick layer of crunchy peanut butter topped with orange marmalade, and—what was this?—two circles of dill pickle wept into the jam.

I felt myself levitating out of my chair and up to the ceiling. From my perch in the rafters, I saw my bent head, my sandwich laid open, my apple with a brown bruise. Next to that, the pink paper napkin and the wadded-up plastic bag that my mother would complain about my not bringing home. My father's note lay on the floor, unread.

My friends plowed through Oreo cookies, potato chips, and bologna with mayonnaise on white bread. Barbara's shining hair plaited into neat braids, Lucy's ringlets unraveled. At another table, Neville wadded spitballs into paper straws and blew them across the table. The boy in black ate alone. The disabled kids clustered beyond. Thuds, grunts, and moans floated up and bounced off the ceiling around me.

The gothic windows swung open. I flew out, soared over the baseball diamond and down Comstock Avenue, lined with towering Dutch elms. I swooped over the Fitzgeralds' yard and into the Rose of Sharon outside our kitchen window. Inside, my parents were holding hands in the quiet of their empty house.

Correspondence

Vienna, 23 April.1939

Dear Harry!

You have already written us two extremely brief letters. Who do you think you are? You have to write at least four pages. Got it?!!! Could you please describe exactly how the farm looks, how you live, eat, and work, what a typical day is like for you?

Otherwise there's nothing more to write about. I hope to be able to go to *ha'Aretz* [Hebrew for "the country," i.e. Palestine] in May. Next time please write more in English and then I'll answer you back with more English!

With a kiss,
Mia

My uncle Rudy worked for Globus Verlag, a publishing house in Vienna. As I found out later, he became an ardent communist after his war experiences (WWI) and may have worked for the Soviet Union. After the Austrian republic was abolished by the Dollfuss government in 1934, he and his family left Austria for Moscow. I recall that my father had to dispose of Rudy's extensive library, including the writings of Lenin. We burned them in our "Kachelofen" in the living room. Apparently, my father felt that it was not safe to keep this "subversive literature" in the reactionary political climate in Austria. For a short while Martin and I corresponded using a secret code we had worked out ahead of time, but then the letters stopped.

From my father's "Notes on Aaron (Rudy) Grünberg"

My father's paternal uncles Rudy, Salo, and Arnold, World War I.

FIFTEEN

"WHAT IS THAT STAR below the moon?" I asked my mother as we walked up to her front door after dinner out, the spring after my father died.

"That's not a star. That's Jupiter," she answered.

"How do you know?" I asked.

"Your father told me." She looked pleased with herself. "Of course, he also told me it's orange, but I could never see that."

"You know, for a long time I thought that being a genius was Dad's job."

My mother laughed. She'd started eating again and her thinking seemed clearer. She was beating me at Scrabble again.

"I asked him: what is it you actually do at work? He told me he spent a lot of time thinking."

"Math and science were your father's natural languages," she said.

That was true. In childhood, when I questioned him again about the stars and the planets, he yanked the living room drapes closed and grabbed the shade off a lamp. He held up apples and oranges to the bare bulb, explaining how the sun cast shadows on the earth and moon, and to show how the moon could eclipse the sun. When I asked him about a math problem, his rapidly executed equations seemed to quiver on the embossed surfaces of our pink paper dinner napkins. Ellipses signaled hidden energy whenever they crossed the x and y-axis.

I wished I'd saved his disposable explanations. Strung together they might have fashioned a guidebook to the world.

Aunt Salomea has dark hair and luminous eyes. Her cakes are a marvel, packed with marzipan and cherries gathered from the trees of her walled garden. Cousin Martin, Harry and I help ourselves to seconds, heaping our plates with heavy cream—*Schlag,* Harry calls it.

He lingers over that word.

Uncle Rudy reaches for another piece.

Salomea slaps his hand. "Enough, Aron!" she says, using Rudy's formal name.

"Does your mother treat my brother this way?" he asks me.

"*Natürlich,*" I answer.

Rudy, "Red" in Polish, is named for his politics as well as his flaming hair. He is not just a socialist, but a real communist. They say he picked it up in a Russian hospital during the Great War, when his leg had to be amputated after shrapnel tore through an artery.

Rudy gets up to light his pipe and tosses the matches on the mantel. He rolls when he walks, smoke billows, and his wooden leg punctuates his movements with a hollow sound. "Harry, you are like your father—always dreaming! Why can't you and Leo see the world the way it really is?"

Harry keeps silent—like Papa does whenever his youngest brother criticizes him for thoughts he hasn't even thought.

After dessert we move to clear the dishes, but Salomea shoos us off. "Martin, take the others outside with Harry's telescope!"

The scope is by the back door, wrapped in an old blanket. Harry gathers it up and Martin's ginger hair briefly lights up under the outside lamp before Harry shuts it off. In the moonlight, a cigarette glows in Martin's hand.

"You're smoking?" Harry asks.

"Papa gave me a pack for my thirteenth birthday—instead of a bar mitzvah. Want to try?"

Martin with his mother Salomea Grünberg.

Harry glances back toward me. "No thanks."

He balances the telescope on the back of a bench at the center of the garden, and he points upward. "These are the constellations—Orion, the Twins, Cassiopeia. The stars shift during the seasons—see? The Big Dipper hangs over the horizon now, but later, it will sit in the middle of the sky."

Harry angles the telescope skyward and bends down to the eyepiece.

I hop on one foot and then the other. "Let me look, let me look!"

"Wow," Harry says, "I can see the rings around Saturn!"

Harry lines up the telescope for me.

"Look," he says.

I squint up one eye and look through the lens. Cosmic dust surrounds the bright light of the planet.

"I see it, I see it!" I laugh.

Martin's big hand pushes us aside. "My turn," he says. He points the telescope down to look into the house. "I can see my mother, upside down, clearing the dishes from the table." He turns the telescope toward the woods. "Perhaps we could set this up on the wall, and *see Gertrude Grüner undress in her house in the Seventh District?*"

Stamps, coins, crystals, and a snare drum—the detritus of abandoned enthusiasms littered Neville's bedroom when we were children. In the ledger my father kept in his desk drawer, red ink tracked my brother's mounting debts.

"All this stuff—he doesn't see his allowance as a privilege," my father complained.

When he was eleven and I was nine, my brother began struggling with his studies. One night, after the evening news, he and my father went back to the kitchen table. From the living room, I heard my father going over and over a math problem, at first patiently but then with growing exasperation. Neville seemed tone deaf to his explanations.

"I talk and I talk and you just don't listen," I heard my father say when I came in for a glass water. He never spoke to me that way.

Sometime after that session, Neville decided he wanted to pursue astronomy. He filled a scrapbook with pictures of the galaxy and the solar system. He left a map of the moon on our father's desk and our mother found notes to Santa next to the kitchen sink, chattily discussing the merits of telescopes. Christmas came and went, but the telescope did not appear. Neville held off on buying *Mad* magazine and board games and saved ten dollars doing odd jobs around the neighborhood. His ledger balance inched upward. By the time April arrived and his twelfth birthday was on the horizon, his account passed zero and our father's resistance began to crumble.

"Maybe it will get him moving on his studies," he said to my mother.

Neville pored over technical catalogues. He and my father haggled over the percentage each was willing to pay. Eventually they settled; my father would pay half, and he extended a loan to Neville to be paid back directly from his allowance over the next year.

When his birthday arrived, Neville blew out the candles and ripped the paper off the giant box. He pulled off the lid and peered inside at tubes and packages of lenses and plastic pieces.

"Where is it?" he asked, rummaging through the packing paper at the bottom of the box.

"I saved the assembly to do together," my father said as he gathered up the pieces. "Let's go down to my workshop." He said it casually, as if the invitation were nothing unusual.

In the years after we moved to Syracuse from Ottawa, where Neville and I were born, my father had spent his weekends finishing the basement of our brand-new house, framing the walls, dropping the ceilings and hiding the wiring behind. He had built shelves and cabinets, an alcove for Nan's sewing desk, plumbed an extra bathroom, and designed his office and a bedroom. My father always worked alone. He never asked my brothers for help. His workshop, a windowless space in the center of the basement, became his inner sanctum. Every kind of tool was arrayed on the wall behind a plywood counter. Screws and nails filled the plastic drawers of the cabinets he took over when Neville gave up his rock collection. I never went into the workshop. I was convinced that the demons populating my vivid nightmares lived on the shelves underneath the counter during the day and crept out to torment me at night.

"Well, come on," my father said.

"Really?" The tip of Neville's nose turned pink, just like Piglet's in *Winnie-the-Pooh*.

My father hefted the box on his shoulder and Neville followed him down the stairs.

My mother, David, and I went into the living room to watch *Walt Disney*. David was in high school by then and even with last summer's tan long-faded, he still looked dark.

"There's a touch of the tar brush in that one!" According to my mother, that's what the delivery nurse said as she swaddled my oldest brother and handed the screaming infant to my father. As a child I had no idea what that meant. David was the baby who stormed all night, the restless toddler and the neighborhood bully. But all that was over by the time he was six and I was born. Learning to read changed him. David opened a book, inhaled fresh ink, and was calmed. In my earliest memories, he is a distant presence. He waves to me from the end of the driveway. He works alone at his homework and never asks for help. Always the brilliant student, he skipped a grade.

David flipped one of the throw pillows in the air when the next commercial started. Neville appeared and sat down next to me."That was quick," David said, flipping the pillow again.

"Is it ready?" my mother asked.

Neville shrugged his shoulders. "He didn't need my help."

As Ed Sullivan started, the back door slammed. My father walked into the living room, his cheeks ruddy from the cold.

"Do you want to come and look at the sky?" he asked.

Neville didn't budge when the rest of us stood up.

"Coming?" my father asked Neville's back.

"No thanks," Neville said, staring at the screen.

My father stood a moment longer, then followed us outdoors.

The telescope stood on a tripod in the middle of the back lawn. The bare branches of the adolescent maples my father had planted creaked behind us. My mother hugged herself and looked up. I shivered. David threw his jacket over my shoulders.

My father directed the telescope at the moon and David took off his thick glasses and leaned in to focus. My father explained how the lenses and mirrors worked to magnify and direct the image onto our eyes.

When it was my turn, the moon filled up the eyepiece, but it still looked very distant.

"Can we see the rings around Saturn?" I asked, hopping on one foot and then the other.

"No," my father said, looking up at the light shining down from the living room window. "Saturn is too far away."

My family: (*left to right*) David, me, my mother, Neville and my father from our 1964 holiday card.

The situation that we hoped to change because it was intolerable becomes unimportant. We have not managed to surmount the obstacle, as we were absolutely determined to do, but life has taken us round it, led us past it, and then if we turn round to gaze at the remote past, we can barely catch sight of it, so imperceptible has it become.

Marcel Proust quotation pasted into my Grandmother Nan's scrapbook

My grandmother Nan and me, 1962.

SIXTEEN

BITS OF MY mother's mother are stored in our attic at Diamond Ledge. I unwrap the clothes my mother and Phyllis wore as children and hang them out to air every summer. Handmade dresses and pinafores with embroidery and delicate tucks, smocked christening gowns in thin cotton—the breeze makes them play like the ghosts of forgotten children.

Nan visited us for months at a time when I was small. My mother tells me that we were great chums and I see that recorded in family albums. Nan sits in a plastic chair in my mother's rose garden, and I stand next to her. Her skirt billows sideways. Her legs are still good, like my mother's, like mine will be. My father posed us for the picture. Nan and I rearranged our faces in anticipation. We gave up by the time he released the shutter.

Nan didn't talk much, but when she did, her Northumberland accent was crisp with sayings, like "both ends of the dog meet," "pull up your socks," and "beware of dark nights and wandering hands." I once opened the bathroom door to find her standing naked at the sink; I let out a gasp and stood transfixed. She closed the door, and her voice comes back to me now.

"One should knock."

When Nan was in residence my mother served tea in the afternoon. She steeped the leaves and poured the brew through a strainer into bone china cups, each unique. Once, I watched from the living room doorway as Nan and my mother settled down to sip. A thin plume rose between them from under the couch, where my mother had shoved her loaded ashtray. I waited for one of them to pull out the ashtray and snuff out the stub, but instead they continued to converse through the haze. My mother raised an eyebrow at me and I moved on.

When I was seven, my mother flew out to British Columbia to collect Nan one last time. My father and I drove out to meet their flight. Nan leaned heavily onto my mother while they descended the stairs to the tarmac. Her skin was gray and her face all hollows. She sank into a waiting wheelchair and leaned forward for a kiss. Her cheeks smelled of lilac.

My father wheeled Nan across the airport and I trotted next to them. My orthopedic shoes clomped and I tripped every other step. I caught my mother's hand and swung from it. At the curb, Nan struggled out of the wheelchair, braced herself against the frame of the door of our boxy Rambler, and fell into the front seat. We abandoned the wheelchair and drove off.

"Won't we need the chair when we get home?" I asked.

No one answered.

Nan took my room at the front of the house. My mother replaced my ballerina pictures with a photograph of the River Eden, near the village in northern England where my grandmother's family came from. My mother leaned a plank against the headboard and placed a pillow on top of that, so Nan could sleep sitting up.

"We wouldn't want water to back up into Nan's lungs, would we?" my mother said. I pictured my grandmother drowning in my bed.

My mother made up the daybed for me in the twilight of my father's basement office. Engineering texts disappeared into the gloom above me. My father's desk hulked against one wall. My mother folded a change of clothes on the chair. It was obvious no one thought I would be down there for very long, but as it turned out I'd be there for close to a year.

That first night, I sleepwalked, as I occasionally did as a child.

David said he tried to wake me up when I came into his bedroom and tenderly lay a bar of soap on his pillow. Back in my father's office, I heard something open the door of the workshop. A young woman walked toward me. She wore an old-fashioned dress like Nan's frumpy outfits and it hung from her thin frame. She radiated light, like phosphorescence collecting around a swimmer in the ocean at night. Her lips moved and I fought terror; her steps whispered against the luxuriant grass that sprung from the rug remnant on the floor.

"Maya!" I said.

My father's sister broke up into fragments and floated away.

Nan improved over the summer, and when she felt well enough, my father and I drove her to the Episcopal Church one Sunday morning. At the curb my father came around to open Nan's door. Nan pulled down the veil of one of her many church hats and clutched it to the crown of her head with one hand and gripped my father's hand with the other. He helped her out of the car. She swayed when he let go of her.

"Thank you, Harry," she said when he slipped her cane into her hand.

He said, "See you in an hour, Mum—right here."

I climbed over from the back seat as Nan inched across the brown grass and into the stone chapel.

My father and I drove to the delicatessen next to the projects. The deli-man rolled up his sleeves and plunged his hand into a glass jar as tall as me. He pulled a bulbous pickle out of murky broth. My father bit the end off while the man stood by.

"*Ach*, nothing like from home," my father said.

But he bought some anyway.

At the Jewish bakery, I eyed the cookies lined up in glass cases while the baker pulled loaves out of the slicer with one hand and slid them into plastic sleeves. My father gave me half of a crust. He ate the other. Bitter caraway seeds stuck between our teeth.

We threw our purchases into the trunk and drove back to St. Paul's. My father let the motor idle and read the front page of the paper while

I pored over the funnies. When Nan shook hands with the minister, I climbed over the back of the seat. My father laid his paper aside and came around to open the door.

After Nan settled and my father was back behind the wheel, he reached over and patted her hand. "How was it, Mum?"

"Just fine, Harry," she answered.

So little was explained to me—I never questioned why it was always my father who drove Nan to church. I accepted that Nan moved in with us because our widowed Uncle Mel didn't need help with his three adopted children now that he had remarried. I assumed Grandfather Alfred was dead, and no one told me otherwise.

Nan's passing came back to me many years later, during a session with a hypnotherapist when my father was still alive. I was trying to find a quick fix for the anxiety that was cutting into my sleep. The session didn't seem very revealing at the time. But I came out of it feeling terribly sad and clutching a memory of sitting beside my mother on Nan's empty bed.

"How were you sure she was dead?" I ask.

"Nan didn't answer when I said hello."

"But how did you know she wasn't just sleeping?"

"I held a mirror up to her mouth and there wasn't any fog from her breath. I checked her pulse."

"Can I see the body?" I ask.

"They took it to be buried."

"Can we come to the funeral?"

"Nan wouldn't think funerals were an appropriate thing for children."

After she died, I returned from my basement exile. I stopped sleep-walking. My nightmares evaporated, though whiffs of them haunt me even now. The delicatessen closed. The Jewish bakery moved to the suburbs. A few months later, my mother stopped smoking.

Nan's homemade felt stockings didn't appear at the ends of our beds that Christmas Eve. The brown paper parcels from Aunt Virginia and Uncle Mel weren't under the tree.

"Why should they go to the trouble of sending presents, now that we aren't really related anymore?" my mother asked.

My father rigged a clothesline near the furnace, and my mother hung her used nylons up. When my brothers and I minced across the linoleum the next morning, the stockings were so loaded they stretched until their toes kissed the floor. I no longer remember what was in them. All I retain is my sense of anticipation when David helped me lift mine off the line. That—and the lingering aroma of my mother's feet.

I found Nan's last diary in one of my files after I started writing. Her entries crowd the top of each page for the first months of 1963. "January 25—Cold—Snow—to Crochet Shop to learn how to knit booties. No satisfaction." Nan complains of difficulty catching her breath. She visits the doctor a lot. My brothers and I rarely come up. My mother is there a little more. But Nan often writes that my father took her someplace—to a friend, to church.

Her last entry reads: "April 28, 1963—Sunday—Beautiful Day—to St. Paul's with Harry." My childish writing surprises me just below. "The last she ever wrote. She died April 30th."

Leafing through the rest of Nan's last diary, I saw why it was among my things. It was also my diary, the only one I ever wrote in. My penciled entries start in May. I mimic Nan's handwriting and format: one line about the weather, one line with the day's activity, a statement about the activity. I don't comment on the oddness of receiving my dead grandmother's last words.

I showed the book to my mother. "Why did you give this to me?"

She turned a few pages, then gave me the answer I expected: "Why would we waste a perfectly good diary that was blank from May through December?"

"How come it was always Dad who drove Nan to church? Did you not want to go to church with her?"

"You know I've never enjoyed driving."

I asked her if she remembered sitting with me on the bed the day Nan died.

"Of course. You asked good questions. I wanted to give you good answers."

"But you weren't sad."

"How do you know?"

"You didn't cry."

"I did cry—later. Ask Neville." A few months after Nan died, my mother cleaned out a closet and found her mother's church hats. "Once I started sobbing I just couldn't stop," she said. "Your brother found me there. He was so sweet, patting me on the back. But it was as much about my sister Phyllis as it was for Nan. I'd never cried for either of them."

I'd told my father about my hypnosis session. "I was surprised by how sad I was when I came out of that," I said. "I don't really remember that much about her."

He looked stricken. He didn't ask why I decided to visit a hypnotist. "We were all sad," he said. "And you must have cried for days."

I could see now. My mother wasn't just doing her duty when she made up my bed and adjusted the headboard on her mother's. That wasn't merely Nan's respect for my father or his kindness toward her that I witnessed from the back seat of our car.

All that was love—plain and simple.

SEVENTEEN

IN AUGUST OF 2006, Martin cut the outboard motor, lowered the anchor off of Church Island, and settled in with his book. I pulled off my sweatshirt. Goose bumps rose on my arms.

"You aren't going to swim?" I asked.

Martin kept his eyes on the book. "You're on your own."

We seemed to be out of sync. When I tried to share my thoughts about Mia, my father's losses, and my writing, I sensed Martin tuned me out. When he tried to share his worries about work and his family, I wasn't always listening.

"Even the best marriage can be a lonely proposition," I said.

Martin didn't look up.

Clamping on a pair of Lydia's old goggles decorated with plastic fish, I straddled the edge of the Zodiac and flopped in. Diving deep, I hovered over boulders gilded by the pattern of the waves above me.

The cold water of the Alte Donau takes our breath away. I pull myself down to touch the sandy bottom. Harry, Uri, Cousin Kurtl, Papa, and Uncle Menio paddle above. When I break the surface, Menio is laughing at Aunt Emka, dressed in an elegant swim costume, poking a toe in the water.

"Come in, Darling," he calls.

"Too cold, Kotek," Emka says, using his Polish nickname, "Kitten."

Menio has laughing eyes and thick lips and dimples like Omama's. He fought in the Great War, but he was an officer, not just a foot soldier like the rest of the uncles. And he has a degree in law from the University of Vienna. He still makes Emka blush when he holds her hand, even though they have been married more than ten years. They have no children, so they treat us as if we are their own.

"Papa, why doesn't family ever visit us at our house?" I ask as we stroll under poplars along the Danube Canal on our way back to Omama Sabine's for Sunday lunch. We are already sweating again.

"We have too many stairs and not enough chairs!" Papa answers, ruffling my hair.

"That's not the real answer."

"What then?"

"We are poor and Mutti's parents are rich and it makes more sense to meet at Obere Donaustrasse."

"Could be," Papa says. "Could be."

At number 65, Mutti's spinster younger sister, Aunt Pepi, walks onto the balcony off the salon. She stares across the canal to the First District.

"Aunt Pepi!" Kurtl calls up to her and waves, knocking off Uri's cap; Harry scoops it up and puts it back on Uri's head, backward. Aunt Pepi doesn't respond. Uri grabs the brim and pulls it around. We pass below her and into the courtyard, then up the winding marble stairs where Uncle Lazarus throws open the door. Lazarus still lives at home with Pepi, Omama, and Opapa.

Lazarus kisses me on both cheeks and asks, "How is my *schönes Fräulein* today?"

I curtsy and bat my eyelashes. "Very pretty and very, very well, thank you!"

Emka offers her cheek and Lazarus gives her a kiss and puts his arm around her.

"I approve of such a sister-in-law," he calls back to Menio, leading her in.

At Omama's, the Yiddish word "*Ess! Ess! Ess!*" is the constant refrain. Everyone is already there, gathered around the polished table. Mutti's cheeks are pink and her worry lines don't weigh down her eyes. Omama signals to me. Her full cheeks dimple when she smiles and pulls me to her. "How is my pretty granddaughter?" she asks.

All the Helwing aunts and uncles live nearby, and today they are all here: Mutti, Menio, Sisko, Pepi, Igo, and Lazarus. Omama pats the empty chair on her other side for Harry and calls to Uncle Sisko to pass down the heavy platter of meat. Opa David shouts from the far end of the table. "How is my *schönes* granddaughter?" Thick glasses magnify his eyes.

Omama's sister, whom everyone calls "Aunt Gittel," sits next to her husband, Simel Blaustein. Uncle Simel owns a huge leather factory and the Blausteins live in a grand house in Atzgersdorf on the outskirts of the city. Uncle Simel is always happy, making jokes, gathering little Gittel in his arms. Their sons, Willy and Ludwig, young men already, argue about politics. Ludwig holds the hand of his pretty fiancée, Rosy Kamil; she was only sixteen when they were engaged. Rosy's teeth flash when she talks. Harry can't keep his eyes off her red lips.

There are so many relatives, we have to eat in two shifts. Theresa brings out more platters of *Schnitzel und Spätzle.* We eat until we have to roll away from the table into the salon, where the grand piano sits and a multitude of faces look back from the gilt-framed mirrors that line the walls.

Omama and Aunt Pepi bring out cakes and strong coffee for the adults and tea for the children. Uncle Lazarus struts around the room, checking his new timepiece and returning to put his hand on the shoulder of his latest *goyische* girlfriend. She peers into a pocket mirror and adjusts her platinum curls. Uri imitates Harry as he considers his next move against Uncle Simel on the chessboard, stroking his cheek and scowling. Uncle Igo and Aunt Berthe fuss over Kurtl, taking turns drying his hair with an embroidered towel. They take off his thick glasses and his eyes look slightly crossed without them. Kurtl bats them away as if they were annoying flies! Uncle Sisko and

My father's aunt and uncle, Emka and Menio Helwing at their wedding, 1920.

Aunt Fanny, quiet and plain, watch from the corner. The telephone rings. Mutti sighs. Is she sad she can't afford to own a telephone? Pepi stares out the window. Perhaps she longs for the stillness of her Monday house when everyone is gone.

Soon enough it's time for afternoon nap. Sisko and Fanny say their goodbyes. Simel and Gittel leave with Rosy and their sons. Opa and Omama and Aunt Pepi all go to their rooms. Mutti and Papa lie on the couches and Uncle Igo and Aunt Berthe go into the guest room. Uncle Lazarus heads out with his girlfriend. Theresa clears the plates.

The grandfather clock bongs twice and the church bells sing. Menio leans over and forks up the last of my streudel and winks at me as he gulps it down. Then he takes Emka's hand and pulls her to her feet. He signals to us to follow them out into the streets and onto a tram to the Prater with its giant Ferris wheel, the Riesenrad.

The six of us stand in a short line and board one of the boxcars. Menio and Emka sit on the bench in the center holding hands. We children run to the windows on the outside and the car drifts up; we dash to the other side to see the view on the way down. We can see the river, the Innere Stadt, the spires of Stephansdom, the Vienna Woods beyond. Menio and Emka disembark but pay for us to take two more turns. They stand below and wave every time we pass on our dizzying trips to the sky.

On the way home, Menio stops at a flower cart and picks out a dozen white roses. The girl wraps them in a cone of stiff paper and ties them up with ribbon. Menio gives a big bill to her and hands the bouquet to Emka. She buries her face in the blooms, then holds them out so I can inhale their sweetness. The flower girl counts out bills and some change into Menio's palm. He stuffs the bills into his pocket, then tells me to close my eyes and open my hands. Paper rustles and then Menio says, "Careful, it's sharp!" I feel the prickle of thorns in one palm and coins in the other. I open my eyes and raise the velvet petals against my cheek and slip the change into my pocket to count when we get home.

Kurtl and Emka stand by the tram while we follow Menio onboard. He pays the fare, then steps off. We run to the back seats and wave from the window until they disappear when the tram turns the bend.

Once home, I take out my treasure box, an old cigar carton covered with glued-on pictures from a magazine. Inside are my prize marbles and a few postcards from Germany from Papa's sister and her family, who visited Vienna when I was very small. I count out my coins and lay them next to the rose. When I place the box back on my shelf, *the marbles roll and knock against the sides.*

My father with three of his paternal cousins, 1928, at the Prater, Vienna's amusement park. *(To the left)* Martin Grünberg, Erna and Henny Aurbach (visiting from Germany). *(To the right)* Uri, Mia, and my father.

Out of air, I broke to the surface. A loon glided in front of the boat and then dove under. It popped up again among the rocks trailing Moon Island. Martin looked up from his book.

"Enough?" he asked.

"Enough."

Martin closed the book and slipped it in the beach bag. He reached over and grabbed my arm and helped me over the side of the boat. He handed me a warm towel. It must have been sitting in the sun.

"Funny how the days are already getting shorter," he said.

"Yeah."

"Sun will go down soon."

"Yep." I dried myself off. The towel was rough, but it felt good.

Correspondence

Vienna, 2 May.1939

Dear Harry!

Even though we wrote to you yesterday, we wanted to answer your letter that came yesterday so that you could answer both of these letters together and consequently save on postage. While I am thinking about it, should I send you pre-stamped postcards? You are surely in need of it in that maybe you are not able to write as many letters as you would like. Thank you for the birthday wishes ... Uncle Simel and Aunt Gittel send their love. Write Gittel—she wants to know whether or not the work there is not too difficult for you after the operation, in other words, if you can perform your duties and especially if you are allowed to do them. Is your face really round and clear of spots? You can write me the whole truth here.

Other than that, there's nothing new here, greetings and tender kisses,

Your Papa

p.s. We have received a ¼ year extension again on our apartment.

Dear Harry!

I already knew that it was cold in the tent and I hope that that won't be bad for you. I stopped worrying when you wrote that you have fat cheeks and feel good.

Is the strenuous work not too much for you? ... Don't they serve meat at lunch? We received a letter from Uri and he writes that he is very pleased to be apprenticing with the master locksmith and he is learning a lot there. We have received a letter from the Herzbergs. We didn't get an answer from Haifa regarding the Technical School. Is there a doctor available on the farm in the case that someone should get sick? What do you wear for work—pants and coat or a training uniform?

Tomorrow is Papa's birthday. Only little Punzi is here but it's better this way. She is very annoyed that her affairs are taking so long and accuses Papa— "It's your fault, you're not taking care of things."

I'm going to close because I need to go to bed.

Tender kisses,
Your Mutti

p.s. We are glad that you have fountain pens again. Which shoes are you wearing for work? Your other shoes are surely worn out.

My grandparents write my father in England. They refer to his hernia operation, and his acceptance at the Technical University in Haifa. Either the visa didn't work out, or my father decided he was giving up his scholarship and would go to a kibbutz if he ever received permission to travel to Palestine.

When we were forced to leave Vienna on account of Nazism, in December 1938, the only port open to us was Shanghai. By the grace of God, we were able to procure tickets for a luxury Italian steamer, which was no easy task, indeed. The preliminary steps of getting passports were horrible beyond description. For many days, we had to stand in line from early dawn, usually until late afternoon, abused and kicked by the executives of the "Superior Race," to be told in the end that we have to come back next day because the quota of applicants is closed. My husband stood it with admirable stoicism, whereas, I got a high fever and had to be under doctor's care for several days and stay in bed. Finally we succeeded in receiving the passports with the addition of a capital "J" standing for Jew ... Was I so happy to have escaped with my own teeth—so many of our co-religionists had them knocked out during those trying months from March to December.

From Emka Helwing's unpublished memoir
My Neighbors and I

My father's Uncle Sigmund (Menio) and Aunt Emka Helwing.

EIGHTEEN

WHEN I WAS TEN years old, my father drove us all to New York City. We visited an elderly couple in a cramped apartment filled with knick-knacks on Cabrini Boulevard. Neville and I took the subway to Yonkers to sit with my father and a skeletal old man in a foul-smelling nursing home. We crowded around a leathery roast and limp vegetables with ancient "uncles" and "aunts" in a fourth-floor walk-up on Coney Island. The highest tracks of the roller-coaster were just visible outside the dining room window, and every few minutes, a loaded car leapt over the sill, whipped around a curve, and dropped out of sight, leaving only screams until the next round. I wasn't clear who these relatives were; now I realize they were mostly from my grandfather's side of the family. They had thick accents and often switched to German or Yiddish. My mother barely said a word.

Then there was family my father seemed to know better. When I was eleven we traveled to Boston to visit Willy Barnes and his wife and daughters. We met Cyril Greenslate in Nottingham, and Rita and Ludwig Barnes outside London on the way to my father's Fulbright year in Copenhagen. I didn't understand our relationship with these relatives. No one told me that their names had been changed, or why. I never saw Willy or Cyril again.

Of all these relatives, only one, other than Uri, was a real presence when I was growing up. That was Sigmund Helwing, my father's uncle, whom we called "Menio." Every year, birthday greetings arrived for my brothers and me, postmarked Salt Lake City. Tucked inside flowery cards were crisp dollar bills—equal in number to our ages—impossible riches.

Menio and Emka Helwing sailed for Shanghai after the Anschluss, one of the few ports that did not require a visa. Once there, they opened a button factory. Menio and Emka were allowed to move to the United States in 1940, sponsored by the Jewish community in Salt Lake City. Uncle Menio's law degree was worthless in America; he worked as an accountant.

I first met Menio in 1965, when I was ten. Our family stood on the tarmac of the Syracuse airport, dressed to the nines, waiting for our widowed great uncle to come off the plane. I had pictured him looking a little like Cary Grant in an elegant suit, with dark hair like my father's. No one of that description came down the stairs.

"What's that thing on your face?" Neville teased me while we waited.

I'd fallen the day before and had a scab on my nose.

"Let me see," my mother said. "Move your hand."

I let my hand go down to my side.

"You can barely see it," she said.

When Menio bounded toward us, I saw I had miscast him. He looked like Alfred Hitchcock, white haired and dumpy. His clean-shaven cheeks relaxed into jowls. Blue eyes twinkled from deep inside lizard-like eyelids. His fleshy lower lip was so thick that it folded over and flopped down onto his chin. Menio embraced my father tightly, then planted a wet kiss on my mother's cheek. My father introduced my brothers and me. Menio shook each of our hands. He held my hand a little longer. "What's that thing on your nose?" he asked me.

We walked into the Skycap Restaurant and sat down at a long table dressed in white linen. Prop planes ambled by the picture windows. Menio ordered whiskey sours for the grownups and ginger ale for the boys. The waiter brought me a Shirley Temple with three cherries on a toothpick. Their juice stained my cocktail red.

"Order an appetizer," Uncle Menio said, opening the menu. My brothers and I moved quickly before our parents could say appetizers were an unnecessary extravagance.

My shrimp cocktail flowered from its crystal goblet. Uncle Menio grabbed a crustacean and dipped it into blood-red sauce. He winked at me when he bit into it. His lower lip jiggled when he chewed; I realized I was staring and turned away. Next to my fork I discovered a velvet box. I pried it open. A ruby chip was set in a gold ring surrounded by tiny pearls. I slipped it on. It fit.

"Wow!" was all I could say.

"That's quite a gift for a little girl," my mother said.

The waiters took the shrimp away and we went to the carving table and filled our plates and brought them back to the table. I admired the way my ruby flashed when I maneuvered the heavy silver. My parents talked with Menio about the weather and complimented the food. There were a lot of breaks in the conversation, filled with chewing.

When the plates were cleared, Menio said, "How about dessert?"

"We couldn't possibly," my mother said as Menio waved down the waiter.

"Baked Alaska all around," he said, "and coffee."

At the end of the meal, he pulled out a wad of twenties and tossed it on the table.

My father drove us home, with me squeezed between him and Menio, and my mother with my brothers in the back. Menio put his hand on mine. His wedding band looked like it was strangling his plump finger. He kept his hand there the entire ride home.

Simel shows his desperation for the first time. He appears terribly upset and agitated and desperately pleads for ship tickets and landing permits for Shanghai. He says it is terribly urgent. My uncle Igo and Bertl had been taken “to Uncle Samuel.” Since Samuel [Simel’s brother] lived in Lvov at the time, this clearly meant they were taken to some place in Poland.

But it was the horror of the experience—which Simel did not want to describe—which colored all his later letters.

From my father’s synopsis of Simel Blaustein’s letters
to his son Willy Barnes.

NINETEEN

In May of 1965, *The Sound of Music* opened at Shoppingtown, a suburban movie theater, and my parents drove me and a couple of the neighborhood girls to see it. My father paid at the ticket booth for me and my mother and pushed through the glass doors. The smell of popcorn wafted back from the concession stand.

Lucy Fitzgerald, who had grown plump in the three years since first grade, dug into the pocket of her hand-me-down dress and found herself short of change. Counting out her coins a second time, a few of them fell to the floor and rolled in several directions. She dived down to retrieve them. My new best friend, Melinda Johnson, took off her white gloves, opened the clasp of her patent leather purse, and discreetly dropped some quarters on the floor; she joined Lucy to help retrieve them. Lucy paid for her ticket and Melinda for hers and her sister's.

"Forget about the popcorn," I quoted David when we passed the concession stand. "My parents think the snack bar is part of some giant capitalist conspiracy."

We leaned back into padded seats and munched on the apples my mother had smuggled in. The lights dimmed. On the screen, Julie Andrews threw her arms out and turned in place. The camera panned back to show her spinning in the middle of a mountain meadow, singing to the heavens, "The hills are alive with the sound of music!" My father shifted in his seat.

During intermission, Melinda and I practiced our ballet steps in the lobby. I was finally growing but I was more legs than anything else. Dance had arrested the inward drift of my toes. Melinda was tall and angular. She held out the skirt of her lavender frock, bought at The Addis Co., one of the fancier stores in the new mall. She was African American, although that term wasn't in wide use at that time.

The Johnsons had bought their house from the Jewish family who lived across the street from Barbara Wallace. Mr. and Mrs. Johnson moved in soon after Nan died and stayed for a couple of weeks to make sure it was safe before the girls joined them. The Wallaces organized the neighborhood to try to buy back the house; my parents weren't invited to the meetings. "I think they thought we were part of some Jewish-socialist plot," my mother said.

For a while, I played with Melinda and her sister on some days and with my friends on others. I know that if my parents hadn't forced me, I would have stayed with my old crowd.

A few months in, the young priest from the local Catholic church visited the Fitzgeralds and the Francinis and advised them to act as if "Christ had moved onto our street." I would meet him after my father died; he'd left the priesthood after a mission in South America where he had fallen in love with a nun. When I asked him if he remembered using the phrase about Christ moving on the street, he laughed. "I don't remember saying that. But it's the kind of thing I said a lot in those days."

The Wallaces wouldn't let me play with Barbara anymore and she stopped showing up at the street games. They sold their home and vacated to the suburbs; I never saw Barbara again.

Once the Wallaces left, Mrs. Johnson left her door unlocked. On her dining table was a constantly replenished supply of snacks and Hawaiian Punch from the airforce commissary. With their new color television set, their house would solidify into the new kid-central on our street. Sydney L. Johnson, Melinda's father, would eventually become superintendent of schools. Percy Hughes would be integrated. One day Melinda walked into the disabled classrooms on the way to

With Melinda at Neville's wedding, c. 1982.

lunch and chatted up those kids. If she had done a series of back flips down the hallway, I wouldn't have been more impressed.

We went back into the theater, munching on the popcorn Melinda bought. The lights went down and the Baron stood up to the Nazis and the Austrian people stoically accepted the German occupation. We breathed a sigh of relief when the von Trapp family sang in perfect harmony as they climbed over Alpine peaks into Switzerland.

"Salzburg is nowhere near the Swiss border," my father mumbled. He didn't join in when everyone else cheered and applauded through the credits. We poured out onto the sidewalk; I joined Lucy, Melinda, her sister and all the children around us, singing and spinning. My father walked ahead to get to the car. On the drive home, he complained to my mother. "Of course, that wasn't how it was. After the Anschluss, Austrians cheered when the Germans arrived. They waved Nazi flags and raised their hands and said, 'Heil, Hitler.'" His voice sounded like a girl's. I wondered if he was mistaken. The Nazis in the movie were clearly the bad guys. Couldn't the Austrians see that as well?

"Now, Harry," my mother said, touching his arm.

I covered my ears and hummed a few bars of *My Favorite Things*. The other girls, crammed in the back seat with me, looked out the windows.

In retrospect, my father's reaction to Hollywood's rewrite of the events he lived through in 1938 revealed yet another crack in the veneer of the stories he had told me in childhood. Growing up, it had never crossed my mind that the Austrians themselves were Nazis. And I always thought the word "Anschluss" translated into a violent, military "takeover." But the meaning of the German word is much more benign. Directly translated it just means "annexation" or "connection."

In my teens, I'd sing a few bars of *Sixteen Going on Seventeen* whenever I wanted to get a rise out of my father. He wouldn't take the bait. "That ridiculous movie—" he'd say, shaking his head. Were his memories of the Anschluss once again suppressed? Or viewed from the safe distance of the 1970s, had that Technicolor Anschluss became just another rerun, rendered harmless by the fuzzy screen of our black-and-white television set?

Correspondence

MINSK, BELORUSSIA

Transport of November 28, 1941	999 People	
Transport of May 6, 1942	994	
Transport of May 20, 1942	986	
Transport of May 27, 1942	991	INCL. MY PARENTS AND MY SISTER
Transport of June 2, 1942	999	
Transport of June 9, 1942	1,006	
Transport of August 17, 1942	1,003	
Transport of August 31, 1942	967	
Transport of September 14, 1942	992	
Transport of October 5, 1942	549	INCL. 5 GRUENBERGS
	9,486	
Returned	9	
Perished	9,477	

List of Survivors: MOTHER (HANNI) WAS SHOT
OLDEST DAUGHTER (REGINA) DISAPPEARED

Edith Gruenberg 1923	DAUGHTER	Lotte Gruenberg 1934	DAUGHTER
Isaak Gruenberg 1891	FATHER	Julie Hochbaum 1903	

Apparently there were ten transports from Vienna to Minsk between November 28, 1941, and October 5, 1942. Of the 9,486 people taken on these transports only nine returned. The May 27, 1942 transport (which included my parents and my sister) had only one survivor. Needless to say, (Schneider's) book does not make easy reading. The last transport to Minsk had three survivors of a Gruenberg family: Isaak Gruenberg (born 1891) and two daughters, Edith (1923) and Lotte (1934). The mother, Hanni Gruenberg, was shot in camp and the oldest daughter, Regina, was taken away and disappeared. Do you remember anything about another Gruenberg family in Vienna? I really don't know anybody else to ask.

A 2001 letter from my father to Rita Barnes (née Rosy Kamil) with questions about Gertrude Schneider's book *Exile and Destruction, The Fate of Austrian Jews, 1938-1945*. His notes above are written on a photocopied page of the book, listing all the transports from Vienna to Minsk.

Erna Jackson and Rita Barnes, 1965.

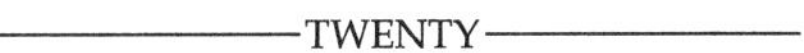

TWENTY

By the time Neville and I first met our London relatives in 1966, Rosy Kamil and Ludwig Blaustein had been Rita and Lewis Barnes for a couple of decades. Only after my father died and most of the letters were translated did I put together that Lewis was the brother of the Willy Barnes we met near Boston, and that their parents, Gittel and Simel Blaustein, were my great grandmother Sabine's sister and brother-in-law. The Barnes' and my father would have all shared the same worry about family left behind, and I sense now the same unspoken grief lurking in the gaps of their often-mundane conversations.

In middle age, Rita was a broad, gray-haired woman who sported a mannish haircut, red lipstick, and an ever-smoking cigarette in a tapered holder. No matter how many times my father told me how dainty and pretty little Rosy Kamil was, I couldn't imagine how that was possible. And my grandmother Elka's cousin, whom Rita called Lewis and my father called Ludwig, always seemed old to me. His hair was colorless and thin. Thick glasses slid down his nose. His hands shook, his feet slid along the carpets when he walked, and he tried to keep a scar on his forearm covered with long sleeves.

"Lewis, you are wrong, darling, it was 1956 not 1955," Rita would admonish him with her thickly British accent.

Ludwig responded in equally thick Viennese, "No, *dahrling*, it *vas* not 1956, it *vas* 1955."

They argued through cocktails. They argued through the pork roast with crackling, the buttered potatoes, the overcooked French beans, and right through dessert—what they called "pudding."

Rita's sister, Erna Jackson, came by with her husband, a Scottish Trotskyite, and their only son Alan, a student at Cambridge University. Rita and Ludwig were childless, but Rita was full of advice for the Jacksons regarding Alan, and for my parents about Neville and me. After one of Rita's stories about how she set Alan right on some matter, Mr. Jackson (I never knew his first name,) leaned over and said in his lilting brogue, "And that's what made him the man he is today!"

I had no sense during these visits that my father had seen Ludwig almost every Sunday at his Grandmother Sabine's when he was growing up. Ludwig never let on that he had been a member of the Jewish elite or that he had grown up in a mansion in Vienna with lovely formal gardens, so unlike their cozy but small semi-detached home with its postage-stamp rose garden.

After reading through the translations of all of Simel and Gittel Blaustein's letters, sent to me by Willy's children, I now knew that Ludwig's parents had been close friends of Eisig and Sali Kamil, Rita's parents. When their grand homes were "Aryanized" the two couples had squeezed into a small flat in the Second District together until their deportation in 1942. I don't remember any of this being discussed at that first visit, and I don't remember hearing about it during my later visits with Rita and Ludwig on my way to and from my Israeli family. Perhaps I was too self-involved to take it in.

"Remember how Kurtl Helwing always brought us chocolates whenever he visited, Harry?" Rita said in one brief hiatus from the usual amnesia. At the time, I was only mildly curious about who Kurtl was; there were just too many relatives to keep straight.

"*Ja, ja*, of course," Lewis nodded. "His foster father worked in a candy factory."

Rita (Rosy Kamil) and Lewis Barnes (Ludwig Blaustein) on their wedding day, June 29, 1939. Ludwig was just released from Dachau.

"What ever happened to him?" my father asked. "He never answers my letters, and I can't find his phone number listed anywhere."

"We haven't heard from Kurtl since the end of the war," Rita said.

My father barely mentioned Kurt Helwing in any of his writings or in our conversations in the years before he died, other than to say he thought Kurt's foster family adopted him, and that he pretty much disappeared after the war. I never heard Uri mention him, even though they were the same age. Did he marry a Christian and raise a happy family, or was he waiting endlessly to be found again?

My last visit with Rita and Ludwig was in the late seventies, when I was a medical student in Tel Aviv. Used to being the darling of my Israeli relatives, it was painful to be constantly criticized by Rita. My hair was unkempt, my dress sloppy, and I didn't shower enough.

"I can't imagine how you got into medical school," she said.

Lewis was silent for most of the visit. Alan came by and took me to a concert—standing room at the Proms. He tried to cheer me up.

"Rita just doesn't like young people," he said. "Give it a few years."

"I should live so long."

We leaned against the railing. "By the way," I said. "She asked me to find out why you've never gotten married."

"Never found the right girl, I guess."

Lewis died, then Rita, then Erna. Years later, Martin, the girls, and I would take a trip to London. I arranged to meet up with Alan and Mr. Jackson for lunch at the Royal Festival Hall, overlooking the Thames. I asked Martin if he wanted to go somewhere else with the girls instead.

"Are you kidding? And give up having lunch with one of the last living Trotskyites?"

We had a wonderful time that day. I remember being surprised by how much Mr. Jackson enjoyed the meal and the wine. I guess I'd always thought of communists as being rather austere—not the kind of people who liked bourgeoisie pastimes like going out to eat in fancy restaurants. I felt a bit guilty that I didn't miss Rita or Ludwig.

Mr. Jackson died not long after that visit, as did my father. I went back to London with Martin on a business trip, and Alan and I met for lunch. He had recently married his longtime partner, Jim. He brought me Rita's wedding band, her gold wristwatch, Ludwig's army medals and honorable discharge papers from the British Army, and his mother's "forever band," a thin platinum ring with tiny diamonds and emeralds set around the edges.

"I can't use these," Alan said, "and I couldn't think of anyone else who would want them."

"Did you find any letters from Lewis's or Rita's parents from during the war?" I asked.

"No letters, just a few telegrams. I suspect Rita pitched the rest."

He handed them over. They included many congratulations

for Rita and Ludwig's wedding in 1939 and a pair of Red Cross telegrams from 1942, set six months apart:

> Inquirer: Blaustein, Rita. Ludwig Erna I healthy and content. Hope with Eisig Sali Simel Gittel the same. We write often and wait longingly for word. Tenderest kiss. Rita
>
> Responder: Simel Blaustein. Very glad that you are well and content. Simel and Gittel healthy with Eisig Sali at home. No news from there. Hearty greetings to all.

"No news from there" refers to all those who had already travelled East.

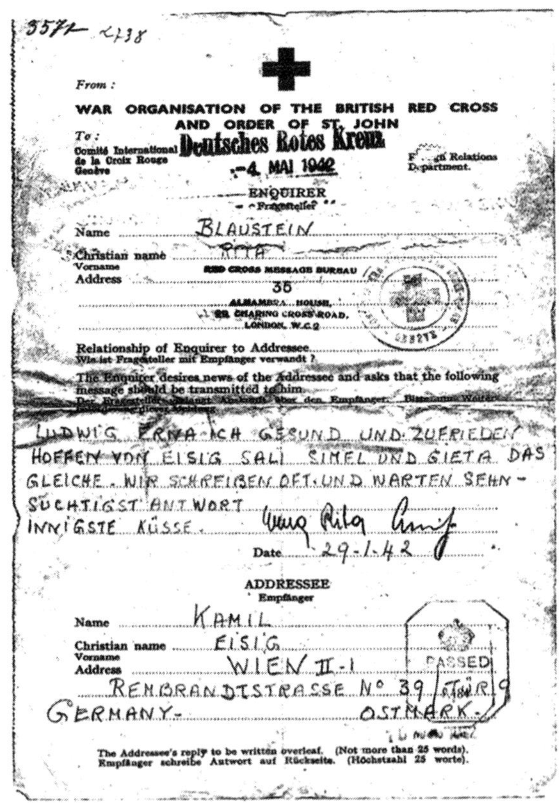

3571 ∠738

From:
WAR ORGANISATION OF THE BRITISH RED CROSS AND ORDER OF ST. JOHN

To:
Comité International de la Croix Rouge Genève

Deutsches Rotes Kreuz
4. MAI 1942

Foreign Relations Department.

ENQUIRER
Fragesteller

Name BLAUSTEIN
Christian name RITA
Vorname
Address RED CROSS MESSAGE BUREAU 35 ALHAMBRA HOUSE, 22 CHARING CROSS ROAD, LONDON, W.C.2

Relationship of Enquirer to Addressee
Wie ist Fragesteller mit Empfänger verwandt?

The Enquirer desires news of the Addressee and asks that the following message should be transmitted to him.

LUDWIG ERNA ICH GESUND UND ZUFRIEDEN HOFFEN VON EISIG SALI SIMEL UND GIETA DAS GLEICHE. WIR SCHREIBEN OFT UND WARTEN SEHNSÜCHTIGST ANTWORT INNIGSTE KÜSSE. Rita

Date 29-1-42

ADDRESSEE
Empfänger

Name KAMIL
Christian name EISIG
Vorname
Address WIEN II-1 REMBRANDTSTRASSE No 39 TÜR 9 GERMANY- OSTMARK-

PASSED

The Addressee's reply to be written overleaf. (Not more than 25 words).
Empfänger schreibe Antwort auf Rückseite. (Höchstzahl 25 worte).

Last telegram exchange, through the Red Cross, between Rita Barnes and her father-in-law, Simel Blaustein.

Correspondence

February 3, 1939

I want to tell you a few things about Vienna after November 10. My parents and I were interned in a school. They took away the keys to our apartment ... we did not get the keys to our apartment back for another 14 days, but then we were forced to give up the flat by 10 December. So we moved in with Omama [Grandmother Sabine]. There, all mirrors, some of the windows, the radio, a table and two chairs had been smashed. [Note: I visited Omama and Aunt Josephine (Pepi) right after Krystallnacht and saw the devastation. The two women were hysterical.]

Your parents were also driven from their home and their keys were taken away. In the evening Göring announced on the radio that all had blown over and so your parents went back home with a second set of keys and went to bed. In the morning the Nazis came back and took away the second set of keys. After about a week they got the keys back [actually, mother had to go Gestapo headquarters to get the keys] and found that the flat had been ransacked. The suitcase from Germany [with presents for Uri], the lamp which Harry had made at school and 1.50 German Marks, which Mia had saved, were all gone. Ludwig, Uncle Sisko [Helwing, my mother's brother] and Uncle Simel were all interned. Uncle Simel was released soon after, but Sisko and Ludwig were sent to Dachau ... Ludwig is still there.

Now I will tell you how I came here. On Sunday afternoon, on 3 December we were all at Omama's ... on Thursday 500 children would be sent to England. Boys on bicycles were going around to pick up the children ... A Dr. Attaman gave me a paper. I was examined, photographed, and then all the children were taken to the Kultusgemeinde [the headquarters of the Jewish Community of Vienna]. On Thursday our luggage was inspected, and we departed at midnight on Saturday. [It always puzzles me why Mia was not included in this deal.] On Sunday, about a quarter to nine in the morning the express train crossed the border into Holland. We received coffee, cake, chocolate, fruit and postcards with Dutch stamps. Passing through Amsterdam we boarded a boat. I had a first-class cabin.

Portion of a letter from Kurt Helwing, to Uri in Palestine. My father translated this letter and the comments in brackets are his. It is the only family letter that mentions the events of Kristallnacht. Although my father's flashback suggested the mirrors at his maternal grandmother's home were smashed during the Anschluss, this letter and most of my father's writing suggested it happened later, during Kristallnacht. My father noted there were many typos in the letter and that 3 December was not a Sunday.

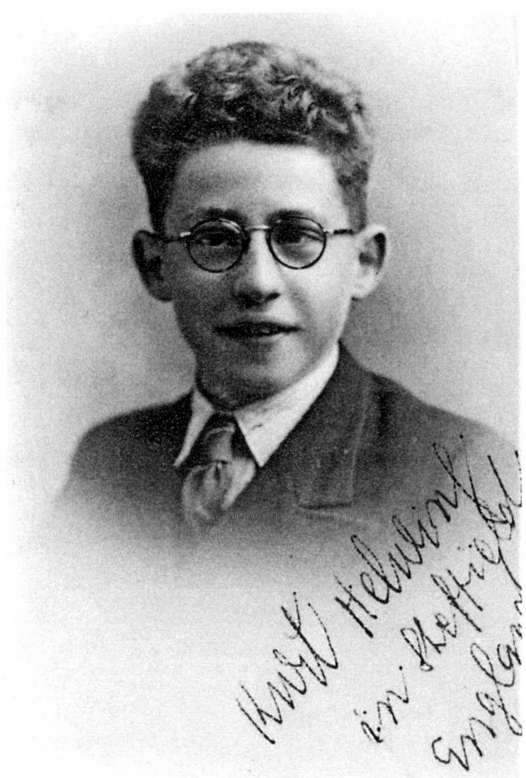

Kurt Helwing, c. 1939.

Kristallnacht ("Night of Broken Glass"), November 1938.
Ransacked synagogue at Seitenstettengasse (1st district)
with defaced ark and destroyed Torah scrolls.

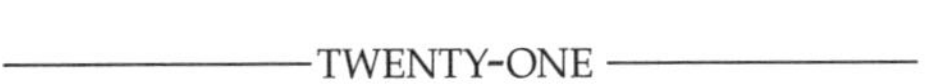

TWENTY-ONE

CRYSTAL NIGHT. I imagine a full moon rising behind Mount Israel and crusted drifts crunching under our boots. Diamond Ledge is dressed in snow and Squam shines like mercury below us. Ice jackets the sugar maples. The scarred trunk of a Hemlock witness tree casts a sharp shadow on the lone glacial erratic standing in a neighbor's field.

Kristallnacht. The language doesn't satisfy. Eerie glow in the sky from burning synagogues, the sparkling of shattered windows, the spreading yellow of healing bruises, the putrid smell of dinners left in haste, the crackle of burning books, the rustle of papers scattering onto cobblestones—the splintering of doors, bones, and dreams.

Washday. Harry and I drag sheets and underclothes down to the courtyard and help Mutti stir everything in the boiling tub. Our hands burn from lye soap and the cold. We haul the clothes back up the stairs to hang on lines strung across the living room and kitchen. The apartment steams with the damp.

The bang on the door. Angry faces of children in brown shirts.

"Give us the keys." A hand thrust out, palm up.

Mutti hesitates.

"GIVE US THE KEYS."

The red swastika winks from a white band around the broad arm of one of Harry's classmates. The palm turns down and Harry's left cheek ignites; his eyes water but he doesn't cry. Mutti reaches into her apron and holds out the keys and another boy snatches them away. The group rushes on to the Harband's door. They pound their fists into the soft wood.

Harry and I skitter to pull a wet sheet off the line and run into the bedroom we now share between the two of us. We throw clothes and books willy-nilly onto it, trying to ignore the banging, now on the Melzers' door.

Harry ties the loaded sheet together and drags it into the living room. "I'm going to help Mutti," he calls back. I spot his paperweight on the desk; its intricate patterns beckon. I pick it up and feel its solid weight.

"Mia, hurry up." Harry cries from the hall.

I get down on hands and knees and wiggle under my bed. Eye to eye with a cumulus of dust, I push the paperweight against the wall.

"Mia, come!" Mutti calls.

A suitcase and the tied-up sheet are at the door. Susi stands in the Harband's doorway, holding a small globe filled with water. The eyes of their goldfish are magnified against the glass.

"Susi, put it back. He'll be fine," Paul says, taking the globe out of her hands and back inside. A tear sidles down Susi's cheek.

Frau Melzer and Frau Harband sob in the hall.

"Stephanie, Olga, what is it?" Mutti asks.

"They took the men," Frau Harband says, her face drawn.

Thank goodness Papa is at work.

Hans and Frau Melzer struggle with a big box. In the end, they pull a few things out and leave the box inside their door.

The priest comes up the stairs. Everyone moves to the side to let him pass. His eyes flit to the corners. His forehead gleams with perspiration. He lifts his key to the latch. Before he turns it, the door is opened from the inside and one of the Fräuleins looks out. The priest pushes her aside and the door shuts behind them.

Mutti brushes the dust off my clothes and hair. "What have you been up to?" she scolds. We leave the apartment door ajar and struggle down the stairs. "We better go to Menio's. Papa will know to come there," Mutti says. There is no time to hug the neighbors when we part on the street.

The tram is closed to Jews, so we walk. Harry hauls the sopping sheet with our belongings. I lug the box of leftover food and the family photographs. Mutti carries one valise. When we reach the Ringstrasse, I realize—"My treasures! I left my treasure box!" I turn to go back.

Harry drops the sheet and grabs me by the elbow. "Mia, come on, we can't go back now."

We pick up our loads again and trudge with hundreds toward the Second District, eyes down. *The heavens combust overhead.*

Correspondence

Our friendship goes back over forty years and never, before or since, have I had such wonderful neighbors and friends. I always loved looking across the street, watching Eden tending to her beautiful garden and Harry washing the car ... We still talk about the blizzard of '66 when Lisa literally swam across the street in the snow and couldn't get home. Funny, the things you remember.

Harry was especially kind when my husband started to fail and was there in a snowstorm to help me take him to the doctor more than once. Harry was what we call a real Mensch. It is a Yiddish word that can't be translated exactly. It means a person of great integrity who deals with dignity and compassion for others. That's how I knew him.

Our neighbor Mrs. Helen Besdin, writes from her Jerusalem retirement home upon hearing about my father's death.

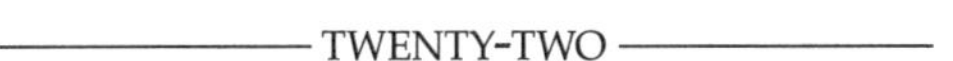

TWENTY-TWO

After exiting the air-conditioned chill of the Syracuse airport, I hit a wall of August heat. David leaned against his mini-van at the curb. When I hugged him, he tensed, pulled away, and patted me on the back.

"David, with you and Neville, I always feel like I'm forcing matching poles of a magnet together—the closer we get, the more we repel."

"We're just manly kind of men, I guess." He opened the passenger door for me, then came around and settled into the driver's seat. I unwrapped a Hershey's kiss and tossed it in my mouth.

"Life among the sugar people—" David said as he pulled onto the road. Like Uri, both my brothers had developed diabetes.

"It's hard to believe Dad's been dead for a year." I said.

David had come up with the idea of having a Jahrzeit on the one-year anniversary of our father's death. That was just like him. Although he was crusty on the outside, my oldest brother remembered birthdays and anniversaries. He called our mother every week and drove the two hours from Albany to visit her every month. We hadn't grown close until I was in high school, when the quiet boy with the crew cut and heavy glasses returned from Cornell as an argumentative man with a lopsided "fro" and wire-rimmed glasses that were always slipping down his nose. We talked on the telephone often. He repeated the same stories over and over but laughed if I

My father and David, Green Lakes State Park, c. 1959.

reminded him I had already heard them all before. We didn't agree on many things; we couldn't talk about politics. But still, he's the person I would call if I ever needed help.

But to really see my oldest brother in that year after my father died, you had to understand he carried unbearable loss. His oldest son had a breakdown after graduating from Harvard. He cut all connections and lived hand-to-mouth somewhere in southern California. It would be years before they reconnected.

"Mom was up for the ceremony," he said. "I called Neville at all his numbers and left messages."

"He left me a voicemail saying he knew it was happening, but I never spoke to him directly," I said. "The usual."

"I think he's having a tough time," David said. Neville and his wife were divorcing and he had custody of their children.

I dialed Neville when we pulled out onto the highway, but the call went directly into voicemail. Shortly after I hung up, a message flashed up on my phone. "He says we should meet him at Starbucks after we pick up Mom."

David grabbed my phone and hit redial, making the car swerve. "Just meet us at Mom's, goddamn it!" He handed the phone back to me.

I heard Neville's voice: "Jeez. Lighten up."

Neville picked us up and the four of us went to the lakes in his car. His right arm was encrusted with a bubbling rash. "I got a little poison ivy when I came out last week to clear a path to Dad," he said.

We emptied out of the car and strolled into the Hundred Acre Wood. Neville veered off into the trees.

"Here it is," he said.

"No, here." He came out and then wove in again. "Definitely, right here," he said, pointing at a small pine. "No, no, it's here." He settled on a scraggly sycamore with mistletoe climbing up the side.

My mother batted a mosquito. Sweat dripped between my shoulder blades.

"I dug a trench here," Neville said.

David and I spoke at once.

"And you just buried the box?"

"You didn't scatter him?"

"Yes, I buried him here." Neville swept his hands back and forth. "I made the trough run exactly east to west."

I held myself back from asking if he'd used a compass.

My mother cleared her throat. "I think we should each say something we remember about your father." She looked down at her hands and then up at us. "What I remember most was his sweetness. He was always so thoughtful. He always remembered things."

David spoke. "Dad looked like he loved me in that album Lisa made for us." I had collected old photographs and chose pictures I thought captured my father's love for each of my brothers. There was a portrait of David swaddled in my mother's arms, and my father looked down on them. His eyes radiated pride.

"I remember how Dad wrote out the solutions to math problems on paper napkins. The embossing always made his lines quiver." I pulled my hair into a rubber band I had found in my pocket. "And he always left me notes tucked into the waxed paper folds of the sandwiches I took to Percy Hughes. Remember the sandwiches?"

David laughed. "Peanut butter with dill pickles on dark rye."

"Bratwurst with limp lettuce anyone?" Neville said.

"At least he made your lunch," my mother said.

Neville shrugged. "I remember third grade at Percy Hughes," he said. "I was looking at those maples outside the windows. I had new glasses, and I was focusing on one particular leaf that was just beginning to change color." He traced the veins of the leaf with an outstretched finger and marveled at the light shining through it. "I was just about to grasp the meaning of the universe." Neville grinned as he held his hand out to stroke the memory of that leaf.

"What's that got to do with Dad?" I interrupted.

Neville dropped his hand.

"You're not the only one who's sad, you know," he said. He took off his glasses and wiped his eyes. "Dad never left me any notes. What did yours say?"

"I really can't remember," I answered.

Diabetes had affected the nerves in Neville's feet, and he and my mother weren't up for going around the lakes, so we went back to the dock to rent them a rowboat. David and I pushed them off and he and I went back to do the walk around the lake.

"Do you remember when Dad was working on the basement?" I asked as we retraced our steps.

"Sure."

"How come you never helped him?"

"I tried," David said. "But I screwed something up early on. Anyway, it was pretty clear he didn't want to teach me."

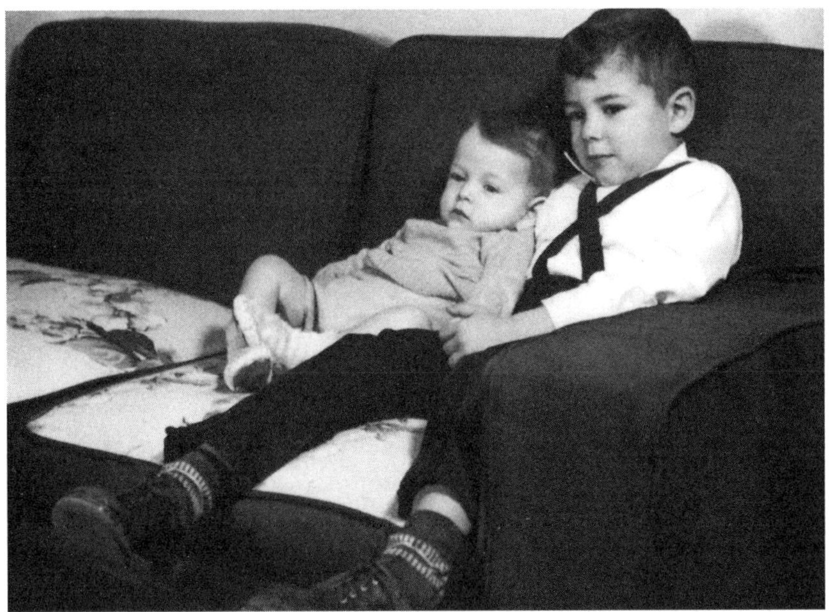

Neville and David, c. 1954.

"Did you or Neville ever read the genealogy he wrote about the family?"

"I never did," David said. "You'd have to ask Neville yourself."

We both avoided looking at my father's tentative gravesite on the way through the Hundred Acre Woods.

"Did Mom and Dad ever talk to you about the Holocaust?"

"Never," David said. "But they didn't talk about a lot of stuff."

We stopped to watch Neville rowing out to the middle of the lake. My mother sat straight in the bow. "Good posture is important," she always said. She waved to us. We waved back.

"It's weird the names they chose for us," I said.

"You mean like naming you and me after no one, and Neville after Neville Chamberlain, the great appeaser of Hitler?"

"Actually, Neville was named for a boy mom took care of after she finished nursing school. He died of tuberculosis. Dad wasn't happy about it, but she got her way. And our Great-Grandfather Helwing was named David."

"You're kidding me," David said. "Does Mom know that?"

"There's the stuff Mom knows and then there's the stuff she knows but doesn't talk about."

"You mean like the fact that her father had another family going in England?" My mother had just received a letter from Grandfather Alfred's great grandson, who stumbled on her and Phyllis while tracing his own genealogy. Nan had apparently been aware of the possibility.

"Yes, like that." We stopped at the end of the lake and watched Neville's awkward rowing.

"I don't remember when I first found out about the Holocaust," I said. "I feel like I inhaled that knowledge, like the radon they discovered in the basement after we all left home."

David's laugh was bitter. He rubbed the dimple in the middle of his chin. "I was twelve or thirteen," he said. "I saw a show about it on television, showing bodies being plowed into a ditch. I found a copy of *The Rise and Fall of the Third Reich* at the library and read it cover to cover."

"Did you ask Dad about it?"

"Are you kidding me?" David answered. "I went across the street and talked to Mr. Rosen." The Rosens were one of the few Jewish families on our street.

"Mr. Rosen turned down the football game and tried to explain World War II and the Holocaust to me during the commercials," David said. "'The war was bad, really bad,' he said. He was one of the only Jews in his battalion, and most of the Southern soldiers had never seen a Jew before. 'They picked up my cap to search for horns.' Mr. Rosen ran his hands over his shiny head when he said that. Once, he was behind enemy lines with his sergeant and another private and they captured a couple of Krauts—that's what he called them. His sergeant told him to keep an eye on the road, and he and the other private took those Krauts into the woods.

He heard some gun shots, and then they came back—without the Germans. The commercial was over then; he wiped his brow with his handkerchief and turned the volume back up. We watched for a few minutes, and then he spoke to the television. He said, 'I never told anyone that story.'"

We walked on.

"You know, some weird stuff came out toward the end with Dad," I said. "He must have told me that story about flushing his last Pfennigs down the toilet on the train out of Germany a million times, and about throwing their hats up in the air. But this last time he said there was a dog with a muzzle and that the soldier had two different colored eyes, which didn't make any sense to me."

"He didn't flush the money down the toilet."

"What?"

"He told me he gave his last coins to some wounded veteran from World War I. He didn't mention anything about a dog—or eyes. But he told me there was a soldier who held back one of the train cars at the border. He played Russian Roulette with those kids for hours."

"That can't be right."

"That's what he told me. He must have been terrified." We stopped and looked down at the submerged trees at the end of the lake. "You know, I couldn't really think what to say back there. That book of photographs you made was the only thing that came to mind. You'd think with everything Dad lost, he would be totally involved with our children and us. But he couldn't have been less interested."

I reached out to touch my brother, but he stepped back. "What I really should have talked about was when Dad took me to Cornell my freshman year. My roommate and his father were already emptying boxes and starting to set things up. Dad helped me bring my suitcases in. He shook hands with me and left. My roommate and his father were together for two hours, putting his books on shelves and making his bed.

"When it came time for his father to leave, they hugged each other and they both cried. They kissed each other on the lips and said 'I love you'—I was embarrassed for them. But now I think maybe *they* were the normal ones, and Dad and I were the ones who should have been embarrassed. I mean, you guys were leaving for Copenhagen. I wouldn't see you for a year. I know Dad was proud of me and that he loved me in some abstract kind of way, but I never felt that love. Then, eight months after you guys left, there was that fire at the dorm." In the middle of the night someone propped open all the safety doors and set fire to the place. His roommate shook David awake. The window louvered from above and there wasn't room to crawl out. They made it down the hallway just before the place was engulfed in flames. David lost everything. Nine people died, mostly on David's floor.

"It's weird we didn't fly home to see you after that," I said. "Did they send you a ticket to visit us?"

"I don't think it crossed any of our minds," David said.

We walked a few steps, but David stopped again. "You know, Dad never once said 'I love you' to me."

"He never said it to me on his own," I said. "But he did if I said it first. Did you ever try saying it first?"

"My shrink suggested I try that. I couldn't explain it to him. It was just something I could never do."

"Maybe the way Dad was with us had something to do with how we echoed his own family almost exactly, right down to the spacing. Boy-boy-girl."

"Sounds a little convoluted."

"Maybe that's why he mixed me up with his sister. Maybe Neville reminded him of Uri—and you reminded him of himself."

"That's a stretch."

We walked out on the ledge at Dead Man's Point. A sign read: "No swimming or wading, fifteen days in jail or $150."

"When we were growing up, this sign said five days in jail or $25," I said.

"Inflation," David said.

We laughed.

"I'm going to ignore that sign someday," I said. "When I'm really old it won't matter to me if I spend a few days in a cell. You can plead my case to the judge."

We peered over the edge together.

"If I knew I'd just have to pay the fine, I'd dive in right now," I said.

Chalky clouds floated in green water, and the cliffs vanished below them. I waited for some sense of my father's presence, but it didn't come.

Correspondence

Vienna, 16 May.1939

Dear Harry!

I'm still here! I'm really furious! Can't you find a sponsor for me? Try your best. I want to leave. Sometimes I just want to scream and cry but I know it won't help and I'm still here! I wait for the certificate every day, but it doesn't come. The only children that get to go are the ones with patronage!!! That's so unfair!!! Please, dear Harry, see to it that I get out of here. Can't I come and live on the farm where you are?

Pretty soon I'll be 14 years old. I promise that I'll peel as many potatoes and work as hard as you like if only you can get me out of here!!!! So Harry, see to it that I get out!!! You were in the English school there—couldn't you go and ask if it would be possible for them to take on another girl? Please go there and talk, talk, talk!!!!! Maybe you could talk to a committee or anything else you can think of ...

I'm really looking forward to getting that little dictionary! I am in dire need of it at the moment. You have to excuse me for not writing in English but sometimes I can't think of the English words and then I can't construct the sentence properly. So please send it to me soon!!!! Now I can't think of any more news to write except that I'm terribly bored and I want to get away from here!!!!!!!

p.s. Take care of it!!!

Many kisses

Mia

Here I have a little bit of space to write! Because I don't know what to write anymore, I'll draw a little picture instead:

 TWENTY-THREE

MY FATHER'S RENDITIONS of his flight from Vienna darkened after his flashbacks, but after talking to David I realized I was still missing many details. Now I imagined him sitting in a third-class seat surrounded by his borrowed valises. Among his things are two changes of underwear, some monogrammed shirts from a family friend, his passport and papers, a parcel of photographs tied up with twine, a slide rule, a compass, his two nineteenth-century mathematics books, and a sandwich of bread and margarine. Also, I know now, he has the small clay bust of an unknown woman and the lenses from his dismembered telescope.

The window next to his seat is so grimy that my father can't see his family watching from the platform. He tries to wipe the glass clean with his sleeve but it remains opaque. He stands up and yanks on the window but it's jammed.

I imagine Mia standing with my grandparents on the platform. She strains to get a final glimpse of him. *Where is he?* The few other passengers in the car stare straight ahead as my father struggles with the window, his sobs breaking against the pane as the train lurches out of the station. He gives up, swallows his tears, sits down, pulls his smallest valise beside him, and shrinks into Menio's heavy army coat. When he wakes, a corpulent woman has wedged him against the window. His legs tingle when he tries to move.

He takes out his sandwich, avoiding the eyes of the little girl who sits with her parents in the bank of seats across from him. He chews and swallows, trying to fill the emptiness growing in his chest. Through the opposite windows, pale green fields replace brown hills. The sky is Syracuse grey. My father is still hungry when he finishes the sandwich. The little girl munches on tiny marzipan fruit from a red tin.

The train stops before the frontier and some passengers disembark. A thick Wehrmacht officer enters the back of the car and walks up the aisle with a German shepherd grinning into its leather muzzle. Then the soldier works his way back. He glances through the papers of the parents of the little girl. He chucks her under the chin. Then, the soldier turns to the woman next to my father. She hands over her papers with a smile. The soldier smiles back.

Then the soldier holds out a broad hand to my father. "Your papers."

My father hands them over. I imagine other passengers turn away when they see the prominent "J."

"Come with me," the soldier signals.

My father puts his papers into the suitcase and closes it up. He steps out into the aisle in front of the soldier and feels the dog's warm breath against the back of his legs. Passengers step out of the aisle to let them pass.

"*Bitte.*" The soldier apologizes to each, indicating my father.

At the next-to-last car, a soldier leans against the door. He holds out a basket with one good arm. The other empty sleeve is pinned up at the elbow. The veteran eyes my father's coat and says, "I am sure my brother from the last Great War will want to contribute to our fund for the Reich's wounded?" He smiles a crooked smile.

My father puts down his valise and reaches into the pocket of Menio's coat. He pulls out his last Pfennigs and throws them in the basket.

"*Danke!*" The soldier salutes my father with his shoulder, clicking his heels together.

In the last car my father joins eight teenaged boys guarded by a German boy-soldier. The train lurches to a stop. My father looks out the window. The big soldier and his dog disembark. The boy-soldier stands with his feet apart and stares at the back of the car. His pink cheeks contrast with the drawn faces of the Jewish boys, who look out the windows at the passengers lining up at a long table to have their papers stamped.

The little girl follows her parents and joins the queue. The soldier with the dog stands and dictates while another officer types and stamps. The line moves through and the passengers board the train again. When the platform is empty, the whistle shrieks. A thud, and my father's car drifts backward. They are uncoupled.

Outside the window, the clerk packs up his papers and the typewriter. The burly soldier climbs back on board. The muzzle is off the dog, and it strains against its leash and draws back its upper lip. In the light of the window the soldier's eyes are two different colors. One blue, one green. He dismisses the boy soldier and settles across from my father. "Let's play a little game," he says. "It's actually a Russian game. Maybe you are familiar with it since your pestilence comes from the East?"

The man opens his revolver and the bullets clamor onto the floor.

"Pick them up," he says.

My father's lips are dry. He tries to wet them with his tongue. He goes down on his hands and knees and crawls around the car to collect the bullets

"There should be eight," the soldier says.

My father reaches around the other boys' legs. One of the younger boys sobs.

My father hands the soldier the bullets, then sits back down. The soldier takes one bullet and puts it back in the gun. He rolls the cartridge, whips around and holds it up to the crying boy's head. It snaps when he pulls the trigger, and the boy faints.

"He played Russian roulette with us for hours," I imagined my father telling David, speaking again in his flat voice. "But at the end of the game, the soldier showed us that the gun was empty the entire time."

"Then what happened?" David might have asked. I wondered how old he was when he heard this.

"That's all I remember about that," my father would have answered.

The caboose is hooked up to the next train coming through. The Jewish boys sit as far apart as possible. The small boy snuffles into his sleeve. They all stare out the windows as they cross into Belgium.

In this version no one cheers. They keep their hats on.

PART III

JOURNEY

Correspondence

Dear Lisa!

Medizinalrat is a very old-fashioned and distinguished title for medical doktors (after about 100 years of practice (especially for the emperor's family)). But medium height and brown hair is okay—it's quite the same with me ... If i am at the airport (which seem to be more likely because i think about a short trip in the same direction in the afternoon with a friend of mine, i'll stand at the exit of the customs on the left side (from where you exit) and i'll improvise a decent white paper with a simple "lisa gruenberg" on it. Behind the paper is probably a dark-red poloshirt with blue jeans (and shoes—for this exceptional occasion). Otherwise we will manage to get in contact soonest—okay? Have a great trip, enjoy lovely Frankfurt and please don't laugh when you see from the plane how small Vienna is. looking forward to meet you in person.

niki

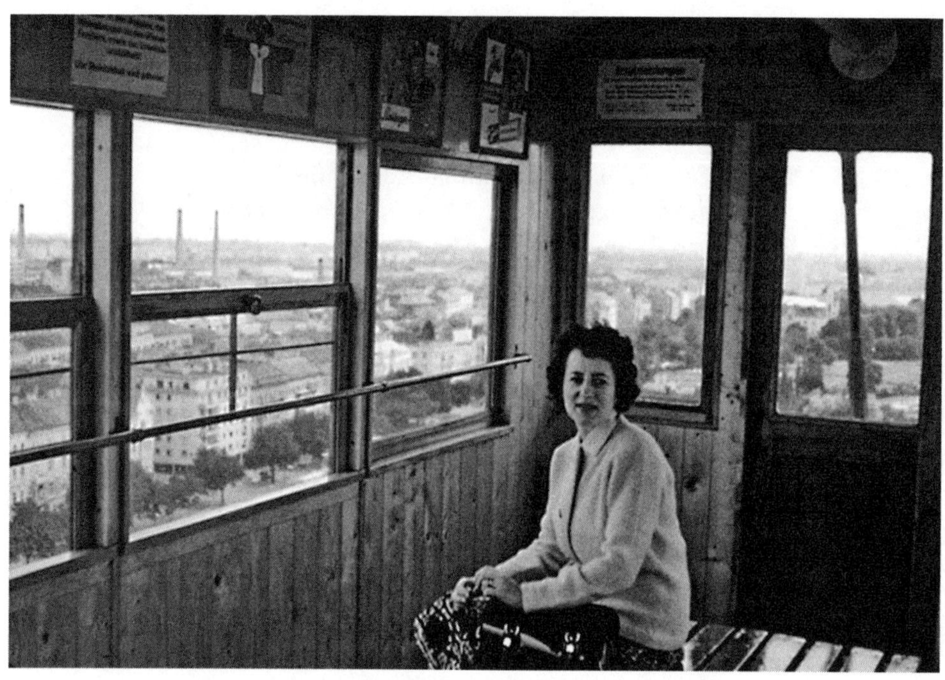

My mother rides the Riesenrad, the giant Ferris wheel at the Prater, on the first of my parents' many trips to Vienna.

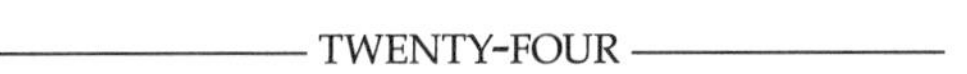

TWENTY-FOUR

After a sleepless night and a long stopover in Frankfurt, my plane drifted over the Danube. The river was a muddy expanse, not the deep blue I'd expected, and I couldn't see the city. I was alone. Martin wouldn't join me for another week and my brothers hadn't wanted to come.

It was September 2006, a little over a year after my father's death. There had been an odd quality to my journey right from the start. Wild opportunities and unlikely coincidences made me think I heard the planets grinding into alignment. Niki, my quixotic tour guide, was drawn into my orbit by one of those coincidences, the death of my childhood pediatrician, Hans Hartenstein.

Despite our differences in age, I counted Hans as a close friend in his last years. He grew up in the Ninth District, just like my father, and also escaped via England. But his family was well off; both his parents got out with him and managed to get sponsors in Milwaukee. Hans was the cousin of a classmate of my father's from Caltech and, oddly enough, settled in Syracuse around the same time we did. Hans read everything I wrote, and we spoke a lot about his experiences before his family fled. He told me he broke his vow never to return to Vienna only once. In the early seventies he went with his wife and teenage daughters.

"I found myself filled with panic," he told me. "Every time I saw someone who looked to be my age or a little older, I wondered where they had been during that year after the Anschluss. I could never understand how your father could go back there again and again."

Hans died on the afternoon of my father's Jahrzeit. His memorial service was held on what would have been my parents' sixtieth wedding anniversary. In the crowds milling around the buffet after the service, I ran into an acquaintance, a doctor who grew up in Syracuse and also practiced in Boston. Her mother was Viennese and also escaped in 1939. I told her about my upcoming trip.

"Do you want a contact in Vienna?" she asked me.

"Absolutely," I answered. "I just have appointments at some of the archives. Only one of my father's cousins is still there, but I haven't reached him yet."

"I have a second cousin there," she told me. "He's the son of my mother's cousin. Niki's youngish; he's never settled down. His family is wealthy—old money. He's the grandson of a Jewish physician on one side, an SS officer on the other."

"Sounds interesting," I said.

"He's not entirely reliable," she said.

I scribbled Niki's email onto my palm.

"The last time I gave his name to someone, he bought them opera tickets and they never showed up," she said. "Promise me you will meet up with him if he answers you,"

"I promise," I said.

After a quick walk through customs, I saw a young man with damp hair holding up a piece of paper with "LISA GRÜNBERG" written in block letters. Under it was the red polo shirt and blue jeans. A day's growth shaded sculpted features. He wore shoes. Some men twinkle, and Niki was definitely one of them.

We shook hands. "*Grüss Gott!*" He gave me the standard Austrian greeting. "Let's run; my friend is parked illegally."

He grabbed my heavy duffle and trotted away. In my hand was his business card. "Mag. Nicolas Macke," it said. I looked up in time to see Niki and my bag fly out the doors. I hobbled after him into the warmth of an Indian summer afternoon.

A dusty BMW purred at the curb. Niki tossed my bag into the trunk. He insisted on squeezing into the back seat, throwing papers to one side. I collapsed next to the driver, who smiled and shook my hand.

"Karin," she said.

Karin was one long muscle clothed in a sleeveless black dress. Without makeup, her pallor revealed the fine bones under her skin. Tucking yellow hair behind her ears, she swerved into traffic. Her bare legs pumped the pedals with black high heels. She and Niki had spent that afternoon mountain biking in the Vienna Woods and Karin's hair was also damp from her shower. She waved to emphasize her mix of clipped German and English.

I angled back to Niki. "So, your family is in renovations?" My friend had told me Niki ran part of the family business. They repainted the opera house after it was bombed by the Allies at the end of the war.

"I don't work so much," he said, "and it's not so interesting."

Niki and Karin flirted and sparred, but their repartee was comfortable, more like fond brother and sister. They had met in high school. Karin was divorced. Niki had never married. Neither of them had children. My new friends drew me in. I felt witty, despite the jet lag.

"My parents met at the first Opera Ball after the war," Niki told me. "I don't think I have met my future wife yet. I think she may still be in grade school."

Karin groaned, "What brings you, Lisa? How can we help?"

"I'm going to some archives to look for relatives and neighbors of my father," I said. "But my main reason for coming is to see some of his old haunts and to try to capture the magic of this city as he saw it." When I explained about my father's romantic stories mixed with the horror of his later outbursts, my father's eyes seemed to gaze out of Niki's face.

We drove over the Danube Canal, wider than I imagined, and onto the Ringstrasse, the avenue built in the nineteenth century to replace the wall that once surrounded the First District, the Inner City of Vienna. Niki and Karin pointed out sights as we passed. The solid buildings glowed. People strolled, still dressed for summer.

I'd chosen my pension in the Ninth District when I saw that it was a few streets away from where my father grew up. When we drove up, I recognized the exterior, but it looked shabby compared to the charming turn-of-the-century building pictured on the Internet. Karin parked illegally. Niki came around and opened the door for me. The key was in the lockbox by the door, as promised.

Niki hauled my bag out of the trunk and slung it over his shoulders and I followed him up the dim stairway. We heaved against the door to open it.

Painted in warm yellows, the apartment was reminiscent of the computer image. But the tall windows faced an airshaft, the living room was dark, and Israeli pop music blared from the opposite apartment.

I caught my tired reflection in the hallway mirror. Through the glass, Niki tossed my bag onto the bed in the room beyond. He ran his finger through the dust on the desk.

"Your clock isn't working," he said, plugging the number on the telephone into his cell phone. He walked back and put a hand on the doorknob, his other on my shoulder.

"You'll be okay?" he asked.

"I'll be fine," I said, even though I wasn't sure I would be. "Can I take you two to dinner sometime? Shall we make a date?"

"I rarely make plans more than a day in advance," Niki said. "But don't worry, I'll call you."

His footsteps receded down the hall.

I sat at the desk and picked up the telephone. It buzzed. I glanced at my wrist and realized I'd left my watch at home. I pulled out my laptop and tried to figure out how to reach the Internet and Martin, but the computer seemed as confused as I was, refusing to connect.

I pulled out the map my father had written on when we did the videotapes, to show me where things were. The lamp was too dim to read by. I went into the bathroom, sat on the toilet, and squinted at the maze of streets around me. The tail of a migraine knocked behind my forehead. I felt as if I had fallen into a nightmare where I didn't know how I arrived or where I was, and that, somehow, I had forgotten to put on my clothes. I only understood a little German; I didn't like traveling alone.

I stuffed the map in my purse and stood up by the sink. Nan admonished me from the mirror. "Come on; pull up your socks!" I grabbed an Advil, showered in lukewarm water, dried off with a thin towel, tugged on fresh clothes, and went out to stroll through my father's city. The skies turned rosy as I walked back to my apartment. Once home, I fell across the bed and tumbled into sleep.

For the first time in years, I dreamt.

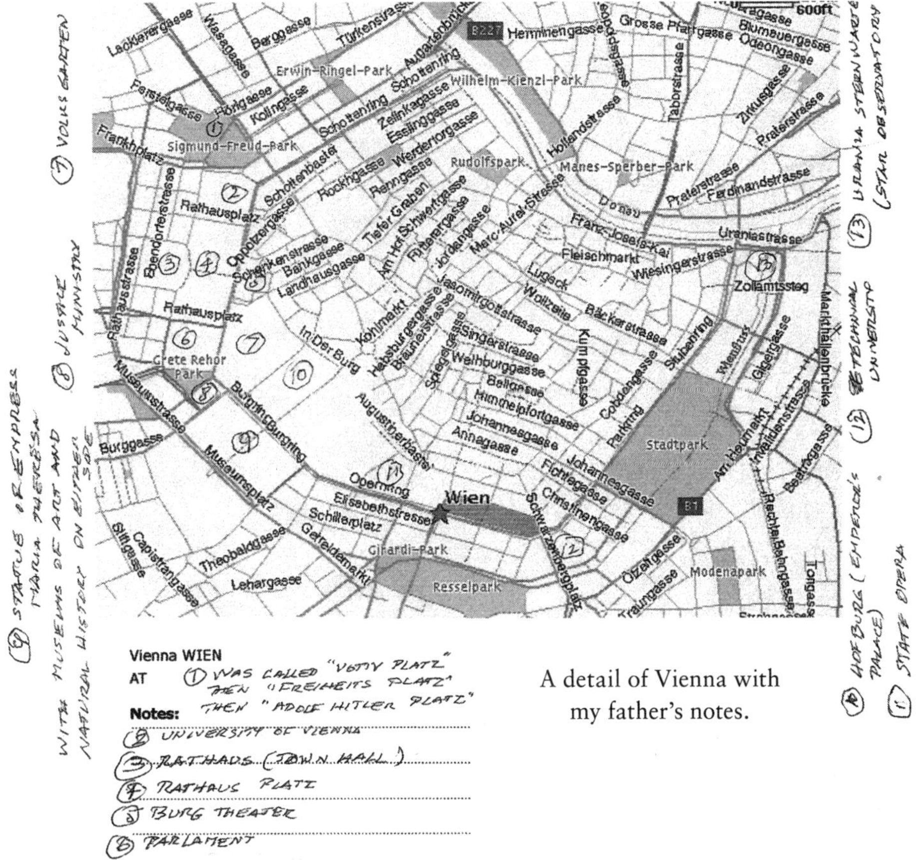

A detail of Vienna with my father's notes.

Correspondence

Vienna, 23 May.1939

Dear Harry!

I'm telling you, it's really frustrating – Mama and Papa both say that you should write <u>my</u> curriculum vitae! But the fact of the matter is I will write it myself! It should read something like this:

I am 13 years old and was born in Vienna on January 26, 1926 and am of German nationality. I have completed four years of elementary school, two years of middle school with excellent grades, and now attend vocational school because it is not allowed for Jews to attend academic high schools. I can speak some English and Hebrew and I am good with small children. I am also talented at drawing and needlework.

I'll try to put it into English now!

I am 13 years ~~old~~ old, ~~and~~ was born in Vienna on the
26th of January 1926 and ~~I~~ am German ~~natio~~
nality. I finished four classes of the elementary school
and two of the higher school with very good result and now I visit
the 3rd class of the normal school, because it is
not allowed for Jews to visit higher school.
I can a little English and Hebrew and I understa
good to keep compost pany with little Children.
Also I have talent to draw and to hand=
needleworks

Mia Grünberg

Did I make many mistakes? Please write them out for me! I was very happy to receive the dictionary and thank you so much! In Mutti's letter I crossed out something (with her knowledge). She wrote that I am "wild with excitement," which isn't true!!!!

Many kisses and see to it that I get out of here,
Your Mia

TWENTY-FIVE

A CHILD SINGING a nursery rhyme sliced through a forgotten dream. I covered my head with the pillow, then lifted the corner to check the broken clock and my empty wrist. After dozing a little longer, I threw off the bedclothes and shuffled across cold floors to yank the drapes open. I leaned out the window, but the small square of gray sky withheld the time of day.

I pulled on my jeans from the flight and slipped a jacket over my T-shirt. I grabbed my purse and went out into the hall, tripping over a plastic basket of butter rolls. I grabbed one, tossed the basket inside my door, and ran down the spiral of stairs in search of its deliverer. Outside, the sun maneuvered onto the narrow street. An olive-skinned woman washed the steps. She dried her hands on her apron while I tried English, then bad German, then hand signals to explain my dilemma with the clock, the telephone and the computer. She shook her head. I pointed to her watch and she showed me the time. Seven o'clock.

"Herr Doktor Grossmannn," she said, and handed me a card. She pointed to Doktor Grossmann's number and pantomimed making a phone call. I tried to gesticulate that the phone wasn't working, then gave up and walked in what I hoped was the direction of the university, gnawing on the stale roll.

I cut through the small streets and found an avenue running back toward the Ringstrasse. Across from the university I turned into a café and took a seat by the window. The waitress wiped my table down with a few swipes but didn't make eye contact.

"*Bitte?*" she asked. She tapped her foot and stared out the window while I stumbled through my order.

She examined me over the glass case of pastries while she steamed the milk. When I caught her eye, she turned back to her work. She returned and plunked down the *café mélange*. She kept her eyes down while she made out the bill and placed it in front of me. My drink was set on an oblong plate with a glass of water and a few chunks of sugar. The thick layer of milk released a rich smell. I looked out at the gate of the University of Vienna while I waited for the coffee to cool. The guidebook told me that with the price of a coffee I owned my seat for as long as I liked. I stared out at students rushing to class.

In the last years of his life, my father remembered a few more stories. They were no longer real flashbacks, but more like flashes of suppressed emotion. Gaping holes of memory yawned between them. He struggled to place when some events happened. He placed one isolated childhood memory in front of the main building of the university in the late winter of 1929, but I am not sure if that was accurate. He also told me that was the year that his grandfather David Helwing died, but my research would place his death in 1934. So, I wondered if this memory, set nearby, was actually from around that time, when the Fascists took over "Red Vienna."

Like me, my father was small for his age when he was young, and I imagined he was swallowed up by his short pants and heavy sweater. Dark curls peeped out under his wool cap and fell over his forehead. His cheeks flushed. A crowd collected by the steps of the university, stamping their feet in the cold. More people gathered. He hoisted himself onto the edge of a fountain to get a better view.

Looking over the heads of the crowd, my father faced a group of men standing on the steps of the main building. The men wore woolen army coats, leftover uniforms from the Great War. One man was speaking to the crowd, his arms slicing the air as he made his points.

His eyes rose up and focused on my father, and he continued to speak as if talking directly to him. My father could only catch a few words—perhaps *Arbeit,* "work," or maybe it was "unemployment." The man's hat slanted across his forehead, and my father felt an urge to reach over the crowd to straighten it out.

But in my imagination, the man's face suddenly clouds and his speech accelerates like the patter of water forced through a narrow sluice. His voice merges with the pounding of marching feet. The crowd turns and faces my father, then looks beyond him. My father turns to follow the line of their eyes. Soldiers pour into the square. They wear metal helmets and their bayonets reach toward the sky. A howl rises from the crowd.

My father's rheumy eyes had looked far away when he told me this.

"Dad, where are you, where were you?" I'd asked.

"I was there, there," he'd said, pointing to the coffee table in front of him.

The soldiers form two rows in the square. The front row drops to one knee, and they bring their guns to their shoulders.

"Dad, did the speakers falter? Were you in the middle of the crowd?"

"I don't know. I don't know."

I imagined my father freezing on the edge of the fountain. The crowd crashes into each other as they try to disperse. And then the sound of the guns—the guns are not as loud as my father expected, but the shrieks fill his ears.

"Bullets hit a woman near me," my father had said. I imagined a small "poof" as a bullet punctures her shoulder and then another hits her abdomen. An explosion of dust flies up from her wounds. Her body spirals to the ground. My father leaps into the bowl of the fountain. It is drained for the winter, but a thin layer of water is frozen at the bottom. When my father hits the ice, it crunches and sends fissures out around him like a spider's web. He gets down on all fours and traces the lace of the cracks with one finger, watching the mist from his breath curl around his face. A few bullets hit the statue above him. As he moves over the surface of the ice, it gives under his knees and hands; muddy water oozes under his fingertips. He sits down and leans against the side, rolls his head back, and looks up at the sky as it begins to rain. He pulls a few coins out of his pocket and fingers their icy surfaces.

The gunshots stop and the screams fade. My father pulls himself over the lip of the fountain. Soldiers amble through the square, stepping over bodies. The veterans are guided into a police van. The leader of the protest is the last into the car; his face blue with bruises, his nose bloody, he looks toward my father as he is pulled in.

No one else notices as a small boy runs across the square.

I left some change on the oblong plate, signaled the waitress I was leaving, and walked to a payphone to call the pension owner.

"Like every hotel in the world, you dial '0,'" Herr Doktor Grossmann said.

"I tried that; it didn't work," I shouted. The connection was poor. "And you should have a ticket for me for an event tonight."

"We didn't receive anything for you."

"I gave them the pension address."

"What was it for?"

I hesitated. "It was from the Jewish Community—for tonight."

I heard a chuckle. "Are you a fellow traveler, Frau Doktor Grünberg? For Yom Kippur services? Just tell them Herr Doktor Grossmann sent you."

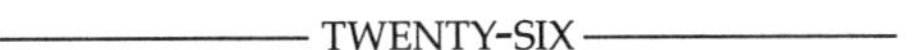

TWENTY-SIX

The orthodox Stadttempel is built in the middle of a city block in the Innere Stadt. It is connected with surrounding buildings on three sides. Visitors have to enter through a small doorway in a wall. This was due to an eighteenth-century edict issued by Emperor Joseph II that only Catholic churches could be entered directly from the street. The building's close proximity to the other buildings actually saved the synagogue from complete destruction on Kristallnacht because the Nazis were afraid the whole neighborhood might go up in flames if they torched the Stadttempel.

Parishioners jammed along Seitenstettengasse, waiting to pass through that doorway under the scrutiny of Israeli soldiers, poorly disguised in suits and ties. When I reached the front of the line, I greeted them in Hebrew, they waved me through. I climbed circular stairs to join the women on the fourth level. Men crowded the sanctuary below me, adjusting blue and white prayer shawls over dark suits. Kippot perched on thick curls and bald heads. Incongruously, a little girl with reddish hair climbed in and out of laps in the second row. The din was overwhelming.

I gave up my seat three times as new arrivals showed me their tickets and claimed their places. Like caricatures of Jackie Kennedy from the sixties, the middle-aged women wore Chanel-style suits and pumps. Sapphire powder wrinkled drooping eyelids, wigs were swept into flips and gold bracelets weighed down their arms. The few young women in the upper gallery appeared fresh and exotic by comparison. I ended up crammed against the front railing next to an aging Kirov ballerina-type with raven hair tied in a low bun.

"Where are you from?" I asked.

"Why, Vienna, of course," she answered with a thick Russian accent.

It was unlikely that there were many Holocaust survivors in the crowd. I'd read that most of the congregation was made up of Russian Jews who came through Vienna in the 1970s on their way to Israel. They learned how to be Jews with the help of the Jewish Community of Vienna. Once they reached the Promised Land, many found they did not fit in. They decided to *yoredet*, to "come down," and return to Austria.

The Kol Nidre smoldered under the alto notes of ongoing conversation. The rabbi added his drone in German. I was pinned against the Russian woman and the railing. I looked for the little girl, but she was gone. The room seemed to tip and I panicked, as if I might pitch over the railing and into the men's section. These people had their own sad stories, but they were not the stories I searched for. I shoved my way back to the stairway, setting off a ripple of complaints. I ran down the steps and out the door. The guards leaned against the wall of the temple, smoking. Their ties were gone.

I aimed toward the spires of Stephansdom. The illuminated steeples came in and out of view as I twisted my way through dark streets. When I entered the bright plaza with the giant church lit up at its center, I imagined the cathedral falling like a fat mother into the center of Vienna. The collision collapsed medieval houses into rubble, leaving her to soar in her own clearing. Teenagers, couples, and families surrounded me as we strolled into the Graben, the broad pedestrian avenue, and past the baroque Pestsäule commemorating the plague of 1679. Tables spilled onto the cobblestones from crowded cafés. The glow of restaurant windows attracted me, but I was repelled by the idea of eating. I ached for Martin and the girls.

A sign lured me away from the crowds, down a narrow side street and into the empty Judenplatz. The moon moved out from behind a cloud and illuminated an immense concrete tomb in the center of the small square. Its walls were carved like bookshelves, but the spines of its books faced inward. Names of death camps were carved around the base—Auschwitz, Theresienstadt, Treblinka. And there it was. Maly Trostinec: a minor death camp outside of Minsk. I'd come across the name only weeks before I'd left for Vienna. One of the few archivists who answered my calls was Christa Prokisch at the Jewish Museum in Vienna. She was interested in Mia and my father, even though she must have heard hundreds of stories like theirs.

"Mia and your grandparents would have been sent on from the train station in Minsk, to a place called Maly Trostinec," she told me.

"My father thought Mia might not have been on that train. He thought there might have been an error in the habitation records."

There was a pause at the other end of the line. I heard Christa typing. "But she's listed here with your parents on the May 27 Deportationsliste. I doubt there was any mistake."

I regretted that I had found this out too late to tell my father. But sorting through his papers again before I left, I had found five printouts of Belarus from MapQuest. Each copy focused closer and closer on Minsk. My father's block letters emerged from the page. "Maly Trostinec"—the words had been made visible only because I now knew what to look for.

> The train rambled through the steppes of Poland
> Towards a bloodbath in the forests of Minsk
> The cries went up to heaven
> But men and God remained silent.

My father must have uncovered the Deportationsliste when he had made his last trip to Vienna—perhaps he found out something more. Had he tried to tell me something? Was I listening? It had mattered so much to him exactly how his family lived and died.

Alone in his city, I found it also mattered to me.

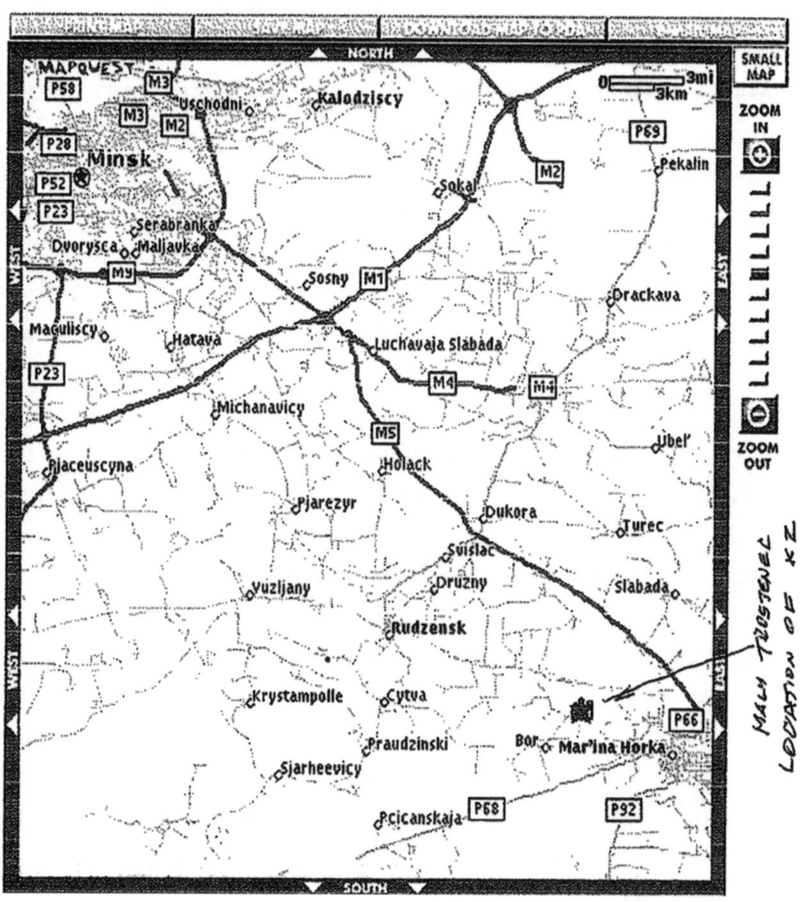

Printout of Belarus from my father's papers.
His block letters on the right read: "Maly Trostinec."

Correspondence

Vienna, 23 April.1940

Dear Harry!

I was glad to receive your letter. It seems that you are feeling comfortable there and also enjoying your work—which is the main thing. This time you didn't write anything about Uri and the others. You haven't received letters from them, have you? ... I wanted to notify you that we will most likely have to move out of our apartment by May 1, so I am searching for a suitable place. Grandmother and Aunt Pepi are planning to travel from Genoa to Shanghai on May 10, but this is still not certain.

I send my heartfelt greetings and kisses.

Your Papa

Dear Harry!

Today I have an awful lot to write to you. So let's put everything in order!

1. Every afternoon I go to the Straub market garden out in the Nineteenth District. One is expected to work very hard there—digging, weeding, harvesting, etc. ... but it's a lot of fun. There are several groups of us girls between fourteen and seventeen from the Youth Aliyah School and we work under the direction of the commanding officer and the assistant commanding officer. The commanding officers are two older gardeners, rather strict but really super. Their assistants are two younger guys, both about seventeen. That makes them feel very high and mighty but I don't mind. I've even become one of their favorites. I didn't scream, for example, when one had to rip a bandage off a wound on my hand in order to replace it with a fresh one. I am as brave as a boy and I do great work. So what do you say about that?

2. I received two affidavits from those nice Californians (Lilly Barker and her brother) but it didn't work out. I can't leave after all.

3. Yesterday I was summoned to Aron Menczer. Earlier I had filled out a form certifying that I have a blood relative in Palestine (Uri). So, I get there, and Aron was—of course!—super nice to me and he told me that, at present, I am not dependent on Uri for help although I could possibly be invited to his kibbutz. He thinks there is a very good chance that I will be able to leave ... Then he told me: "I know you so well and anyway you are such a good student in school, etc., that if there is ever a possibility for someone to leave, then you will be at the top of the list." What do you say to that?!

4. Next time I'll tell you in detail about the Pesach gathering. It ended on the 6th already and Mutti wants to write something!

Many kisses.
Mia-Neomi
Answer my questions!!!!
Plus the old questions!!!!!!

Dear Harry!

We enjoyed reading your last letter and this time you wrote us a detailed report, however, you didn't answer my questions. Are you still the accountant on the farm? We are glad that you are able to study the language more intensively. Are you in good health? Will you be able to observe the high holidays there? We haven't heard anything from Uri—I just don't understand why the boy doesn't write.

I will close by sending you tender greetings and kisses and pleasant holidays.

Mutti

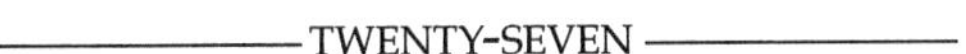

TWENTY-SEVEN

ASIDE FROM THE archives at the Jewish Museum, where Christa Prokisch always gave me a warm handshake and invited me into her office for tea, each of the many archives had its own peculiar code of conduct that only became clear after I had erred. The Archive of the City of Vienna, the Staatsarchiv, was sterile. They provided a lab coat and assigned me an assistant. He handled microfiche with cotton gloves. I directed him with whispers. At the Landesarchiv, the archivists stood behind a desk as tall as my forehead. I shouted up my requests, as if I were at the deli counter.

"You need to have an appointment," they called down, sternly.

"But you never answer the telephone," I called up, crossly.

The Archives of the Jewish Community of Vienna, the IKG, was buried in a warren of rooms in the basement of the Stadttempel. The director wrangled leather-bound records out of rickety cabinets. My father's family and neighbors crammed into columns and boxes, all written in the same spidery hand. The archivist pushed me away when I tried to look through the books myself. "These are fragile!" he scolded. He cradled his cell phone in the crook of his neck to free up a hand. His cigarette spewed ashes as he turned the pages for me. He couldn't direct me to the Holocaust Victims Information and Support Center, but it turned out they were right around the corner in a modern apartment building.

"We can't help you," the archivists at the Victims Center told me when I finally found them. "We only deal with compensation issues." But they called me back within a week. "Could you stop by this afternoon and pick up a few papers?" They handed me a stack thick as a Bible, each person housed in a separate plastic folder.

And I was warned not to expect a warm reception at the Dokumentationsarchiv des österreichischen Widerstandes (DÖW), the Archives of the Austrian Resistance. The name struck me as an oxymoron. Was there an Austrian Resistance? I'd only seen pictures of Jews being humiliated in the streets after the Anschluss, Jewish windows broken and paint-drizzled writing on the doors of Jewish stores.

But the DÖW (pronounced "dove") had to be visited. I was told it was the source of the deportation lists released in the late 1990s, confirming Mia and my grandparents were on a transport together, leaving Vienna for Minsk on May 27, 1942. The office didn't answer my inquiries, so I simply turned up.

A circular stairway ended at a bolted door. I buzzed and somebody buzzed back. Inside, a receptionist peered at me over wire-rimmed glasses. A stripe of crimson coursed through her gray crew cut.

"It was for the election," she said when I stared at the stripe. "I think it helped."

I couldn't come up with a response. "I'm a Communist," she said. "The election was yesterday." She shrugged when I still looked blank. She pointed at the sign-in list and asked for my passport. I left my cell phone and jacket in a rusty locker and took my notes with me. I followed the communist receptionist though a series of windowless rooms lined by files and books.

A pale woman my height and age stood up when I passed through the last door. Precarious towers of papers and documents covered every inch of her desk. On the shelves behind her, a zigzag of books and boxes looked as if an earthquake had just hit.

"Dr. Elisabeth Klamper," she said. She gripped my hand across the table. Her skin was as arid as her manner. One of the piles on the desk rang. She left my hand extended and deftly wrested the receiver from underneath the pile. She plunked into her seat and swiveled to look out the window. She spoke in rapid German; a hint of a smile on her lips. I sat down in the hard chair across from her. In the corner of the office, a ponytailed young man sat at a computer. He flushed scarlet when I caught him staring at me. He cast his eyes back to his screen. His blush faded, but two bright circles remained on his cheeks as if he had been slapped. I pulled papers out of my bag and piled them on the floor next to me. I thought about how to best frame my requests.

Dr. Klamper finished her call. "How can I help you?" She drummed her fingers on the arm of her chair.

"Well, I'm looking for a number of things," I rushed, hoping to capture what seemed to be her limited interest. "For one, I want the actual documents that confirm my Aunt Mia and my grandparents were deported together, and I was told those documents would be here, at the DÖW. I'm also hoping to connect with someone who might have known Mia. My father didn't seem to remember that much about her, even though her letters implied they were very close."

"There is nothing here that will help you, nothing at all. Those documents are at the Staatsarchiv." Dr. Klamper turned her swivel chair toward the young man, and his forehead clashed with his strawberry blond hair again. "Print out the directions to the Staatsarchiv for Frau Doktor Grünberg!" The young man typed furiously and then ran out of the room.

Dr. Klamper's eyes receded behind her glasses. She seemed to be waiting for me to pull my things together to leave.

"But there is a bit of a mystery to all this—let me explain." I willed her not to turn from me. I pulled out the police documents from my father's files.

"You see, my father obtained these documents in 1946. This first one is probably correct. It shows my father's departure on March 12, 1939." I put the copy on her desk. She barely glanced at it.

"And this one says my father's sister left for Minsk on April 27, 1942."

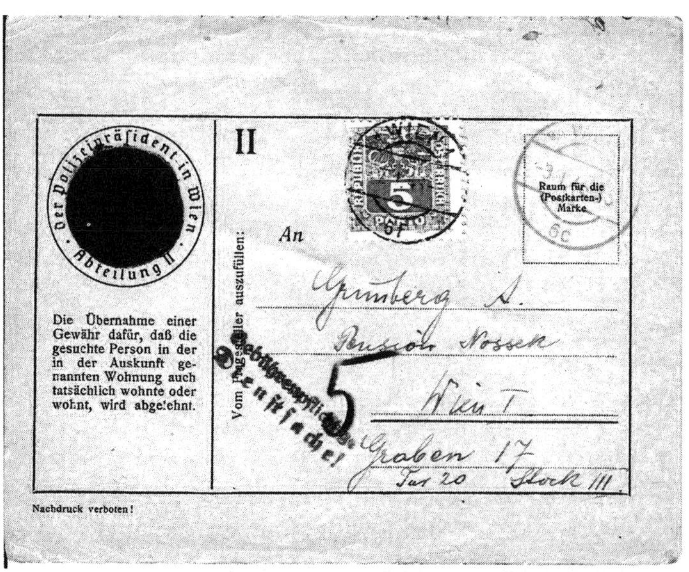

Der Polizeipräsident in Wien
Abteilung II

Die Übernahme einer Gewähr dafür, daß die gesuchte Person in der in der Auskunft genannten Wohnung auch tatsächlich wohnte oder wohnt, wird abgelehnt.

II

Vom Fragesteller auszufüllen:

An

Grünberg A.
Pension Nossek
Wien I
Graben 17
Tür 20 Stock III

Raum für die (Postkarten-) Marke

5

Nachdruck verboten!

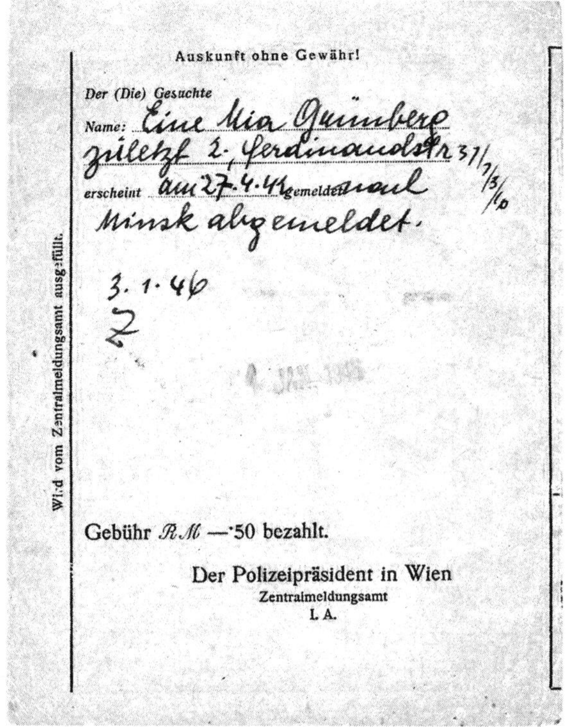

Auskunft ohne Gewähr!

Der (Die) Gesuchte
Name: Eine Mia Grünberg
zuletzt 2, Ferdinandstr 37/7
erscheint am 27.4.42 gemeldet nach
Minsk abgemeldet.

3.1.46

Wird vom Zentralmeldungsamt ausgefüllt.

Gebühr RM —·50 bezahlt.

Der Polizeipräsident in Wien
Zentralmeldungsamt
I. A.

Police documents obtained by my father's Uncle Rudy in 1946 showing Mia's deportation to Minsk.

"There wasn't a transport on that date."

"I know. Maybe that's one of the reasons my father doubted she went to Minsk with my grandparents. And these show my grandparents left for Minsk together, on May 27, 1942." I lay down their cards.

Dr. Klamper leaned in to see the documents, and then her eyes lit up and she laughed. "Left—they left? They didn't 'leave.'" She pointed at the German word *abgemeldet*, then tried to pluck the translation out of the air with her hand. "They didn't leave—they moved on, no, they 'vacated'—no, they were 'cancelled,' *cancelled* to Minsk."

She chuckled and turned to her keyboard and began typing fast. "These bureaucrats," she said as her fingers hammered. She turned the screen so I could see. "Here they are on the May 27 transport." I saw Mia, Leo, and Elka clustered together on a long list of names. There were numbers next to them, consecutive numbers.

She shouted in German, and another boy flew in and replaced his blushing colleague. This one was a brunette with one gold earring. He typed a few strokes and ran out of the room. The first boy returned with a printout and laid it across two piles on Dr. Klamper's desk and scurried into his seat again.

I continued. "But, you see, it is this document that made my father think maybe the police were mistaken, and that Mia wasn't actually with her parents at the end. This and a letter he remembers getting from his father that said Mia was taken separately in 1941."

I lay down the police record that showed Uri leaving on the same train in 1942. "My uncle left on a children's transport for Palestine in 1938, and survived, so there is no way he could have been on this train."

Dr. Klamper leaned in to examine the copy. Her eyes captured mine. "They didn't make many mistakes, you know," she said. "At least, not with things like this." She picked up the copy to examine it more closely, then she turned back to the computer and typed again.

The second boy returned with more papers and pitched them on the growing pile.

"These habitation records are all stamped 1946. Where did your father get these documents?"

"My father's Uncle Rudy got them when he came back from the Soviet Union after the war. He tried to trace everyone. He told my father that he found out that my grandparents and Mia were gassed at Auschwitz.

"Is his name also Grünberg? Was Rudy a nickname for Martin Grünberg?"

"It was Martin's father, Aaron Grünberg. Aaron was my grandfather's youngest brother. Rudy was his nickname, because he was a redhead."

"Communists?"

"Yes. They fled Austria for Russia around 1934 or 1935."

Dr. Klamper swiveled slightly and, without looking, pulled a booklet from the shelves behind her. She opened it up and offered it to me.

"This is Martin Grünberg. Is this your father's cousin?" The black-and-white picture was of a slim man in his forties.

"It could be."

"This is a small town. My ex-parents-in-law were communists, so, of course, they knew Martin and his father. Aaron and Martin Grünberg were spies, you know, KGB," she twirled her hair around her finger and fixed me with unblinking eyes.

"I don't think so," I said. The light from her desk lamp was too bright.

"Well—maybe not," she turned to type again, then swiveled back. "But we displayed Martin's passport in one of our exhibits about communists in the thirties and then after the war. It was definitely KGB issue. We had to take it down."

Dr. Klamper took up the police documents again. "But who is this, this Raimund Nechmac. Is this another relative?"

"No—Uncle Rudy tried to trace the manager of the building at my grandparents' last address through the Red Cross, to see if he could find out what happened to my grandparents." I held out Raimund

Nechmac's affidavit. Dr. Klamper read the original while I looked at my father's translation. I marveled at how even my father's writing was before his Parkinson's forced it into a slant.

"'The Gestapo forced me to cooperate?'" Dr. Klamper said. "'A thousand people came through my house?'"

This is a letter by somebody named FIOLA to my uncle, Aaron (Rudy) GRÜNBERG concerning NECHMAC RAIMUND, the former caretaker of the house where my parents lived before the were removed from Vienna. It states:

NECHMAC was until 1944 caretaker of the house on FERDINANDSTRASSE 31. According to him he was forced to cooperate with the GESTAPO. Through that house passed about 1000 persons – mostly Jews – on the way to Buchenwald or Theresienstadt [Terezin in Czechoslovakia]. He cannot remember any names. There was a list of all who "passed through". These lists were kept by "house inspector" LEOPOLD HÖHN, an illegal Nazi. Where Höhn is now he does not know.

NECHMAC could not recall the name GRÜNBERG. He (NECHMAC) makes a harmless impression. He has told neighbors repeatedly that he has helped many Jews and that some of them have ~~told him~~ promised him that they would take care of him should they ever come back.

NECHMAC presently (January 1946) lives in Vienna XXII, LOBAU AM SCHILLERWASSER 115 as sub-tenant. He is alone.

NOTE added by me: According to the police NECHMAC RAIMUND moved to the SCHILLERWASSER address on 26 APRIL 1944. (see police report)

en 19. Jänner 1946.

ünberg

, I., Fleischmarkt 3-5

1944 Hausbeorger im Hause
ft war er nach seiner eigenen
er seinerzeitigen Gestapo.
e des Nechmac etwa 1000
henwald - Theresinstadt
mehr erinnerlich. Es waren
gelegt worden. Diese Listen
n, ein illegaler Nationalsoz.
ute aufhält ist ihm nicht

Iamen G r ü n b e r g nicht
harmlosen Eindruck.
iederholt, daß er vielen
dass ihm einige versprochen
kkommens für ihn sorgen werden.

, XXII., Lobau am Schiller-
lleinstehend.

Fiola

Affidavit by Raimund Nechmac, manager of the building at my grandparents' last address, obtained by my father's Uncle Rudy through the Red Cross.

I couldn't tell if she was laughing. "Are you talking about the building manager?" I asked.

"No, no!" Dr. Klamper smiled and tried again. "It's not the 'manager.' It's more like the cleaning person—and thousands of people? The Gestapo forced me?" She turned and typed. Six young men now surrounded the desk behind her, talking to one another in low voices. Dr. Klamper stopped typing, swung around, and jumped to her feet. I was amazed how tall her petite form appeared.

"Go back to work, or better yet, go to the kitchen if you want to talk about the cinema!" The boys scattered.

"This is who I get to help me here. They do civil service to avoid the military. They are nice boys, but really!" Dr. Klamper sat back down.

"I am hoping you can help me with some details about my Aunt Mia's life here before she left for Germany," I said, trying to get us back on track. "She left the Jewish school in the Ninth District. Apparently it was overcrowded and didn't even have enough chairs. She started up in the Youth Aliyah School in the First District sometime late in 1939 or early 1940. She talked about Aron Menczer, the leader of the school and the Youth Aliyah in Vienna." I handed over one of the last letters my father would have received before his arrest on the farm in England.

"I wrote a book about Aron Menczer and the Youth Aliyah School." Dr. Klamper turned back to the shelf and plucked a paperback volume and handed it to me.

I went on while I flipped through the book. "I have a letter sent from Holland to my father from 1939. It is signed 'your friend, Aron.' I am wondering if it could be from Aron Menczer. My father worked for the Youth Aliyah, he was training to be a *madrich*, a group leader. So maybe he and Aron were friends. And my father's neighbors had a similar last name. It's spelled several different ways in the letters, mostly Melzer. I thought maybe Aron Menczer might have been related to them." I handed Dr. Klamper the letter. "My father never translated this," I added.

Werkdorp (Work camp), Holland, 22 July.1939

Lieber Harry!

I received your postcard and was pleased to receive your news. I also received the card you sent me quite some time ago, only I could not answer you because there was no return address.

As you know, my hachshara in Ellguth didn't last very long. After only three days, we were taken in trucks to be transported into Poland, even though we were all German. Naturally, things didn't go entirely smoothly, and nobody got away without a beating; not even the girls were spared.

We had to line up in a row in the courtyard and on command they began to beat us. Then a whistle sounded and the commandant made a speech in which he particularly emphasized that he was sparing our lives, even though nobody would punish him if somebody were killed. Then off we went to the border.

The border police realized the impossibility of this plan and sent us to Opole. The girls were freed there. The rest of us stood around for an entire day in the prison and then were evacuated on a special train. From the direction the train was going we could tell where it was headed: to Weimar, therefore Buchenwald.

In Weimar we were greeted with a big *Hallo* and immediately brought into the camp, where the conditions were no better. We were not made to work but the hygienic situation was nonetheless abominable. Two thousand men lived in one barracks and in the four weeks that we were held there, we were not allowed to wash ourselves a single time. There were also no outhouses, so that there were five or six persons per tin pot.

In spite of all this, our people withstood the imprisonment very well and after four weeks, by way of interventions of the *Hechalutz* Berlin, we were able to continue our "hachshara." I put this in quotations because there was practically no work going on at all.

In early February we received our entry permits for Holland and went to the Werkdorp. Except for myself and one other Viennese, all from Ellguth have left on Aliyah. Until a month ago I worked in farming. Then, someone in Vienna recommended me for this locksmith apprenticeship. We have 250 hectares of land with tractors and fourteen horses. Besides a locksmith workshop for forty people, we have a carpentry workshop for thirty people and 100 people work in agriculture. The girls work in the kitchen, washroom, fabric workshop and garden.

Next time I'll go into detail about the conditions here in the Werkdorp.

Heartfelt greetings from your friend, Aron

Dr. Klamper read it through and looked up. "That's quite a letter," she said. "You have to wonder if 'Aliyah' was code for being sent east—to get by the censors."

"I did wonder about that."

"There was a 'retraining camp' at Ellguth in Upper Silesia, which is now part of Poland. The Gestapo did send Jewish children to work there, and other places. Aron Menczer did sometimes go with them. But I don't think he was ever in Buchenwald, and he certainly never went to Holland."

"Mia writes about the Stadtkibbutz, where my father also worked. She loved the school and working the fields with her friends. She writes about Aron Menczer and the group leaders in her letters."

Dr. Klamper went directly to a box in the file-stacked cupboard across the room. She reached in with both hands and retrieved a slim volume.

"This is the 1941 membership book for the Youth Aliyah School. It should have gone to Jerusalem with the rest of the documents of the Youth Aliyah, but somehow it was left behind."

She opened the book to the G's and laid it in front of me. There she was, listed with several other Grünbergs, including an Edith Grünberg, perhaps one of the survivors of Maly Trostinec listed by my father in his letter to Rita Barnes. Mia's entry listed the address her family was forced to move to in May, 1940. It listed her party affiliation, T.L., the Tchelet-Levan, the Blue-White, and the Hebrew name: Neomi, not the Miriam my father remembered.

Grünberg Edith	1. Nibelungeng. 8/8	21.12.23.	DR	NZ
Grünberg Eduard	15. [illegible] 8/2	25.2.30.	DR.	NZ
Grünberg Elfriede	2. Blumauerg. 22/16.	1.4.29.		NZ
Grünberg Mia	9. Boltzmanng. 12/9.	26.1.26.	DR.	NZ

Excerpt from 1941 membership book for the Youth Aliyah School.
Mia's name is listed fourth row down.

Seeing Mia's name made me feel like the walls were closing in on me; the room was suddenly claustrophobic. I excused myself. In the WC, I threw water on my face and onto the back of my neck.

When I returned, Dr. Klamper was just getting off the phone.

"I am sorry, Dr. Klamper," I said.

"Call me Elisabeth." She blinked when she handed me her business card. "I just spoke with Martin Vogel. He is the only one of two *madrichim* from the school who survived the Shoah, and the only one still alive. Why don't you bring your letters tomorrow around one o'clock. Aron Menczer was his good friend. He will be able to tell you what you want to know."

"And maybe he remembers Mia?"

"Perhaps," she stepped back. "But be cautious. These survivors can be very fragile."

Correspondence

Vienna, 12 July.1941

My dear Willi!

We are in good health. Your dear mother was sick for a short time and was confined to bed. Once recovered, she tried to get under the wheels of a bicycle where she suffered abrasions on her hand, her leg and her nose. Furthermore, her dress was badly torn. At the same time, she should consider herself lucky that she got away without suffering serious injuries and without being seen by a policeman. She could have gotten a fine because it was all her fault.

Aunt Sabine had an operation on her eyes this week because she could barely see anymore. Let's hope that her vision will be better now.

We have received photographs from Menio and Emka, and we find them very nice ... We don't know what happened to Uncle Samuel. We wrote a postcard to him on June 12 and it was returned to us on June 28.

Please write more often.

Sending our kindest wishes and kisses. We embrace you.

Your parents

I have nothing to add in particular because your father took up the page. So, I am writing these few lines to give you at least a sign of life. We are full of confidence and we hope for better times to come in order to be happy with you. Only God knows when this day will come. I am embracing you in my mind.

Sending best wishes and dearest kisses.

Yours, Mother

1941 letters from Simel and Gittel Blaustein to their son, Willy Barnes in New York, after Simel's sister Regina and my father's Aunt Berthe and Uncle Igo were deported to Opole, in Poland.

TWENTY-EIGHT

BY A FEW DAYS into the trip I had developed a routine. Each morning I went back to the café near the university. The waitress almost smiled when she brought me my coffee. I wrote up my notes, jotted down memories, sketched out a few stories, and planned which archives to visit that day. Midweek, I looked up from my work to watch a family with two small girls sit down at the table next to mine. The older girl reminded me of Heather.

When our daughters were small, and another New Hampshire winter finally drew to a close, we hiked up the Old Sandwich Notch Road. The girls held hands and skipped ahead of us on the rutted path, throwing their hips from side to side and flinging their outer arms wide. Heather turned around and smiled back at us to make sure we were keeping up. The Notch was once the main route from Canada down to Portland, heading past our home on the way to our village, a bustling town in the last century. Traffic continued through the winter, with sledges drawn by horses or oxen. The walls and cellar holes of the farms in the Notch are still visible in spring, but the dense green of summer will hide them. The rows of crops from that time, and the people who farmed them, have long since vanished.

Before the Anschluss little Hans Meltzer skipped between the stalls at the Naschmarket. Susi caught up with him and they circled their inner arms around each other and threw their outer arms out extravagantly. Uri, Paul, and I ran after, veering around shoppers on the way. Hans looked back, then Susi. We zigzagged around pungent sacs of spices in shades of persimmon and orange, pumpkin and sable.

But now Vienna is no longer our playground. Boys who once flirted with me now wear the uniform of the Hitler Youth and don't look me in the eye. Papa lost his job with the rest of the Jews at the bank, then was rehired at half the salary to work at night, liquidating accounts.

After Harry and Uri left, Paul Harband and I joined the Youth Aliya and went to work at the Stadskibbutz growing vegetables for the community. The *madrichim* cleared the Rothschilds' topiaries to make room for our fields. The assistant gardeners are two younger guys, both about seventeen. One is tall, and whenever you ask him a question, even a question like, "Where should the potatoes go?" he puts a long finger along the side of his nose and ponders. I have become one of his favorites.

After our friend Hafner left on hachshara over the border in Ellguth, we have a new *madricha* for the Tchelet-Levan. Lily's glasses make her look more serious than she is. She is a sunny girl with a ready smile. She teaches us Hebrew songs, and the backbreaking work is made bearable by singing and comradeship. We spread across the fields based on ideology, left to right. Gordania, Ha Shomer, Tchelet-Levan. The religious girls stay at the far-right side of the fields.

I stand for a moment and lean back with my hand in the small of my back and watch my friend, Trudy, lean into her hoe. Paul comes alongside me and props himself up against his shovel.

"Do you hear from Harry or Uri?" he asks.

"Not much. They're busy, I guess." I flick away a fly.

"They are going to force us out of the apartment soon." Paul kicks the earth. "I can't wait to get out of here. I'll go anywhere." Paul is seventeen now. The boy we grew up with is almost a man. "Are you leaving soon?" he asks.

"I'm still waiting. I got affidavits from those nice Californians, but it didn't work out."

One of the Ha Shomer boys watches us a few rows over. His hair is thick and has the most startling color, almost magenta, like the borscht Omama's cook used to make on Sundays. I catch his eye and he turns away.

"Where is Susi?"

Paul shrugs and turns back to his work. "It will be time to go soon," he says.

I wonder: Maybe she was sent to Poland to be with Mrs. Harband's Christian relatives.

Without the tram we have a two-hour walk ahead of us, and we must be home before curfew.

The boy with bright hair keeps watching me as I make my way down the row.

Lily starts singing again and Trudy smiles at me and we all join in. *We are, after all, still young.*

Correspondence

Hi Lisa!

I tried to call you since saturday because i found something in my office that i wanted to borrow you (an old mobile phone of my company which still works—just for easier phoning around for all your dates) ... (and to be found ...) and there is still a bike available (which also could be stolen without too many tears). And something i want you to know: there is really enough space in my flat if you are fed up with the wall or if you just want more space AND my parents went to Krete—so i'll be in their house most of the time unable to disturb you ... So please let me know if this offer is interesting—you would not bother me at all and i would love to house you (especially after thursday when the cleaning-lady has come) Could you call me—i don't want to wake you ... GOOD MORNING!!

niki

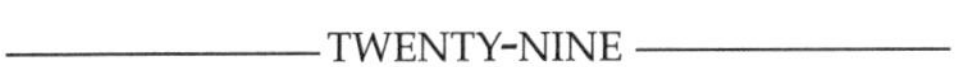

TWENTY-NINE

I WAITED FOR Niki under a street lamp on Wipplingerstrasse in the Innere Stadt. I recalled that my father had tutored a wealthy boy whose home had been on this street. After the Anschluss, he had ignored the sign posted on the front gate: *Eintritt für Juden Verboten*— Jews Forbidden. He climbed the grand staircase. "This way," I imagined Hermann calling down, hanging over the polished railing. He had been one of my father's least promising students, but also one of his wealthiest.

After Kristallnacht, my father had screwed up his nerve and asked Hermann's father for a raise.

"You people are always working the angles," Hermann's father had said.

"This seemed an odd statement," my father had told me. "Hermann's father was Jewish. He had converted when he married and then had Hermann baptized. It didn't matter. I found out that they were both deported anyway."

A few minutes late, Niki pulled up beside me on a motorbike—no helmet. His hair still looked damp.

"Was I in the wrong place?" I asked. "You said Wipplingerstrasse, right?"

He'd laughed at my pronunciation and made me repeat it over and over for him—"Wipplingerstrasse, Wipplingerstrasse!" I couldn't get it right.

He handed me a cell phone and I tucked it in a pocket. "Climb on," he told me.

I hiked my skirt up and straddled the seat behind him. "Put your arms around my waist!" he shouted. The bike jerked forward and we wove through traffic to the Ringstrasse and alongside a tram to the Musikverein, where he parked on the sidewalk.

A redheaded woman waved from the entrance. I smoothed my hair down.

"This is Andrea," Niki said as we came up the steps.

Andrea smiled, offered her hand and said. "I may not see you again tonight, so just in case, let's say hello and goodbye!"

We shook hands and then she sauntered away, pulling a clip out of her hair, which unraveled and rippled down her back. She turned and waved, then folded down onto the cobblestones and leaned back against the sun-warmed brick.

"I'll wait twenty minutes, okay?" she called, and Niki took my elbow and steered me into the hall.

"I don't want to take her ticket," I said.

"Don't worry about it." He flashed two tickets at the usher.

We came out into the crowded hall. A wrought-iron fence caged us to the back. "The standing section used to be my second living room when I was a student," Niki said. The gilded boxes beyond were filling. Everyone was formally dressed. The small stage was already jammed with the warming orchestra. "Okay. I go get Andrea. If we get caught, I will pick you up out front at the end of the concert." Niki vanished.

Students sat with their backs to the fence, defining their territory with books, papers, and musical instrument cases. They protested when I approached, so I walked to the very back and leaned against the gilded mirrors. Martin and I always bought good seats at the symphony. The thought of standing for an entire concert was a disappointment, even though they were playing one of my favorite pieces,

Beethoven's Ninth. Then I smiled, thinking of my father lip-synching along to the choral movement. He would throw his head back, open his mouth wide, and set his eyes in a rapturous expression.

My father and Uri once got tickets from his father's boss to hear the symphony in this hall. They sat in the tenth row. "What a thrill," my father had said. After his outbursts began, he would add: "of course, that would have been long before the Anschluss. After that they closed the concert halls to Jews."

Niki and Andrea emerged from the opposite entrance. Andrea was as tall as Niki, and her red dress seemed to change shades as she approached. The crowd parted, as if my new friends were some kind of rarified species that needed space and oxygen.

"Maybe you are getting too old for this," Andrea said to Niki when they got to me. I nodded my head, thinking of going to all this effort to save the three-euro price of a third ticket.

"But I have done this since I was a student. If I stop now, it will be a sign that I have given up on life." He took Andrea's hand and she leaned back and coiled next to the mirror. I slithered down next to her.

"My voice teacher is singing the solo tonight," Andrea told me. The applause exploded. Niki left us and moved up by the fence, where the students opened up a space for him.

As the familiar notes of the first movement rolled over me, I lay on the floor next to Andrea with my purse pillowing my head; I was sixteen again, lying on my unmade bed, listening to an LP of Toscanini conducting Beethoven's brilliant last symphony. Over and over, the arm of the record player picked up and swung back, overlaying music on the footsteps of my family. There was something wonderful about just listening without straining to look at the orchestra. I ruminated on the last few days. Jet lag, fair weather, disorientation, and loneliness left me wavering on the edge of the past, both my own and the city's.

I stood up at the beginning of the fourth movement. Andrea's eyes were still closed and her thick hair spread onto the floor. I joined

Niki by the fence. He put his hand on my shoulder. Notes gathered on the ceiling, then floated down, like sparks from fireworks raining harmlessly around us. I was filled with an adolescent certainty that something important was about to happen.

Alle Menschen werden Brüdern. All men become brothers.

When we jostled our way out of the hall at the end of the concert, Niki handed me a key.

"I suggest you take my bed when Martin arrives. You are married, after all, and a big bed is best in such situations. Eat the food, drink the wine! I'll be in and out." He pulled the motorbike off its stand and got on. "Your bicycle is on the landing," he shouted over the engine.

Andrea climbed on behind him and wrapped her slender arms around his waist. Niki waved and made a wide arc onto the road. I watched Andrea's bright hair stream behind her until they disappeared.

Correspondence

Concerning my "sin register," it looks as follows: 1st marriage: Lia, born Glesakowa, 1918, Moscow; divorced 1943; son Felix, born February 10, 1942—2nd marriage: 1944 "Katja," actually Szigne Valalyk, born 1919; divorced 1948; lives in Budapest; pensioned Russian teacher—3rd marriage: Leopoldine, born Zeman, 1924 in Grinnenstein; died 1967; divorced 1956—4th marriage: Renee, born Goeth, 1925 in Vienna; divorced 1983; daughter Christa, born 18 Mar. 1959 in Vienna—5th marriage Fritzi (Friederike) born Kohn, 1920; wedding March 6, 1984, Vienna.

A letter from Martin Grünberg from the 1990s in which he answers my father's genealogy questions.

Visiting Martin and Fritzi Grünberg.

We visited Martin and Rudy on our first overseas trip on the way to Israel. Coming back to Vienna was painful enough for me but arguing with what had been my favorite cousin was worse. We had to stay away from political topics to avoid serious clashes.

I went back to Vienna by myself for a few days early in 1967 while we lived in Denmark. We stayed away from politics and things went quite smoothly. I was glad I went because it turned out that was the last time I saw my uncle alive. Martin was at the time married to his fourth wife, Renee. They had a little daughter (Christa) but I had a feeling that things did not go too smoothly in the marriage. I also had the impression that Uncle Rudy had a domineering influence on them. Some of my former friends who had embraced the party line and had returned to Vienna after the war, dropped the party after the uprising in Hungary, others were disillusioned after the six-day Arab Israeli war in June 1967, or after the brutal suppression of the Czech revolt. I believe that Martin only began to change after his father died.

From my father's "Notes on Aron Grünberg."

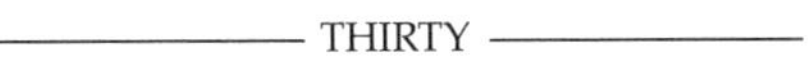

THIRTY

"SLOWLY, WITH BRITISH English," Martin Grünberg's nasal voice repeated.

I mustered my best Tony Blair imitation and shouted into the cell phone. "It was a shock. Your voice reminded me of Uri."

"Ring me up when you arrive in Vienna," he said.

"But I *have* arrived. I'll come by around 1:00."

"Do you have my number?" he asked.

"I just called you."

"What number did you dial?" he asked. I read it out to him in German.

"That's not correct, it's 2997."

"But I just called you on 2979."

"Ring me up when you arrive. And speak slowly, British English." The line went dead. I stared at the buzzing phone for a minute and then closed it. I pulled together my things to leave, but then opened my computer and went through my father's notes about his cousin and his family one more time.

Martin had studied mathematics at the University of Moscow in the late thirties. When the war spread to Russia, his parents, Rudy and Salomea, were moved east beyond the Ural Mountains to some sort of forest operation. Rudy had a desk job, but Salomea, according to my father, had to fell trees, which took a heavy toll on her health.

Because of his language skills, Martin was involved with reindoctrinating Austrian POWs before their release. Rudy and Salomea moved back to Vienna in 1946 and Martin in 1948. My father thought Rudy became the general secretary of the party and that Martin became active in the Soviet-Austrian Friendship Society when he returned home. Martin also ran a very extensive Russian Language Science Library and acted as official translator at state functions and on visits of Soviet dignitaries. Salomea died in 1948 after a reaction to nitrous oxide during a dental procedure, so my father never saw her again.

My guidebook said to bring a small gift when invited to visit someone's home in Vienna. It didn't instruct me as to what I should bring an eighty-seven-year-old-diabetic-ex-Communist-second-cousin whom I'd never met before. I picked up a bouquet of red roses on the way into the S-bahn. When I came out of the station in the Thirteenth District, the glare of sun on white concrete buildings made me blink. It crossed my mind that Viennese architects imitated the style of Israeli architects in Nahariya. Of course, it was the other way around.

I was buzzed into the building. At the fourth-floor landing, Martin and his fifth wife, Fritzi, stood at their door. Martin was thick around the middle and his hair was scant. Blue eyes flashed behind bifocals. He gripped Fritzi's hand in a wide paw. She was like a little doll. The corners of her lips turned up and lit her features. They both reached to me and pulled me into a tight embrace. "*Velcome, velcome*," they said.

The scene inside Martin and Fritzi's home felt as familiar to me as the buildings outside. Tile floors and midcentury-modern furnishings echoed Uri and Sahava's apartment and my father's office. Books lined one wall and the dining table was already set for midday dinner with chicken soup steaming in china bowls. We settled in at the table. Fritzi spoke to me in clear German, encouraging me to eat and drink, asking me about my trip. I completely understood her and Martin translated what I said for her.

"So, what brings you here?" Martin asked.

"I'm hoping you can tell me what you remember about my father's family."

"You'll have to speak up." Martin slurped his soup. "I'm deaf." He stopped to pour me a glass of wine and watered his down with seltzer water, just like Uri used to. "I don't remember very much," he said. Was it possible to have a German-Russian-English accent?

After soup, Fritzi brought out salads and chicken on a platter. She indicated I should help myself. They watched me arrange the food on my plate. Then, she and Martin put the chicken on the plate and the salads into glass bowls next to their forks. They eyed my empty bowls. Rules were in play.

"Do you remember my grandparents?" I asked.

"Leo and Elcia were very good together," Martin said, "but your grandmother wasn't well. I don't know what the problem was." He took a sip of his wine. "Your grandfather was a marvelous conversationalist, and they were both really good listeners. They came to our house on Sundays, or we went to theirs, but we only ate together at our home. Your father's family was very poor, you see. My father sent a third of his salary every month to Leo."

"Do you think that might be because your grandmother, Sarah, lived with them until she died?"

"I don't remember," Martin answered, pushing back from the table and taking another sip of wine.

"Did you know she was called "Pious Sarah?"

"Was she called Pious Sarah?"

The longer Martin and I spoke, the more I realized that his apparent fluency at the beginning of our phone conversation was the result of advance preparation, drawn from a dictionary and remnants of grade-school English. Talking in person was slow going.

"Did you spend time with the Helwings?"

"Who?"

"Elka's family—I mean Elcia—Kurtl, Menio. My father said they spent most Sundays there."

"I don't recall them at all," Martin said.

"And their neighbors? Paul and Susi Harband? The Melzers? He also had a friend named Aron who wrote to him from Holland."

"No, I don't think I ever met them."

I took a few bites of food. "What do you remember about my father?"

Martin folded his hands over his paunch. "We got along very good. Even when we met up again after the war, we got along."

"Didn't you argue about politics the first time you saw each other again in the sixties?"

"No, not at all,"

"Do you remember Uri and Mia?"

"Uri—yes. He hung around with Harry and me. Mia—no, not at all—she was blond, I think—but I don't really remember. She was too young when we left."

"She would have been nine or ten already when you left for Russia. My father said her hair was reddish."

"I don't remember her."

"My father used to confuse our names. He said I looked like her."

Martin looked at me, then turned back to his food. "I don't see it," he said.

The sun passed behind the building across from us. Fritzi got up to flip the switch on the wall.

I tried to match the teenaged Martin my father knew with the old man in front of me. "How did your father know it was time to leave Vienna?" I asked.

"Papa was—I don't know the word—a person who could draw conclusions."

"A realist?"

"Exact."

"My father said your mother was very beautiful."

"Yes, she—" Martin's eyes misted and cleared. "No, not beautiful—just very nice." Martin drew a "z" sound over the "c" of nice. He mopped chicken grease up with bread. "Of course, your father was very serious, even as a child. We made an amazing telescope together; my father got him the lenses. But Harry was really the brains behind the whole business. Your father had a mind

My father and his cousin Martin Grünberg, c. 1924.

that was—unusual—yes?" He poured more wine in my glass. "We could see the moons circling Jupiter with that telescope. But I was just the person who brought him the pieces. He put it together."

"My father said you taught him to read."

"Maybe."

"He said you were quite the lady's man."

Martin smiled, and translated for Fritzi, who laughed.

"Didn't you used to write to my father in code after you went to Moscow?"

"I don't remember."

I asked Martin what he remembered about his parents being sent to Siberia, and his mother being sent out to work in the forest felling trees.

"I didn't know about the trees. Whatever it was, it ruined her health," Martin said. "When my parents returned to Vienna in 1946, my father tried to find out what happened to everyone. Only his sister from Germany, my Aunt Ester, survived the camps. My father tracked her down and brought her home to live with us. After my mother died, she stayed on and kept house."

"My father said Aunt Ester was very frail. Did you get along?"

"We were very good together," Martin said.

"My father said your father was a difficult man, very demanding," I said.

"Difficult? Not at all. We all got along very good." Martin took a sip of wine. "I was asked to stay on in Russia, to work with the German POWs after I finished with the Austrians in 1948. I refused, of course, and came home."

"What is the difference between Germans and Austrians? They were both Nazis, weren't they?" I asked.

Cousin Martin gave me a look. "*Nazzis?*" His Russian accent took over. "The Austrians were victims of the Nazis. There was a world of difference." He opened his arms wide and his hand caught his goblet, sending it spinning. A maroon puddle seeped into the white tablecloth. Fritzi leapt up to blot the stain.

"This never happens," Martin said, his rosy face deepened to crimson. He poured himself another glass. "I was the head of the Soviet-Austrian Friendship Society in Vienna for years. I brought over the ballet companies and the orchestras. I think people here thought I was a spy, KGB." He chuckled. "Of course, I lost my job after Prague Spring. I was a little too vocal about my disapproval. They didn't fire me right away, but within a year, I was out."

Fritzi cleared the dinner plates and put a colossal piece of chocolate cake in front of me and a pear in front of Martin. When she went back to get the coffee, Martin grabbed my fork and broke off a chunk of cake, popped it in his mouth, winked at me, closed his lips, gulped, and smiled.

Fritzi came back with the coffee and a bowl of chocolates. She looked at my desecrated cake and back to Martin. She picked up his napkin and wiped a bit of frosting off his lips. When her husband reached for a chocolate, she slapped his hand.

"Do you treat your husband this way?" Martin asked, unwrapping the candy and popping it in his mouth.

"Of course." I took a bite of my cake. The chocolate was rich and there was a tinge of cherry flavor in the icing. "Do you remember my father getting caught in the current of the Danube and being dragged under the Reich's Bridge?"

"We swam across the Donau all the time. The current picked us up in the middle and we really struggled to get over to the Donau Island. But we never got as far as the bridge."

"Did Uri and Mia swim with you?"

"Uri, yes. Mia, I don't remember."

We sat for a while, listening to Fritzi washing dishes in the kitchen.

"Of course, the old Reich's Bridge is gone now," Martin said. "It collapsed sometime in the seventies." He took a sip of black coffee. "But why do you ask all these questions?"

"I'm writing about it and I'm trying to figure out what it was like. And I want to know what happened to everyone, especially to Mia. My father said he received a letter from Leo that Mia was taken to Germany in May 1941. But after my father died, I realized the letters stopped in January of 1941, before she would have been taken. But my father must have heard that somewhere. Maybe he destroyed the last letters, or maybe he hid them. Anyway, he couldn't understand how Mia got back to Vienna to be on that transport to Minsk in 1942."

"But that's wrong. They were all taken to Auschwitz and gassed." Martin's voice was loud and high. Fritzi came back in and put her hand over his.

"*Was ist los?*" she asked.

"My father doubted she was gassed at Auschwitz," I said. "I'm still figuring out what might have happened." I pulled out the Deportationsliste from the DÖW and handed it to Martin. Fritzi peered over his shoulder.

He took a long look and sighed. "May I have copies of these?" he asked.

"Of course," I answered.

Fritzi finished clearing up. "*Zeit zum Schlafen*," she lay her head on her arms and indicated the couch to me. I got up and sat down on the edge. Martin walked to the bedroom door and turned to look down at me.

"And your father was religious," he said.

"My father was an atheist."

"Not then. He used to pray all the time. He wore that shawl and wrapped the leather things around his arms and put that thing on his forehead."

"Tefillin?"

"He even prayed when he visited our home. He had a Bar Mitzvah."

"Maybe you're thinking of someone else?"

"No."

I swallowed this image.

"Don't you ever think about how much was lost?" I asked.

"No," Martin answered. He disappeared into the bedroom. I heard the bed creak. "What is past is done. I guess I'm not so sentimental."

Fritzi threw a pillow at one end of the couch and signaled that I should lie down. I put my head on the pillow. She pulled a throw off a nearby chair and spread it over me, and then sat down next to me. She traced my face with her hand. "She looks like Harry," she called to her husband. "I see it around her nose and mouth." She pulled the blanket around my shoulders.

"*Träum süß*. Sweet dreams," she said.

She went into the bedroom. They spoke for a few minutes and then all was quiet. The sun found its way between two nearby buildings and sent a shaft of light against the wall.

Frau Harband cradles the match and the flame makes her palms glow. Waving her hands over the candles, she looks at each of us. Then, she covers her eyes and recites the blessing, so as not to see the candles again until she completes the mitzvah. Even Cousin Martin is here, because Uncle Rudy and Aunt Salomea are too communist to celebrate the second Seder. The Melzers stand with their two sons, tall Kurt and little Hans. The Harbands' Christian and Jewish in-laws line one side of the table. Paul's friends from Hebrew school, Harry's from the Youth Aliyah, are along the other.

Harry pours water from a china pitcher over his hands and then dries them with a towel. He drips a little over my hands and Susi's. The towel scratches as he helps me dry off.

After the Seder and the enormous dinner that follows, Susi and Hans Melzer curl up on the couch together and fall asleep. Grown-up talk moves to politics. Mutti signals to Harry, Uri, and Cousin Martin. "Take the young people to our flat," she says.

"But I want to talk politics," Harry says.

Mutti insists.

The older kids continue the discussion about Schuschnigg and the fascists around our kitchen table. There is Hafner, intense, a Zionist. We call him by his last name. Sonja's black hair is clipped like a boy's and her hands chop the air. Pretty Helen is quiet but listens intently to what everyone says.

"What do you think?" Helen asks Harry after everyone else has spoken. Harry, who was talking great guns at the Harbands', can't bring himself to answer her.

Martin pulls a cigarette from his pocket, lights it, and holds it out to Helen, who shakes her head. Hafner takes it and inhales deeply and exhales slowly. Sonja takes a puff and gives it back to Martin, who matches Hafner, sucking the smoke into his lungs in what seems like an endless stream. The conversation stops until he finally exhales.

"They won't like it if we smoke," I say.

"They don't need to know," Martin answers.

He offers the cigarette to Harry and Uri, who shake their heads, but Paul Harband takes a drag. They all have to clap him on the back to get him to stop coughing. Conversation peters out with the last of the smoke.

"*Flaschendrehen*, spin-the-bottle, anyone?" Martin holds up an empty milk bottle.

We pull the table back and sit around him on the floor. Martin gives the bottle a tap and it makes a half turn to Sonja. He rubs his palms together, leans across the circle, and puts his hand on the back of Sonja's head. He kisses her hard on the lips. Helen flushes. Paul and Uri clap and whistle.

Sonja gives the bottle a wild spin and it careens across the floor, knocking me in the knees and bouncing to point at Hafner. Sonja reaches out and grabs the back of Hafner's head and pulls him to her. Hafner closes his eyes while Sonja plants an equally long kiss. Sonja's eyes are locked on Martin's the entire time. Hafner spins and the bottle points to Harry. He spins again—Paul. The boys clap and boo. Martin lights another cigarette. On the fourth try, the bottle points to Helen. Hafner leans across the circle, closes his eyes, and puckers up. Helen leans toward him. Her curls fall across laughing eyes. She pecks Hafner on the cheek. We all laugh, even Hafner.

Helen directs the bottle to Harry. She jumps up. "We're going in the other room." She takes Harry's hand and pulling him to his feet. She leads him into Mutti and Papa's bedroom and closes the door.

The circle exhales. Martin sits down in Papa's chair and blows out a smoke ring. It floats to the ceiling and breaks apart. Paul and Uri lean their ears against the bedroom door.

"Hey! What's going on in there?" Uri calls out.

The grown-ups are suddenly saying noisy goodnights in the hallway. Martin leaps out of Papa's chair, opens the window, and tosses his matches and cigarettes outside.

Paul throws the bedroom door open. Harry and Helen's faces almost touch. Helen's hands are on Harry's shoulders. Harry's hands hang by his sides.

"Come on, Romeo," Paul says, grabbing Harry's arm. "Your parents are here."

Papa tries not to laugh when he sees Martin trying to fan out the rest of the smoke. Herr Harband cuffs Paul on the ear and sends him back home. After Martin, Hafner and the girls leave, I pull myself into Papa's lap and tell him about spin-the-bottle. Harry busies himself with a book.

"Helen wanted to kiss Harry," I say.

Papa smiles at the back of Harry's head. "Just a piece of advice," he says. "If someone offers you something for free, you should always take it. *If someone tries to take something from you that's yours, scream like hell until they give it back.*"

Only five percent of the young people recorded in the membership file of the "Youth Aliyah" in May 1941 survived the Shoah.

From *We'll Meet again in Palestine: Aron Menczer's Fight to Save Jewish Children in Nazi Vienna* by Elisabeth Klamper

THIRTY-ONE

A GANGLY MAN sat behind the desk with his hand on Elisabeth Klamper's arm. His white hair floated over his wide forehead and patrician nose. As soon as I entered, he bounded up with an outstretched hand.

"Martin Vogel, former madrich of the Youth Aliyah." He shook my hand vigorously. "Did you bring the letters?"

We settled into our seats. I handed over the letter from "Aron" first. Martin Vogel took it in his right hand, and while he started reading, he fumbled in the pocket of his jacket with his left. Not taking his eyes off the page, he unfolded the glasses with his teeth and put them on.

"It's quite a story," he said when he was finished, "but it is not Aron Menczer. He did sometimes accompany his students on these Gestapo work details, but he never went to Buchenwald. And he always signed his letters with his real name."

"What was that?" I asked.

"Adolf," he said with an impish smile.

"Everyone who met him said Aron was an extraordinary person," Elisabeth Klamper said. "There will never be another like him."

Martin Vogel's eyes filled. "Aron's family went to Palestine very early on and he had an entry visa to join them. But he told me his work was here, with these children. In the end, he gave his visa away."

Aron Menczer (*center front*) and the leaders of the youth associations. Only Martin Vogel (*third from left*) and Mirjam Neumann (*second from right*) survived the shoah.

From *We'll Meet Again in Palestine: Arom Menczer's Fight to Save Jewish Children in Nazi Vienna* by Elisabeth Klamper.
Photo courtesy of Rita Vogel

"Do you know where he lived?" I asked.

"I think in the Second District somewhere," Martin Vogel answered.

"Not the Ninth?"

"No, definitely not the Ninth."

Elisabeth rubbed her lenses with a Kleenex and held her glasses up to the light.

"How long did the school run?" I asked.

"Didn't you read the book I gave you?" Elisabeth swiveled her chair toward me and put her glasses back on.

"I haven't had a chance yet," I said. She gave me a look like a disappointed schoolteacher.

"Aron ran the Youth Aliyah until the school was abandoned in May of 1941," Martin went on. "Those of us who were left behind arranged one last meeting. It was very dangerous. Aron told us to have faith—that we must survive to build a new Jewish society in Palestine."

"Do you remember when you discovered what was happening in the camps?"

"When the letters stopped coming we thought that was just the chaos of war. I don't remember clearly when I first understood what was happening. It could have been 1941 or 1942."

Elisabeth put her hand on Martin Vogel's arm as he sat back.

He looked out the window for a moment. "My mother was Christian. She stuck with us. That meant she got full rations for a time and that my father and I weren't arrested. I am the only one of two from the madrichim who survived and the only one still alive. The rest of us were slaughtered." Martin Vogel looked back to me. There was nothing I could think of to say. I looked down at my papers.

"Would you like to see one of my aunt's letters about the school?"

"Absolutely!" Martin Vogel said.

I read a translation while he read the original.

Vienna, 16 April.1940

Lieber Harry!

This is really the last time that I'm going to write you such a detailed letter. You need to answer my questions and generally, to write me! Do you understand?

"I remember that," Martin said. "Always desperately waiting for an answer to our letters. We had the sense everyone who left had taken on their new lives and forgotten those they had left behind."

So now, I'm going to tell you about the Passover gathering. On Saturday, April the 6th, at two in the afternoon, all of the groups went into the social center. We were all dressed in blue and white. Then the older ones decorated the hall, and then we all rehearsed ... Finally four o'clock came and all the honorary guests arrived: the representatives of the individual associations, Aron Menczer, Lily Szuran, Kiki, Barry, Tasso, etc. We stood at attention and sang hymns. Then one of the honorary guests gave a welcome speech, and then gave us a lecture. Then we were told our new obligations ... handing over of the flag—speech of thanks—hymns, of course, this is a very brief description. Then Aron led a great discussion, and others gave lectures. Then it was over. Sunday, we all gathered together and discussed everything and how we thought things should go from there, and much more. The honorary guests told us that they were very pleased with the ceremonies. Naturally afterward, Aron stayed with us and we sang. Fantastic!!!

End, Kiss, Mia

View of the Youth Aliyah exhibition.

From *We'll Meet Again in Palestine: Aron Menczer's Fight to Save Jewish Children in Nazi Vienna* by Elisabeth Klamper.
Photo courtesy of Rita Vogel

"Oh, my goodness, Lily, Kiki, Tasso," Martin Vogel beamed. "It was wonderful what the children did for that celebration," he said.

"What did they study in the school?" I asked.

"They studied English and Hebrew, literature, mathematics, and art." Elisabeth held up her book. "The school was nearby, on Marc Aurel Street. And, of course, they learned how to farm at the Stadtkibbutz."

"Most importantly, the school gave them hope and a sense of purpose," Martin Vogel said.

"Aron Menczer gave the children back their childhoods for a few hours each day," Elisabeth said. "They had comradeship. They even fell in love."

"We had affairs," Martin Vogel said, sitting back. The boyish smile returned.

"When Mia talks about the school in her letters, you can tell what a wonderful place it was," I said.

"That's why they risked the trip into the First District, past the German check points and over the canal. They often arrived bloodied and bruised, but they came alive within the walls of the school," Martin Vogel said.

"But how did the Nazis know they were Jewish?" I asked. "I thought they didn't wear the yellow stars in Vienna until September of 1941."

Elisabeth and Martin looked at each other and burst into laughter. Bitter tears flowed down Martin Vogel's face.

"They had dark hair," Elisabeth said.

"They had big noses!" Martin Vogel managed between guffaws.

My father hated it if my brothers and I described anyone as looking Jewish. He refused to admit the possibility.

"Anyway, even if the Nazis couldn't see it, they could smell it," Martin said.

"Do you remember Mia at all?"

Martin Vogel ran a long finger down the side of his nose. "I don't think so; do you have a photograph?"

I handed over the few that I had. "I don't know how good a likeness they are," I said. "My father told me she was pretty, with reddish hair and intense blue eyes. He thought she looked a lot like me at that age."

Martin Vogel absorbed the pictures, then looked up at me. He took off the glasses and put them back in his pocket.

"I don't recognize her, I'm sorry." He handed the pictures back.

"My father said her Hebrew name was Miriam, but she signs one of her letters Neomi."

"It doesn't ring a bell." Martin Vogel shook his head. "What happened to her?"

"My father says she was taken to Germany in 1941. But she was listed on the May 27 deportation to Minsk with my grandparents in 1942."

"I'm so sorry." Martin Vogel flipped through the pages of Elisabeth's book. It fell open to a page with children from the Tchelet-Levan. "Look, this is Lily, one of the madrichot!" He pointed to the girl with glasses. "Here is Katri, he lives in Israel. And look, this is Trudy." He turned the book around so I could see it, holding his finger next to the face of a pretty young woman with dark eyes. "She still lives in Vienna."

I looked at the pictures. A girl in one looked like a Helwing and maybe a little like my cousin Maya. "Do you know this one?"

Martin Vogel took the book back. "No—of course, I was in the Ha'Shomer party, so I wasn't as familiar with the Tchelet-Levan, the Blau-Weiss." He flipped through the pictures. "I don't recognize anyone else." He handed the book to me.

I looked again at the black-and-white photographs of the children of the Youth Aliyah School. And then I saw her. A girl in the first row on the far right looked up at the camera. It could have been me as a teenager, down to the skinny wrists and the long slender hands. It could have been one of my daughters looking at me from across the kitchen table. Was it her?

"This one?" I pointed her out to Martin Vogel.

Members of the "Tcheleth-Lavan."

From *We'll Meet Again in Palestine: Aron Menczer's Fight to Save Jewish Children in Nazi Vienna* by Elisabeth Klamper.
Photo courtesy of Rita Vogel

He fumbled for his glasses again. "No, I can't say I know that one either, I'm sorry. I'll call the IKG and get Trudy's number. Maybe she knew your aunt and would be willing to meet with you. And I'll get in touch with Katri in Israel."

"My father worried that Mia might have been the subject of medical experiments," I said, gathering up the letters and photographs, "or that she might have been forced into prostitution."

"Well, we know she wasn't a prostitute," Elisabeth said.

"How do you know? My father said she was developed for her age. She was taken when she was fifteen."

"The Germans didn't sleep with Jewish women—or at least, it was very rare. It was illegal."

My research had shown me she was wrong on this point, but I didn't say anything.

"She could have been a prostitute for the Kapos, the Jews who did the dirty work at the camps. That is possible," Martin Vogel said.

"The other thing is, my father couldn't understand how she could have been in Vienna in 1942. He remembers getting a letter through the Red Cross when he was interned in Canada. His father said she was sent to a camp in Magdeburg in 1941."

"Did you say Magdeburg?" Martin Vogel asked.

"Well, this makes perfect sense." Elisabeth folded her arms across her chest. "You really should have read my book. In May of 1941, the Gestapo sent one hundred fifty girls from the Youth Aliyah to Magdeburg Province to harvest asparagus." Elisabeth flipped through my copy of her book, then passed it back, open to a photograph of girls and young women standing in the fields.

"There was an outbreak of scarlet fever among some of the laborers," Martin Vogel said. "The IKG negotiated for the Viennese girls to be sent home again. I was at the train station when they arrived. It was in July, 1941."

"So Mia could have gone to Magdeburg and then come back to Vienna," I said.

"Yes. And then she could have been on the train to Minsk in 1942," Elisabeth said.

Martin Vogel left, promising to get me Trudy's and Katri's numbers. Elisabeth watched me pack up my things.

"Don't give him the rest of your aunt's letters," she said.

"But he asked for them."

"He seems strong, but he isn't."

"I'll ask him again before I send them."

"You should leave it alone."

I didn't answer. Once I gathered my things together and stood up to go, she came around the desk and walked me down the hall.

"Where should I look for records that Mia actually went to Magdeburg and then returned again?"

"Inquire at the archives in Jerusalem," she said. Her eyes seemed cold. "They will have some record of your aunt, I am sure, Dr. Gruenberg."

"Thank you, Dr. Klamper. Thank you for everything." I shook her hand and nodded goodbye to the receptionist, whose crimson stripe was already beginning to fade.

Correspondence

Vienna, 3 April.1939

Dear Harry!

... In regards to your aunt, her situation is the following: she would like to obtain a position as house maid or nanny. The announcement should read: Pepi Helwing, 40 years old, studied culinary arts at the *Kultusgemeinde* [Jewish Community] with good grades ... When your things arrive, Kurtl and his foster-father will visit you on a Saturday. Have you been to visit Rosl? Ludwig is departing tomorrow—thank God—but unfortunately he won't be in London. He will write you as soon as arrives. Write to me how and where you spent the high holidays.

Some news—Uncle Sisko has discovered a Menkes, a publisher in Manchester. My mother had a brother born in Lemberg, a certain Selig Menkes—maybe it's her brother or one of his children. Supposedly he runs the largest publishing house in England. Could you find out more about this? It could be useful. Maybe he could help Mother and Aunt. You'll let us know, I trust. Miracles do happen. It's all so overwhelming, I know, but we would be so grateful to you if you could try. You could write something like this: "I am the grandson, Harry Grünberg and have been in London three weeks by way of [*illegible*.] My grandmother is Sara [Sabine] Helwing, married to David Helwing, first residing in Kolomea and presently residing in Vienna. Their children had to leave the country, etc."

Are you in good health? That naughty Uri hasn't written to us and we are getting rather worried.

Tender kisses,
Your Mutti

THIRTY-TWO

WITH THE DANUBE Canal on one side and whizzing traffic on the other, I walked to the Second District and my great grandmother Sabine's former home. Posters from the recent election lined the walls, and their anti-immigration slogans screamed at me with yellow letters.

Cracks fissured the façade at 65 Ober Donaustrasse, perhaps left by mortar fire when the Second District became the battleground between German and Russian troops toward the end of the war. The remnants of an eighteenth-century frieze scalloped the sky and the balcony where my father had witnessed an old man's murder still extended off the second floor.

My father's recollection was that his Aunt Pepi was always timid and withdrawn and "a little pathetic." But Pepi had written to my father in England right after he fled, and the letter belies my father's description of her as entirely addled and incapable in the early years of the war.

Dear Harry!

I have a big favor to ask of you—if you would be so nice as to follow the advice of Mrs. Novak, who lives in our building, by going to her son and his cousin, Alfred Eiberschütz, so that, with his reference, I will be able to obtain a house maid or nanny position in England. Mrs. Novak's son is a British citizen and, according to his mother, a nice young man. He is 24-years-old and married to a British woman.

Mr. Alfred Eiberschütz is a member of B'nai B'rith and would be very helpful if you needed anything. Mrs. Novak asks you to give greetings to her cousin and her son and daughter-in-law from her mother, Frau Dr. Clara Kraus, and from Mrs. Novack as well.

Dear Harry. I hope you are in good health and write to me soon.

Greetings
Your Aunt Pepi

From Menio and Emka's albums. *(Left to right)* My great-grandmother, Sabine; Pepi Helwing, and Sabine's sister Gittel, in Kolomea before World War I.

When Pepi wrote this letter, she and Sabine hadn't yet been forced out of their grand home, but eventually they would be moved to a small flat a few blocks in from the canal. They had to share it with another family. After my father fled, visas became harder to come by. Thousands would be deported and murdered because countries like Britain and the United States did not allow them entry. Aunt Pepi was one of the many relatives writing my nineteen-year-old father and asking for a way out. It's not clear how hard he tried, and then Britain declared war, and he was arrested and deported.

Pepi was admitted to the mental hospital on the outskirts of Vienna, Am Steinhof, in March 1942 after attempting suicide by throwing herself in the Danube Canal. Am Steinhof had been Freud's institution, and was at the forefront of modern psychiatric care at the beginning of the twentieth century. But with the rise of National Socialism, the doctors there took a wrong turn. It became the site of active euthanasia, particularly of children with disabilities. Pepi died less than two months after her arrival, and was buried in a pauper's grave by the Jewish Community just a few weeks before my grandparents were deported east.

My father worried Pepi might have been raped early on, and that later she might have been a victim of medical experimentation or actually murdered at Am Steinhof. Elisabeth Klamper, and many others who researched the Holocaust, said it would have been unusual for a Jewish woman to be raped by a Gentile during this period, but I wondered. It is clear that both Pepi and Sabine had been badly beaten, probably on Kristallnacht.

Christa Prokisch, my friend from the Jewish Museum, suggested I go in person to Am Steinhof: to locate Pepi's medical record, to see an exhibit on Nazi euthanasia, and to visit the Otto Wagner church built on the grounds. I took a cab from Sabine and Pepi's home and was dropped inside the entrance of an enormous compound. A patient interrupted a conversation with himself to ask me for a cigarette. I realized then that Am Steinhof was still in use as a mental hospital. I headed uphill, past locked wards. I tried to catch my breath as I walked into the vast gallery of the exhibit hall. Dozens of children stared at me from photographs. Some had cleft lips, others the features of Down syndrome. Many looked perfectly normal. The captions told me that several hundred children had been murdered at Am Steinhof as part of the Nazi euthanasia program designed to purify the "Master Race."

At the end of the hall was an office and sitting at the desk was the red-haired boy from the DÖW. He turned to his books when I came to the door, but his burning cheeks gave him away.

"Hello, again! Can you tell me how to find the central office?" I asked.

"I have no idea," he answered without looking up.

"Perhaps you could look up the phone number for me?"

"There is no way to get this information."

"But surely you could tell me where the administrative offices are?"

The boy looked up at me finally, with an expression that clearly communicated he thought my request was inappropriate or even perverted, a look I was getting used to. I wonder if this attitude had kept my father from pushing for more information about his family. But perhaps my father's reticence went beyond politeness. He grew up in a world where getting on the wrong side of a bureaucrat could get you killed.

By the time I had wandered the grounds and found the main office, the doors were locked; Wednesdays they closed early. A young woman was getting into her car and I ran down the steps to her. "I came a long way—I'm trying to locate a medical record from wartime."

The woman smiled as if this happened every day. She handed me her business card and waited for mine; when I didn't hand it over, she said, "I will contact the medical director, Dr. Eberhard Gabriel. He will be more than happy to locate those records for you." She hesitated, as if still waiting for the card. "Call me tomorrow," she said finally.

There was nothing left to be done. I went back up the hill, following the signs to the church. The guidebook said that they allowed Otto Wagner to build here because he was too radical for the time. What better place for the building of a madman than on the outskirts of the city on the grounds of a mental hospital? I walked into the soaring white nave, sparsely trimmed in gold leaf. I sat in one of the pews. It was hard to feel meditative when I thought about the children who had been murdered nearby. Eventually I just got up and left.

An elderly couple approached me as I exited. Big hands and feet hung from the man's narrow limbs. I refit my father's small smile into the man's round face. He held the elbow of a woman with mirthful eyes. They struck up a conversation with me.

"Don't you love Vienna?" the woman asked. Everyone in Vienna asked me this.

"Yes, yes," I answered. I couldn't explain to her how Vienna's beauty lacerated me or that I was horrified that life went on here as if nothing ever happened. I couldn't explain to her how guilty I felt about not coming here when my father was still alive. The couple said goodbye and supported each other as they walked up the steps and into the church.

Without the Holocaust my father might have married this woman with merry eyes and lived out his days in this city. He would not have met my mother. My brothers and I would not exist. I walked out of the back of the compound into a wide park with a gentle view of the Vienna Woods beyond. Couples and families walked hand-in-hand, enjoying the sun slanting on lush fields and lighting up Vienna in the distance.

I'd thought my father had invented the late-afternoon stroll; our neighbors in Syracuse had eyed us as if the activity were somewhat suspicious. But those walks were yet another preserved island from my father's former life. The memory gave me the odd feeling I had arrived home.

Correspondence

Vienna, 24 July.1939

One good thing is that I still have my job so that at least we don't have financial worries. On Sundays Aunt Bertl and Uncle Izio (Igo) come to visit and we build "castles in the sky." Maybe one of our wishes will come true.

Letter from my grandfather Leo to my father.

THIRTY-THREE

THE NIGHT BEFORE Martin arrived in Vienna, I dreamed of Diamond Ledge. Through dusty screens, clouds kaleidoscoped silver and mauve. Red Hill was umber against a turquoise sky and Squam Lake was an afterthought of blue. I dreamed the smell of mown grass and cocoa shells on the flowerbeds, the bright white of the fence around the paddock and Mozart on the radio. Martin looked up from his book and reached over to touch my hand.

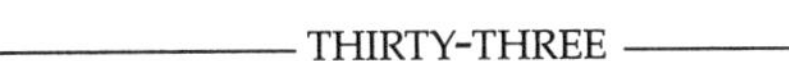

On a spring day in 1941, sunlight warms the walls of the Yeshiva the Gestapo had commandeered to process Jews. After Uncle Igo and Aunt Berthe were deported to the ghetto in Opole, the remaining Jews of Vienna were told to register. We stand in a line that snakes around a corner, waiting with the other G's and H's.

"There is Herr Doktor Grüner," Pepi mutters. "Not so high and mighty now."

"Stop, Pepi." The bones on my grandmother's face tent her skin and her right eye is completely clouded over.

Pepi picks at the rough threads of her ragged sweater, running her hand through hair that hasn't been washed in days. Papa leans against the building and supports Mutti on his arm.

A soldier works his way down the line. "Stand up, you two!" he says.

Papa shifts off the wall with Mutti, revealing a young woman standing behind. Her hair is paler than I remember, and her curls have relaxed into gentle waves that seem to be brushed to a high gloss. Her skin is not so much white as transparent. Blue blood courses through her veins.

"Susi!"

Susi's pale lips don't smile. Her eyes don't seem to see. Mutti drags her into an embrace. Susi's arms hang by her side.

The toothless man behind us grips Susi's arm and lisps, "Go to the back of the line, young lady."

Mutti puts her hand on the man's elbow until he releases Susi. "She's with us."

"Where are you living?" I ask, but she continues to stare across the street. Aunt Pepi picks up a pebble from the sidewalk and rolls it between her fingers, then tucks it between her molars and her cheek.

Hours later we reach the front of the line with our silent friend. Mutti pulls Susi's papers out of her pocket and hands them over with ours. We take her home. Our single ration card will have to feed four instead of three. But it hardly matters. *Susi will leave most of her share uneaten, as if her silence no longer requires sustenance.*

Correspondence

Vienna, 4. March. 1941

Dear Willi!

I wrote to you last week and requested that you immediately send us strong affidavits, one from you and another from someone else. We also asked you for boarding passes for the ship [to Shanghai] with exact dates on them. We ask you one more time to take care of these documents and to send them to us, as this is now a question of life or death for us ... I have to tell you that this is very urgent ... Aunt Regina [Simel's sister], Igo and Berthl and other friends have left to go to Uncle Samuel. We are healthy, and our only concern is to leave the country, rather to you than to Uncle Samuel. As you know, I don't get along with him very well. I like him, but only from a certain distance.

Vienna, 27. April. 1941

Dear Willi!

Another disruption must have occurred with the airmail service because we haven't received a letter from you in weeks. We are deeply longing to hear from you, but we hope that you are in good health and doing well. Last week we were summoned to go to the emigration office (Prinz Eugen Street) in order to get registered for our emigration. We stayed there standing from 8 AM to 4 PM. The result was that in order to get passports we have to pay a sixth additional fee of 500 Reich marks. No one has contacted us regarding the affidavits or the tickets yet.

... Leo hopes to achieve a very well paid and honorable position very soon ... Unfortunately we only have very sad news from Aunt Regina She lives in one of these mass quarters, is starving and has gotten lice. I have no possibility to send her something, therefore I wrote to Uncle Samuel and Gisela [Simel's actual relatives, in Hungary at this point], so that they can send her something.

Aunt Sabine is with Pepcia and they live very far away from us on Bocklinstrass. She is almost blind. She looks miserable ...

I wish I could see you to tell you everything that has happened, because I can't write you everything. Yes, occasionally, I could become mad or take my own life if I didn't have to fear God and wasn't hoping for better times. But I keep on telling myself that God must and will help us.

Much love, Your father

Simel Blaustein writes to his son, Willy Barnes.

In 1986 my parents visited the Barnes and Jacksons in England. *(Left to right)* Mr. Jackson, Erna Jackson, my mother, Rita and Ludwig Barnes (Simel Blaustein's son), 1986.

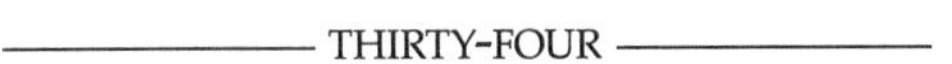

THIRTY-FOUR

THE MORNING AFTER Martin's flight arrived, we awoke intertwined on Niki's bed. Sunlight poured through the skylight and spread across honeyed floors.

"I dreamt again last night," I said.

"About what?" Martin asked.

"I don't remember now."

But I did remember. I was dressed in hospital pajamas, trapped between stiff sheets in a room with ecru walls. The padded door swung open and a snowy-haired doctor entered. He raised a dark revolver to my temple with his pale hand. The click of the empty chamber woke me.

"I had a dream, too," Martin said, "that my dad called."

"What did he want?" I asked.

"He wanted me to help him become a member of the Massachusetts Bar Association."

"You always were his can-do child."

"I didn't want to wake up. It was kind of nice hearing from him, even though it was just like him to ask me to do something really difficult as if he were requesting something really easy. I asked him where he was calling from. I was already trying to think of whom I could talk to about making the arrangements. Then I woke up, and now I feel bad about resenting his call."

"My father doesn't visit me in dreams," I said. I disentangled myself, stood up, and pulled on pants from the heap on the floor.

Martin looked me over. "You've lost weight. What's with that?"

"I guess I haven't had much of an appetite. I've been busy." I pulled Martin's shirt on, opened the sliders, and walked onto the balcony and looked down at the peaceful garden below.

Niki's home took up the fourth and fifth floor of a building in the Fourth District. He ran his business out of the garage and first two floors. His loft had the superficial tidiness of a space that hadn't been enjoyed for months. Dust accumulated inside closets and under the beds. His longtime girlfriend had moved out months earlier, taking most of the furniture. Niki's clothes took up one drawer of the bureaus that lined a wall of his bedroom. A few shirts hung in the closet. I walked back through the bedroom and down railingless stairs into the two-story living and dining rooms.

A grand piano dominated one end. A Brahms Intermezzo was open on the music stand and stacks of jazz and classical sheet music stood next to the piano bench. On a table nearby was a jumble of instrument cases; I guessed clarinet, flute, saxophone, and maybe a trombone. Books and LPs lined one wall. Another long wall was hung with canvases of Vienna scenes, all painted in red. They were all signed "Macke."

I walked down the hall and peeked in the other bedrooms. An architect's table angled under a skylight; another room had a computer, a third was devoted to bicycles. Some were rusty, some sleek; there were a couple of mountain bikes and a tandem.

In the kitchen, a pot of coffee steamed on the counter next to a bowl of fruit and a loaf of brown bread on a cutting board. There was a plate of pale yellow Turkish delight. "I thought it might bring back happy memories!" Niki's note said. Every kitchen implement I could think of and some that I couldn't identify, lined up on a magnetic rack. A metal mesh glove hung menacingly under my nose.

"It's for holding onto oysters when you pry them open." Martin put his arms around me. "How 'bout we go to Prague or Budapest today?" he said.

"How 'bout we stay here, instead?" I said. "I've still got stuff to do." I popped one of the candies in my mouth. It exploded into the essence of lemon and vanilla.

We set off after breakfast and zigzagged through quiet neighborhoods and across the broad avenues that spoked from the center of the city. Martin caught me up on what the girls were doing and his work. I tried to tell him about my discoveries.

"Cousin Martin said my father was religious. Can you imagine?" I said.

My husband had that look on his face. I could tell he wasn't really listening.

"This is Mariannengasse," I said. "It runs along the back side of my father's building. My father walked to elementary school along here." We continued toward Alserstrasse. The roar of traffic shattered the quiet, and the trolley clanked by.

We counted down to number twelve, missing it on the first pass. Walking back I saw the outline of a bricked-off archway with a frosted-glass doorway cut into it, labeled with a tiny number twelve. It was locked.

The first floor of my father's building housed a men's clothing store. "Do you want to go in?" Martin asked.

I was suddenly reticent. "Let's look from the other side first."

We wove our way across the wide avenue. On the opposite side, my father's childhood home was reflected against a row of plastic derrieres in thongs in the window of a lingerie shop. I turned back and tried to erase the stores and the booming traffic. Soot stained the carved stone façade of the building and I imagined I could see little Mia skipping at the end of my father's hand, through the archway and out of sight. Martin took a few photographs, and then he took my hand and we crossed back and entered the shop.

A string bean of a man with tangerine-streaked hair jumped forward to offer Martin assistance. I went to the older man standing behind the cash register. His toupee was slipping, making it hard to focus on his eyes.

"My father used to live in this building before the war," I said. "Would it be possible to get into the courtyard?"

The man pulled keys out of the drawer and signaled for us to follow him to the back. He unlocked the metal door and pried it open with both hands. He bent under a stone archway. We followed him. "Knock when you want to come out again." The man left us.

The stones of the courtyard were lumpy under my feet. Just as my father described, the horizontal piece of the building, where his apartment had been, was like the bridge of an H dividing the courtyard into front and back. Martin took some more photographs, and I walked up to the door of the stairwell and pulled. It was locked.

In one of the few photographs my mother ever took, my young father leans far over the banister at 12 Alserstrasse and smiles down at her. It was his first trip home.

"We went upstairs and knocked on the door of my flat," my father told me after his outbursts began. "No one was home. But on the way down, an old neighbor stood waiting for us in the hall."

My father introduced himself and a flicker of recognition passed over the man's face. "I remember your family," he said. "They moved away."

"Moved away"—my father's mouth smiled; his eyes did not. "I waited for some question about what happened to them. None came."

I walked through the center archway and into the second courtyard, and Martin came up beside me. "There used to be a horse in this courtyard," I said.

We looked up to the fourth floor.

In each window a face pressed against the glass. In what could have been my father's home, an old man opened the window.

"*Was ist los*?" he called down.

Martin answered the man in prep school German.

"Come out, okay?" The man in the toupee stood in the center archway. "One of the tenants called to complain."

We went back into the shop and Martin bought a tie from the man with the orange hair. We walked back toward the First District.

"Well, thanks for doing that with me," I said.

Martin didn't answer.

"I'd like to go up to the Prater and ride the Riesenrad, and then to the Alte Donau and see where my father learned to swim," I said.

"Couldn't we go to the Kunstmuseum and see the Breughels?" Martin asked.

"You can go," I said. "I hoped to be done by the time you came, but I keep finding more leads."

Martin looked at me. "So we're just going to do archives and see places your father was? We're not going to go over to Budapest or anything?"

"Martin, I can't be a tourist right now," I said. "You know, you don't listen to me when I talk about what I'm doing here." We came up to the lights near the Ringstrasse. "It makes me feel like you find me tedious."

Martin rubbed his head again and adjusted the strap on his camera. "I'm just afraid you're going off the deep end again with all this stuff."

"I'm not going off the deep end. I feel pretty together right now. I'm just sad. But you're making me feel like—"

"Like what?" he said.

"Like I'm being incredibly self-indulgent."

Martin's cheek twitched. "Well, what do you think? Are you being incredibly self-indulgent?"

"Maybe I am, who knows? But I have to do this now. I should have come here years ago—with my father—and I didn't. And I need you to be here for me."

Martin took my hand when the light changed. "I'm here, aren't I?"

The Jewish section of the Central Cemetery, Vienna.

THIRTY-FIVE

SATURDAY MORNING, Niki, Karin, Martin, and I walked through the first gate of the Zentralfriedhof, Vienna's sprawling cemetery in the Nineteenth District. We strolled down the gravel path that marked the border between Christian and Jewish gravesites. To our left, families scrubbed headstones with buckets of soapy water, and worked around their ancestors with garden forks and rakes. Flowers smiled among the gleaming graves.

We turned away from the bustle and color of the Christian side and down an uneven path into dense green and gray. The Jewish side of the old cemetery sucked the sunlight and sound from the day. Smashed headstones piled along the western wall, broken monuments erupted through matted grass like misshapen molars, and vines mounded over uneven rows of graves, building walls of foliage.

"It makes quite a statement, don't you think?" Niki said. "No one is left to take care of the graves, so they are left the way they were at the end of the war." He stopped and turned abruptly into high grass.

"Ah, so—here we are," Niki said.

Niki's Jewish ancestors had their own section. He ripped vines off the surface of his grandfather's grave. The carving was mostly washed away; the writing barely whispered.

"How did your grandfather survive the war?" Martin asked Niki.

"I think it was my Christian grandmother who saved him. The

Nazis came for him a couple of times, but my mother's mother was a very difficult woman. They say she refused to let them in the door, so they left. My grandfather was a well-respected doctor and his Christian patients continued to see him for a time. Maybe one of them hid him in the last months. No one really talks about it."

"Is your grandmother here?" Karin asked.

"No, she is over on the Christian side, with her family."

"Does your mother remember much?" I asked.

"She was old enough to remember Kristallnacht. A storm trooper came to our house and was told to wait for my grandmother in the dining room. My mother was playing with her dolls under the table, and she watched the trooper's boots pace back and forth. My grandmother came in and shooed the man off. The Nazis were more lenient with mixed couples at the beginning, especially if the Jewish partner had converted." Niki knelt down to yank out some weeds at the base of the grave. "Shall we move on?" he asked.

I'd obtained the coordinates of my relatives. My great-grandmother Pious Sarah Grünberg, my great-grandfather David Helwing, Pepi Helwing, and my father's and Cousin Martin's Aunt Ester were all buried here.

We tried to count from the few row and grave markers that were left. We waded through thick grass and ripped vines off stones to find names and dates that were no longer readable. In defeat, we went back to the main gate to inquire.

"These people are all in the New Jewish Cemetery—Door Four." The cemetery director pointed. "About a kilometer down, past doors two and three. But they will be closed today. It's their Sabbath. You'll have to come back another day."

"Will we go to see your Christian family?" Karin asked Niki.

"I never go there," Niki answered. "But we must pay our respects to Beethoven and the others before we leave." We walked together into the Christian section, like walking from twilight into day.

"The Youth Aliyah used to farm behind Door Four, after the Rothschild estates were taken over," I said. I thought about the possibility that Mia might have stood in a clearing out of view, beyond the chapel and the walls of this section.

To meet his eyes, I have to tip my head back. Beet-colored hair lights up his pale face.

"Shall we go through 'the park' on the way home?" he asks. Jews can no longer enter city parks, so we have made our own among the graves behind the Fourth Door. His voice is deeper than I imagined when I caught him eying me from his group in the fields. He looks back down to the row of beans he was tending. Soil is thick under his nails. His rough hand takes mine. How does he know I am willing?

"Is it allowed for a boy from Ha Shomer to fraternize with a girl from the Tchelet-Levan?" I ask.

He smiles. "Ideologically, we could align."

Gangly wildflowers scramble between untended markers as we walk. Bumblebees hum from bloom to bloom on azaleas gone wild. He bends to pick a violet and tucks it behind my ear.

"Do you have anyone buried here?" he asks.

"Grandparents," I answer. "And you?"

"My family is all in Poland."

We walk under ancient oaks and out among younger graves near the eastern wall. He slips his arm around my waist and we continue between two rows of stunted markers. We stop and face each other. His lips are chapped and sweat beads on his upper lip.

The hum of the mourning prayer makes us move apart. A scruffy rabbi mumbles over an open grave. He doesn't look up when we pass. Church bells toll the hour.

"We'd better get home," he says. "It's a long walk to the Second District."

He takes my hand again. We don't speak, but the walk that usually seems so tedious flies by.

When we approach the Donaukanal, he stops and moves away.

"You should go ahead of me," he says.

"I want to stay with you."

"No, it is better if you go ahead." He indicates his bright hair. "It seems to attract them like bees to flowers. And you don't look so Jewish." He gives me a push. "I mean it. You go ahead and don't look back."

After I pass the soldiers on the bridge over the canal, *I do look back, but he is no longer there.*

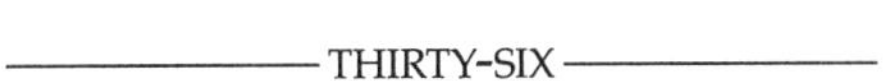

THIRTY-SIX

IN THE MONTHS after that first trip, I was left with more questions than answers. It seemed most likely that Mia had returned to Vienna in the summer of 1941, but I had no proof. It also seemed that despite the habitation record my father received from his Uncle Rudy showing her deportation date as April 27, 1942, it was more likely the date was an error, and she was deported from Vienna to Minsk with her parents the following month.

My cousin Maya visited several archives in Israel, looking for the list of girls sent to Magdeburg. She only found an affidavit Uri filled out in 1982, saying that Mia was likely gassed at Auschwitz. Maya also called Katri, the survivor Martin Vogel mentioned.

"Katri was happy to talk about the Youth Aliyah School," she told me during one of our Skype calls, "but he didn't remember Mia at all."

Niki emailed the provincial archives in Magdeburg but received no response. The city archivist in Vienna searched the police habitation records for him, to see if there was something documenting Mia's return to Vienna in 1941. They turned up nothing. Niki also called Trudy, the other survivor Martin Vogel had mentioned.

"Her children wouldn't let her come to the phone," he told me. "I sent her your letter with Mia's photographs. The letter was returned, unopened."

I tried calling Trudy's number myself. To my surprise, she answered the phone immediately. She spoke English with a young voice. "I think I remember Mia, but we lost touch," she said. "Her hair had reddish highlights and she had blue eyes, is that correct? Give me a minute; her married name is just on the tip of my tongue."

"I don't think she survived," I said.

There was a long silence at the end of the line. Then I heard voices speaking urgently in German. Trudy came back on. "I have to go now," she said. The line went dead.

Another possible source of information was the archive at Bad Arolsen in Germany. This giant collection of Nazi documents from the war years was in the news. Germany argued that the files contained confidential information about people who were still living, and therefore the documents couldn't be released until everyone mentioned in them had died. I contacted Bad Arolsen by email and letter, telling them what I knew and requesting information about slave laborers near Magdeburg and the deportations to Minsk and Maly Trostinec. Months later, I received a curt email with a copy of Mia's information from the DÖW website, explaining to me that she was taken to Minsk on May 27, 1942, not acknowledging that I had sent them this information myself.

I also traveled to Washington to visit the giant archives at the United States Holocaust Memorial Museum. I timed my visit to attend the presentation on a momentous discovery—boxes and boxes of records from the Jewish Community of Vienna, found in an abandoned apartment in the outskirts of the city. The records were out of order, the pages water-damaged and moth-eaten, but they documented each family in the community, their resources, and their connections for emigration.

Most of the panel was made up of Holocaust researchers who could barely suppress their excitement at this discovery. I recognized this excitement—I felt the same guilty pleasure whenever I followed some tangential lead and discovered the fate of a distant relative or someone mentioned in the letters.

The last panel member to speak was not a researcher or academic but rather a lone survivor who was the same age as my father had been when he left Vienna. The auditorium and the museum were scheduled to close ten minutes after he started speaking, but he settled in to tell his entire story. He was interrupted after the Anschluss by the guard at the door and then after Kristallnacht by the head of the panel, who apologized profusely.

"We have to go to questions from the audience now," he said. "Just a few."

But the audience was full of survivors, each wanting their time with the mike. Despite the guard's protests they continued to file up. One survivor began speaking about Theresienstadt only to be heckled after only a few sentences: "*Terezin*? Terezin? Terezin *vas* a country club compared to Auschwitz!" at which point the entire audience began shouting and gesticulating.

I tried to imagine my father at the microphone. Of course, he would never have stood on that stage. The guard cleared the hall.

A month later, my phone rang and a woman introduced herself. Ditta Lowry saw my search for Mia in *Together*, the print publication of Internet searches from the Allgenerations website, an internet community that serves survivors and their descendants. Ditta told me she saw the name "Mia Grünberg" and my aunt's face popped into her head.

"I have not thought of Mia Grünberg for the past seventy years!" Ditta said. It turned out Ditta lived ten minutes from my home.

Ditta did not know Mia well, but they were classmates at the Jewish School in the Ninth District in 1939. She did not go on to the Youth Aliyah school when the Ninth District school was closed by the Nazis, but she did work in the Stadtskibbutz, and later, in the gardens at the Zentralfriedhof.

"Mia was a tall girl, very pale, quiet and intelligent. She wasn't really pretty in a conventional sense. Her nose had a slight bend to it." She confirmed what Martin Vogel told me: that even in the desperate conditions in Vienna, teenagers continued to be interested in friendship and love.

Ditta's father was deported early and did not survive. Ditta was deported with her mother, her grandmother and her mother's sister to Theresienstadt in 1942. There, she met Aron Menczer and her future husband, Louis Lowry. Ditta and her mother survived Auschwitz, slave labor, and the Death March.

She told me her mother had an uncanny ability to tell when people were being lined up and sorted to live or die. If her mother sensed they had chosen the wrong line, she would just pull Ditta from side to side, again and again, until they ended up in the group that would live.

"I remember every detail, every moment of my horrific experience—except for one thing. I cannot remember the trip from Vienna to Theresienstadt in 1942. That memory is completely irretrievable. Isn't that strange?"

Anticipating another trip back to Vienna, I went back through everything I had to see if I could find something to confirm Mia had gone to Magdeburg and then returned again. Uri's letters, like my father's, broke off in 1940. It seemed unlikely that all the later letters would be missing by chance. Had Uri destroyed or hidden his later letters as well?

But finally, buried in a June 1941 letter from Simel Blaustein, I found: "Mia was sent to the Altes Reich last month." The "old" Reich—that meant Germany. Simel's letters cease at the end of 1941, when the US entered the war. Mia is not mentioned again.

In early 2007 I caught up on my writing, looking out at snowflakes hitting the windows at Diamond Ledge. Lydia was spending her junior year in a high school program in Spain. Heather was home from college for the weekend. After clearing the walk to our side door, she and Martin came to sit by the fire. Their faces were rosy from the cold, and they warmed their hands around mugs of sweetened tea, pulling out a deck of cards for a game.

"Mom, take a break and join us," Heather called. She was a sophomore in college, planning to go to medical school.

"Come on!" Martin patted the seat beside him.

I put aside my notes and joined them.

"Now, Mom, where *are* you?" Heather asked, doing a parody of the family therapist we saw for a few months when my father and Marty were still alive, and Lydia and I were struggling.

"I'm right here," I patted her cold hand. "I'm right here with you." It was true. Even though I was absorbed with research and writing, I was exploring going back to paid clinical work, and felt more connected with my family and with the present than I had for years.

In the evening of May 16, 1941, the members of the "Youth Aliyah" met in Marc-Aurel-Strasse to say good-bye to the girls ... Menczer tried to bolster up their courage and suggested that they should see their work as a kind of Hachshara. He took leave of them with the words "We'll meet again in Palestine."... The girls also drew courage from what Aron wrote into their *kvutzah* (group) book: "This is a decisive moment ... Almost all of you are going to the camps. You will be working hard in the weeks to come, but in spite of all the trouble and hardship you must not forget what unites us, and should try to strengthen the bond between us. I have confidence in you all, and I shall be happy if you live up to the trust I have in you, by hard work and good behavior. Be strong!"

From *We'll meet again in Palestine: Aron Menczer's Fight to Save Jewish Children in Nazi Vienna* by Elisabeth Klamper

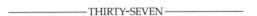

THIRTY-SEVEN

Hunger takes me in its jaws and drags me from sleep. Papa and Mutti curl together, lit up in moonlight, their filthy blanket thrown off. Papa sucks his cheeks between his gums and releases a snore. The corners of his mouth turn up—I hope he is in the middle of a happy dream.

We had discovered the trapdoor to the roof when the heat of an early summer drove us upward. For a few nights we were alone, but then other families emerged to lie under the stars. One night it rained on our outdoor bedroom, but most of us stayed, even though our rags were soaked through and we had to huddle together for warmth.

I feel faint when I stand up and have to grip a chimney coated with soot. I wipe my hands on my threadbare blanket and fold it, but then I unfurl it again and lay it over Papa's thin shoulders and across Mutti's arms, to cover her bracelets of bug bites.

The spires of Stephensdom grow pale with twilight; I lower myself through the door. Gravel cuts into my forearms and clatters to the floor while I circle my foot to find the chair with the tip of bare toes. I ease myself off it and descend the stairs to our apartment.

Dirty drapes cast muddy light on the mattresses on the floor and the stink of unwashed bodies almost knocks me over. The families we share with sprawl like corpses under moth-eaten blankets. Susi is curled up in a corner, her skin so pale she seems to glow. I pull on my dress with the Mogen David stitched loosely over my heart. We sold Omama's wedding ring to buy the star for the trip to Germany. We couldn't afford more than one, so I will need to move it from dress to dress.

We have no mirrors. The ones that weren't smashed were collected by our neighbors, along with our radio. I stand in front of Susi and run my hands though my hair and tie it back from memory. She opens her eyes and gazes beyond my shoulder and out the open window. I look down at the garish yellow star on my chest. One of the threads has come loose, and it angles dangerously. I try to straighten it out and another thread snaps. I work my finger through the rest of the stitches and yank the star off and throw it to the floor. I kneel down and press my lips to Susi's temple. I pull back again, straighten out one of her curls, then turn and walk out the door.

The boulevards of the Second District are empty, but I avoid them anyway. I walk north and west, divining a way through narrow streets and alleys toward the fields along the broad Donau. The tall grass rustles and he stands next to me, thick hair off his thin face. A bruise marks his left cheek, and I see the muscle twitch below it. As the sun elevates, the downy hair on his face glints. Behind him, the river slides by like the back of a lazy snake.

I pull my dress over my head and lean over to unbuckle my shoes. I fold my dress and put it next to the trunk of an oak. I unclasp my locket, with my brother's pictures within, and put it inside my shoe.

I walk to him in my slip, feeling damp air on my arms. I unbutton his shirt and help him pull it off. Keeping my eyes on his, I fold the shirt and lay it down with my dress. He sits down in the tall grass and yanks at his shoes. His lungs draw in the skin between his ribs. He stands again, and I take his hand and lead him to the water.

Our feet sink into mud and the river swirls around us. He puts his hands on the sides of my face, then kisses me on the forehead, and then moves down to my lips. His tongue is sweet and salty. I lie back and wrap my legs around his waist and smile to the sky. His hand moves under my slip and along the concave surface of my stomach.

The river lifts me, and I unlock my grip. I hover next to him for a moment.

"Mia!" he cries, as I slip away.

The sound of my name wakes me as if from a dream. I flip over and throw my arms out and try to grab his outstretched hands, but the current drags me out. I fight a little, but I don't have the strength I had when I swam here with Martin and my brothers. I float beyond a bend and the sound of my name becomes the sound of the waves hitting the banks. I lie back and let myself drift into the center of the river. Clouds roll over me, and hunger and time fall away. I am like a bird caught in a warm updraft, suspended over an ocean of sky.

Buildings line up on the water's edge. The sun moves behind a cloud and the air around me chills. I sense the Reich's Bridge is accelerating toward me and I am falling toward it, as if back to the earth.

If I smash into one of the buttresses I will die instantly, but if I go through the arches then the whirlpool beyond will drag me under and drown me.

I pull myself upright and tread water. Soldiers run onto the bridge. I aim for the wall of stone between the arches, then lie back again and close my eyes. The soldiers' voices are above me, shouting, "It's a woman—a woman." I open my eyes again and see their faces in a line peering over the railing. I see the girders of the bridge as I shoot through. On the other side their faces hang over, open-mouthed. The weight of the water sweeps me around and it looks like their heads snap upside down, *and then they vanish as I am pulled under and far below.*

Correspondence

... I asked our common friends in Israel whether they can remember Mia Grünberg. Unfortunately not ... I can remember the transport to Siems (near Magdeburg) for the asparagus harvest very well, especially that we tried to get the girls back to Vienna as soon as possible when they got sick. I was amongst those who picked them up at the Westbanhof when they returned. But I can't remember any details.

2007 letter from Martin Vogel.

THIRTY-EIGHT

NIKI DECIDED TO close his business in the spring of 2007 and take a year or two off to travel the world, starting in the U.S. "You need to come back to Vienna before I sublet this place," he told me during one of many phone conversations. "I have lots of time right now. I can help you with your research."

"I called Bad Arolsen to arrange for a visit to the archives but I couldn't get through." I said. "They finally called me back last week. They said they'd be happy to give me the tour but that they wouldn't be able to find the documents on such short notice."

"I didn't have any luck with the Magdeburg archives either. I'll try again," Niki said. "When I come to the U.S., you need to help me buy a used van to carry my bike. We can fit it with a mattress in the back."

"Won't you get lonely?" I asked.

"I like being lonely. Anyway, Karin or Andrea may join me for a few weeks in Arizona, and meanwhile I meet another young lady—" His voice trailed off.

I groaned. "Just one bike?" I asked.

"Okay, okay. Maybe two."

A few weeks later he met me at the Vienna airport and we went to his apartment by cab. There was a hint of green in the fields on the way into town. "I think I'm just going to go finish up here and then go up to Germany and rent a car and just show up at Bad Arolson,"

I said. "Things seem to happen when you show up. Maybe I'll just drive around Magdeburg, too."

"Let me try calling for you again today."

After a week we still hadn't heard back from any of the archives and I made plans to take a train up to friends in Berlin and work from there. The morning before I left, Niki and I finally walked through the Fourth Door of the Zentralfriedhof into the "New" Jewish cemetery. The graves were well tended near the door; small stones adorned many of them. But when we moved on to the markers from the first half of the twentieth century, we found, once again, that many were shattered or covered in weeds.

The row where my maternal great-grandfather Helwing should have been was smothered in vines. The vegetation made a wall as tall as a man. I gave Niki my bag and got down on my hands and knees and crawled under the shadow of a woody canopy. The modest stone listed to one side, but I could just make out the name, "David Helwing," "February," and "1934." I crawled out and Niki patted the dirt off my clothes.

"The lucky ones died early," he said.

Pious Sara Grünberg was absent, as was her husband, my father's namesake, Henoch. We found Pepi's section and row. But her pauper's grave was missing.

"So many missing pieces," Niki said. "Both here and in Germany."

A clamor of church bells marked four o'clock. As the last toll faded, Niki's cell phone played a phrase from a Chopin nocturne.

"*Ja, ja,*" Niki said into the phone. "*Gut.*" He turned to me.

"They found Mia. She is listed in the provincial archives at Magdeburg."

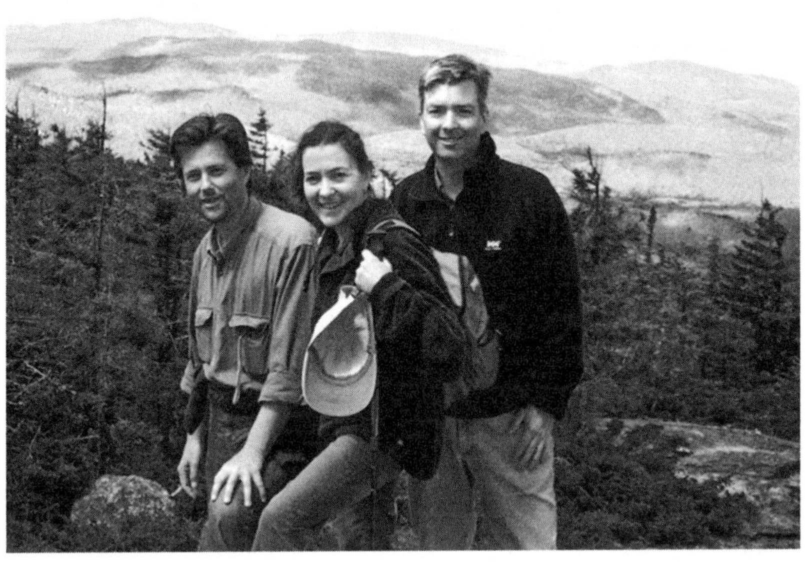

Hiking in New Hampshire with Niki *(to my right)* and Martin.

Correspondence

Vienna, 6 June.1941

Dear Willi!

We are in good health and are patiently waiting for better times to come. I don't lose hope and even encourage everyone to live on and hope ...

Aunt Regina doesn't stop lamenting and we can't do much for her. In her last letter she told us that she received a food package from Uncle Samuel. This gave her some confidence. He is rather more able to send her packages from there than we can do from here.

As I mentioned to you, Aunt Sabine stays here with Pepcia. She is almost blind and had had several surgeries on her eyes but they didn't help much. Her children don't support her, therefore Leo and I have no other choice than to support her. God will help us that we won't have to depend on anybody.

Leo is part-time, or rather, occasionally employed in a bank. He makes 100 Reich marks a month. As a wounded veteran he also receives a payment of around seventy Reich marks. In addition, he makes some money with other jobs. So, he gets along with things.

Otherwise, nothing new.

Sending our kindest wishes and kisses. We embrace you.

Your parents

PS: Mia has grown up already. She is currently in labor service in the Old Reich. We are happy that Ludwig wrote a detailed letter to you about his doing well. Please send him and Rosl our kindest regards and our congratulations on their wedding anniversary.

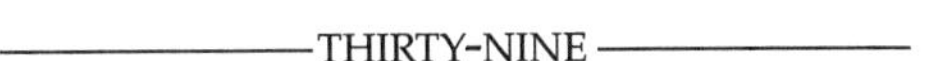

THIRTY-NINE

SONJA GRABOWSKY WAITED for me outside the train station at the town of Magdeburg, in the former East Germany. Her short hair was dyed pitch black to match black jeans and leather jacket. She ground a cigarette into the sidewalk.

"Those are bad for you," I said.

"You Americans," she grinned and shook my hand.

I had "met" Sonja months earlier on the Allgenerations web site. Sonja was neither a survivor nor a descendant. She was a German PhD candidate who was interviewing children of mixed marriages who had survived the war. I had emailed her about Niki's mother, and we corresponded for a while. When I told her I was coming to the archives in Magdeburg, she had offered to take the train up from Cologne and accompany me, acting as my translator.

In the flat light the worn buildings and the unfashionably dressed passersby made me feel like we had stumbled onto a black-and-white movie set of 1950's East Germany. After some searching and misdirection from locals, we found the street for the Magdeburg Landesarchiv. But every time we thought we had arrived, the address numbers skipped up or down by fifty or one hundred.

"*Ach*, the former GDR!" Sonja said.

Eventually the brick building, unlabeled, was in front of us. Sonja and I walked up the empty stairway and tried to find the office of the woman who had contacted Niki. When I had called to set up an appointment, the phone just rang and rang. Then the answering machine picked up and told me: "Don't leave a message."

A woman in her thirties rushed by us, then turned and smiled.

"May I help you?" she asked.

Sonja told her whom we were looking for, and the woman indicated we should sit on a bench. She disappeared down the hallway. Twenty minutes later she returned.

"She is busy in a meeting. She said you should have called and made an appointment. But the document is here in the library. Unfortunately, we close in half an hour."

"May we make copies?"

"No, there are strict privacy laws in Germany. But you can list the pages you want, and, if it is all right, we will make copies and mail them on."

She led us into a hushed room with towering ceilings. On a long table, an uneven stack of documents was bound together with a frayed cover. Osterberg, the name of a nearby town, was written across it in large letters. Sonja ran her fingers over the edges. "It's titled 'Jewish Education, State of Magdeburg, 1882–1941.'"

She leafed through the pages, translating as she went. It was a hodgepodge of documents having to do with Jews over the course of a century. But toward the end of the stack was a list of one hundred and fifty names with dates of birth; all were girls and young women from Austria sent to towns around Magdeburg Province. Mia was on the list. She was sent with fifteen others to the village of Rönnebeck, working for a firm called "Friedr. Vinzelberg."

Other documents outlined who qualified for labor and how the women were to be treated and what they would be paid. "The workers could only leave their barracks two hours a week. They could not enter stores or the cinema or the homes of their hosts," Sonja translated. She paused. "The language is so chilling," she said. "It's so bureaucratic."

"How do you mean?"

She pointed to the top of a document. "I can't exactly explain. The formality of the language just doesn't translate. This one is from the Office of the National Police. It's titled Announcement or maybe it's Dictum? 'In this province there will be arriving a large number of female Jews, especially for the upcoming harvest to supply labor. In anticipation of all the dangers to the German people that could occur because of these Jewesses you must: 1. Go to the elders of each community and make sure they understand the dangers of racial mixing.' They use the term 'Rassenschande.' That translates, I think, to 'racial stigma,' but I think it's the term for the prohibition against relations between Jews and Gentiles—that any kind of interaction is dangerous and forbidden." She turned the page. "Look at this, they had two hours off on Saturday and another two hours Sunday morning and then three hours in the afternoon. I guess that was so their managers could have some time off." She pointed at number seven. "And this. They said the girls shouldn't wear the star or anything else that would identify them as Jewish because it might cause unrest. It could lead to riots."

"So there was the possibility of opposition then?"

"I didn't think so, but maybe so."

The archivist returned. "The building is closing," she said. She took the book from us but promised to send copies of the documents on. "But I will have to cover the addresses and birthdates of the other girls. I am sorry."

"There are no dates on these documents, and it doesn't say how long the girls stayed in the province," I said.

"Maybe at the provincial archives at Stendal—the habitation records would be there."

I couldn't articulate my disappointment. I realized I still hoped that the habitation records and the deportation lists in Vienna were wrong and that Mia had made it to Magdeburg Province and stayed on when the other girls were sent back. Even though I knew it was ridiculous, I still hoped that, somehow, she had survived.

Sonja and I walked back to the station. She had to get back to

Cologne, and I would spend the night with friends in Berlin. We called the Stendal archives for an appointment. No one answered the telephone.

"Just take an early train out from Berlin," Sonja advised. "Show up and demand the records. Then go on to Rönnebeck. That's your best bet. Good luck." She took a last drag on her cigarette, cast it to the ground, and climbed onto the train without looking back.

380

Geheime Staatspolizei
Staatspolizeileitstelle
Magdeburg
- II B 4 - 176/41 -

Magdeburg, den 23.Mai 1941

R u n d s c h r e i b e n Nr. 41/41.

Betr.: Einsatz von Jüdinnen im Reg.-Bezirk Magdeburg.
Vorg.: Ohne.

Im Reg.-Bezirk Magdeburg gelangen in grösserer Zahl Jüdinnen, insbesondere zur bevorstehenden Spargelernte, zum Arbeitseinsatz.

Um allen Gefahren vorbeugend zu begegnen, die durch diesen Einsatz dem deutschen Volk hierdurch entstehen können, gebe ich die nachstehenden Richtlinien zur Beachtung :

1. Die Ortspolizeibehörden setzen sich im Falle des Arbeitseinsatzes von Jüdinnen mit den Dienststellen der NSDAP und ihrer Gliederungen in Verbindung, damit diese ihrerseits die Bevölkerung auf die Gefahren, die hierdurch entstehen können, insbesondere Rassenschande, nochmals durch entsprechende Aufklärung hinweisen. Auch die örtlich zuständige Dienststelle der DAF. ist mit hinzuzuziehen, damit diese gleichermaßen eine entsprechende auf

Detail from a page of the police announcement from the Magdeberg Documents, c. 1941. For translation, see page 323.

Gemeinde R ö n n e b e c k.

69.	Adler	Grete		
70.	Berger	Hedwig		
71.	Baumfeld	Hertha		
72.	Bäckermann	Käthe		
73.	Fischer	Fanni		
74.	Finkel	Laura		
75.	Grünberg	Mia	26. 1.26	Wien
76.	Herzka	Jrene		
77.	Hauser	Sara		
78.	Kral	Edith		
79.	Krieser	Käthe		
80.	Meisels	Zelda		

List of names of women and girls assigned to Rönnebeck from the Magdeberg Documents.

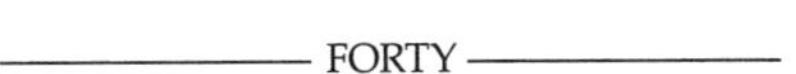

FORTY

I SUPPOSE THE ASPARAGUS *fields outside of Rönnebeck could be lovely,* but it is still raw. The fields that stretched outside our windows on the train to Magdeburg had fueled our hopes, but hunger still sits with us like a constant, complaining companion.

Our hands are rough and fissured; we slide in the mud and wind burns our faces. They say we will stay long enough to harvest the asparagus and put in the potatoes and beets. But Herr Brünn, the overseer, sneers when we talk of returning to Vienna. We start each day at sunrise, take a short break for a meager dinner, then work again until sunset.

Today we plod through flooded furrows between the rows of plants. Asparagus must be cut precisely, but we leave some stalks behind to flower and seed again. Weeds multiply after the rains and must be yanked out before they strangle the tender vegetables. We bend and straighten over and over. At the end of a row, I stand and hold my hand against my back to ease the ache. Clouds roll over a field of rapeseed beyond the wall; the yellow buds have fallen to the ground. Scarlet poppies bloom among the green and gold, and their colors match Herr Brünn's handkerchief. He signals me to get back to work.

I turn to start another row, following Laura and Grete. Herr Brünn comes behind Grete and directs her, letting his hand glance against her full breast. She stands straight and stares at the horizon while he leans against her. A thin blush adds to the sunburn on her cheeks.

I pass them and continue down the row behind Laura, who is tiny, but the oldest among us at twenty-four. My knife slips on a tough root. I don't feel the cut in my numb fingers, but blood leaks into the crusted dirt on my thumb. I bring it to my lips.

At the end of the next row, the shepherd guides his sheep along the wall to graze in the fields behind the Vinzelberg Schloss. His daughter follows him. Her cheeks are rosy from the cold. I imagine good farm butter makes her face so round. She splashes in the puddles on the side of the road, then climbs up on the wall and watches us work. Poppies weave through her fair hair.

"Ursula, come along!" the shepherd calls to her.

My knife slips out of my hand and I walk toward the girl. Herr Brünn barks "*Nein*!" and the girl jumps off the wall and back on the road. She skips along the puddles again, chasing a butterfly and scooping it up in her hands. She carries it with her for a few steps, then opens her arms wide to release it, looking back at me under her eyelashes.

The sun reaches its zenith, and Herr Brünn signals us to quit work and walk back to dinner at our barracks behind the shepherd's cottage. We eat outdoors. Through the trees we can see the carved fountain that stands in front of the Vinzelbergs' grand house.

Laura puts a bunch of poppies in a jar at the center of the table and squeezes my shoulder when she sits next to me. We sip thin soup made of asparagus stems and gnaw on our weekly ration of bread. We wrap the loaf in damp rags to try to ward off staleness.

We reread letters from home. Mutti says they have lost touch with Uncle Samuel, so no word from Uncle Igo and Aunt Berthe in the east. Mutti hopes I enjoy the small cake she sent. I wonder who is eating it. We rinse our bowls and fill them with translucent coffee made of acorns.

Grete asks Laura, "Have you seen your monthly?"

"I've not seen it for almost a year. It's the starvation, Grete. It happens to all of us."

Before we finish our coffee, Herr Brünn calls us to the fields again. The clouds hide the sun and the wind flails us. The rain starts and plasters our hair onto our cheeks. Herr Brünn has to give up and leads us back to our barracks.

I am weak and too tired to pull off my wet clothes. My throat hurts. I lie down on my straw mattress and watch the rain run down the cracked glass of the window. We haven't been able to pull it all the way closed, and the water comes under the edge of the window and onto the sill. A cricket alights on the bed and flexes its wings. I pick it up and make a cage with my hands and feel it flutter. I begin to shake and drop the cricket back on the bedclothes.

"You're flushed," Laura says. She feels my forehead. "You're burning up." She and Grete pull off my clothes and pile their thin blankets on top of me. I rest my head on the pillow and the cricket crawls next to me. *The next thing I know, I am dreaming of home, long before our world fell to pieces.*

On the road to Rönnebeck.

FORTY-ONE

EARLY IN THE MORNING, my old friend Dan O'Connor and I set off for Stendal. He was a retired professor from my alma mater, Williams College, and had studied philosophy and music in Münster after the war. He and his wife were spending the year in Germany in order to be close to their daughter and granddaughter, who had settled with her German husband in Berlin.

The weather in Austria and Germany had been unseasonably warm and sunny, but on this one day, rain threatened and the breeze left me shivering in my thin coat. The tires of our city bicycles bounced off brass plaques imbedded among the cobblestones. These markers—thousands of them—carried the names of former citizens of the city with the date and location of their deaths under the Nazi terror. They were among the many tactile reminders of Berlin's past. It was so unlike the unmarked sidewalks of Vienna.

At the station, we pulled our clunky bikes onto the train for the two-hour ride to the west. City streets transformed into flat fields stretching to a gray horizon. I told Dan what I knew about Mia's story. At Stendal we pulled the bikes off and rode into town. We found the archives, but discovered that the habitation records had been destroyed in firebombing at the end of the war.

"On?" Dan asked. Dan was more than twenty years older than I, but every time I saw him, he just seemed to get younger and fitter.

"Yes, let's go," I said.

It looked a short distance on the map, but once we hit the outskirts of the town the road changed from pavement to gravel and then to narrow dirt and sand lanes running through wide fields. The wind resisted us at every turn and the sky turned the colors of an old bruise. Dan pushed ahead, sitting rod straight. His large ears seemed to grow under his wool cap; I imagined they gave him an aerodynamic advantage as he disappeared over the horizon. A sea of glowing rapeseed rolled in great waves around me, and sand blowing off the road sent clouds across the fields. The heavy bike seemed to sink with every circle of the pedals. The horizon fixed, and I felt as if I weren't moving at all, but rather was tossing in an ocean of sickly yellow and green. On a sunny day, I imagined the fields would have been glorious and the pale blossoms on the wild fruit trees picturesque. But the gray skies closed in and cast everything in twilight. The fields oppressed, gnarled limbs threatened, and roots spread under the surface of the road like knotted hands. I pulled over and propped the bike against a stone wall, pulled out my thermos and took a long drink. Dan reappeared and flew back to me. His ears and nose were blue from the cold.

"We're on the edge of Storbeck. It's one town away from Rönnebeck."

I put the thermos away and climbed back on the bike and bore down on the pedals. On the far side of a muddy asparagus field we passed a brick church and a few farms with high walls running close to the narrow road.

A man rode toward us on a rusty bicycle. He was young but with skin aged by sun and tobacco. He smiled at us with brown teeth. Dan stopped him and spoke in German. "I am telling him about your search," he told me.

The man straddled his bike while he listened to Dan, and then he pulled a pack of cigarettes out of his pocket and offered it to us. When we said no, he shrugged, pulled one out, and lit it. In one breath, the cigarette shrunk to nothing, as if the man inhaled the collective memory of the village.

"I don't know anything about slave laborers," Dan translated. "The Vinzelbergs were a big family, not a firm. For generations they farmed all the fields around here. In 1941, most of the fields would have been planted with asparagus. The Vinzelbergs were very wealthy. They lived in the *Schloss* at Rönnebeck." The man cast the stub of his cigarette on the ground and ground it in with a muddy shoe. "The soil here is good. There is plenty of rain." He lit another cigarette. "But I am too young to know anything about the war."

The man squinted at me while Dan finished translating. Then he pointed to the church and at a large brick farm building across the road. "That belonged to another Vinzelberg, and there are plenty of them in the graveyard." He pointed the other way. "Rönnebeck is just a few kilometers more." He eased himself onto the seat of his bike and rode on, still smoking. "Good luck with your search," he called back.

We went back to look at the Vinzelbergs in the churchyard, then got on our bikes to travel on. When we rode down the road, there was an old woman standing at almost every door, watching us pass.

We missed the unmarked turnoff to Rönnebeck and it was almost four o'clock by the time we retraced the road and inched across newly planted fields into the village. The single street was lined by low walls, a few houses, and a church. Fields surrounded us as far as we could see.

We rode up and down a few times in search of the Vinzelberg Schloss. Remembering what had happened here, I grew angry at the bland scenery. We had not passed a car or a person since Storbeck. I rode toward the open gate of the churchyard.

"Lisa, come back," Dan said.

I turned around. Dan stood with an old woman propped up on two canes. She had materialized out of nowhere. "This is Ursula," he said. "She was twelve years old in 1941. She remembers."

Ursula led us into a tiny yard and the threshold of her modest cottage."You were lucky you caught me," Dan translated for me.

Ursula's voice was almost a whisper. "I was just trying to get in my daily constitutional." She leaned one cane against the stucco wall of her house and ran her hand through her thin hair. "The Schloss was right back there." Dan translated as Ursula pointed behind the property with the other cane. "But when the Russians came they kicked the Vinzelbergs out. The Russians took their home apart, brick by brick, and moved the fountain to Osterburg, where it now stands in the town square. The girls from Austria lived in a barn next door," she indicated the direction of the nearest field, "but it has long since burned down."

Ursula opened the door and looked directly at me and spoke in heavily accented English. "Come in. I'll show you something."

We entered her dim kitchen. She switched on the lights, but the room was still cast in shadow. She opened a cupboard door and pulled down an old cigar box covered with peeling magazine clippings. She lifted the lid and pulled out black and white postcards. A few marbles rolled when she put down the box. She arranged the postcards on the checkered oilcloth on the kitchen table. They were multiple views of an eighteenth-century castle with an elaborate fountain in front of it. Ursula's pale eyes watched me out of her weather-beaten face.

"Does she have family pictures?" I asked Dan.

"All lost in the war."

"Did she know the Vinzelbergs?" I asked.

Ursula laughed when Dan translated. "They didn't socialize with the likes of us."

I laid out the photographs from the Youth Aliyah and the few pictures I had of Mia. Ursula barely looked at them. "They were always too far away," Dan translated. "We weren't allowed to go near them, and we children couldn't ask any questions—the grown-ups couldn't talk about it. If someone approached the girls or was kind to them, they could be taken away themselves, so we stayed away. We were told they went back to their homes after they worked with us, and that they were paid for their labor."

As Dan translated, Ursula and I watched each other.

"Did they get sick? Is that why they left?" I asked.

Ursula answered Dan with a rush of speech. He struggled to keep up with her.

"They left after the asparagus harvest was finished. They were here six to eight weeks at the most. Italian girls came next—then the Ukrainians. It was cold that following autumn, and they had no coats or shoes. They were beaten in the fields."

Ursula's words fueled a growing ache. How could I have hoped Mia might have spent some months in a place where she was treated with kindness? How could I have imagined I would find her here, miraculously missing her deportation from Vienna and, somehow, waiting for me to find her?

"She remembers one girl," Dan said. "She says it was hard to look away from her. Even though she was starving, she had the most beautiful face." Ursula looked out the window. "Then the firebombing started in the towns—then the Russians." Dan's voice trailed off. Ursula's ancient refrigerator hummed.

Ursula avoided my eyes and gathered up the postcards.

"What happened after the war?" I asked.

Dan translated and Ursula's face seemed to turn inward, as if the flood of recollection about the slave laborers in her town brought with it painful memories about the Soviet soldiers, rape, and plunder.

"I had to leave school at fifteen. I joined my father as a shepherd." Ursula put the postcards back in the box. "I need to stop now," she said in English. She fingered my pictures, then piled them up and handed them to me. She smoothed down her housecoat and picked up her canes.

"Thank you for coming." She opened the door without looking at us. "It was good to talk with you."

Dan and I stepped outside. We walked our bicycles through the empty main street.

"What were the odds of that? Of her being the only person outdoors today?" I asked.

"It was as if she were waiting all these years for us to show up," Dan said.

We mounted our bikes and the wind propelled us through the village and over an irrigation canal. Outside of town, I pulled to the side of the road and looked back across a field of wheat to the low line of houses and the church steeple of Rönnebeck. The sun broke through the clouds and the sky turned sapphire and white. Poppies seemed to bloom out of nowhere.

We set off for Osterburg, gliding past a nineteenth-century fountain and into the shabby train station. We boarded a train back to Berlin and arrived just in time for the opera.

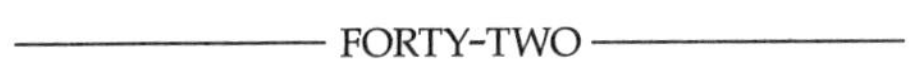

FORTY-TWO

LATE THAT NIGHT I called to check in with Martin from Berlin.

"How's it going?" he asked.

"Missing you."

"Likewise."

"How's the weather?"

"Weird. The apple blossoms were out and then it snowed. I'll send you a picture."

"It's full-blown spring here."

It was silent at the other end of the line, then Martin asked, "How are you holding up?"

"I'm good, I guess. Yeah, I'm fine, really."

"Good."

"You guys?"

"All good here. Home soon?"

"I think so. I think I'm done here. I haven't decided if I need to go back to Vienna again."

"Let me know."

"Love you."

"Likewise."

The house was quiet when I hung up; the O'Connors had already gone to bed. I turned off the lamp next to the bed, then turned it on again, pulled my notebook into my lap and opened it to a blank page.

A freak storm hit after the trees budded on Obere Donaustrasse. By late afternoon, traffic froze and fat flakes blanketed the branches, weighing them down with snow on top of early blossoms. Around suppertime, someone decided that the "useless Jews" should clear the streets. They rounded up the old people and the children and sent us to work.

Uncle Simel hobbles through slush in his bedroom slippers. A prayer shawl drapes over his shoulders for warmth. He bends to collect snow in his arms and slides to the side of the road. He smiles when the policemen laugh at him, maybe hoping they won't notice poor Gittel with her useless arm. Mutti, Papa, and Susi's faces are the color of the snow gathered in my skirt. They push at the ice with their shoes. My heart, unreliable after my fever at Rönnebeck, flip-flops inside my chest. I am hungry for air.

Omama leans against the wall of her old home, and her sightless eyes seem to follow the falling snow. Skeletal hands pick at her clothes. Her ring finger is indented where her wedding band used to be. Aunt Pepi comes up beside me. She pulls a handful of snow out of my skirt and tosses it in the air, then licks her fingers.

"Be careful, Pepicia, the policeman will see you," Mutti says. She lays a hand on Pepi's shoulder, but Pepi shrugs her off and Mutti falls back.

"Pepi!" I shout.

Pepi fixes me with her eyes. "The insect speaks," she says.

Mutti says, "Shhh."

Aunt Pepi keeps staring at me, and it looks like the whites of her eyes entirely circle her irises. The end of one sentence runs into the beginning of the next, making her words sing. "My husband ran off with that woman—that whore. They took the children, all six of them. Even little Kurtl, my baby, has gone off to New York."

"My darling Kurtl," Omama mutters.

"I told the cook to bring me a nice schnitzel, a nice schnitzel from the market." Aunt Pepi eyes me again. "I never married—I am married, but I can't say when. My husband is in America with our children and his bride. Our youngest is ten years old. My mother makes me nervous." Aunt Pepi points at Omama, "I am too intelligent and she does all kinds of things to irritate me. She is making us both *meshuga*."

A policeman comes toward us, and we all bend to our work. All except Aunt Pepi, who walks past him and toward the Donaukanal.

"Halt!" the policeman shouts. Aunt Pepi keeps walking.

The policeman pulls out his gun and lets off a wild shot. *Aunt Pepi disappears into a swirl of snow.*

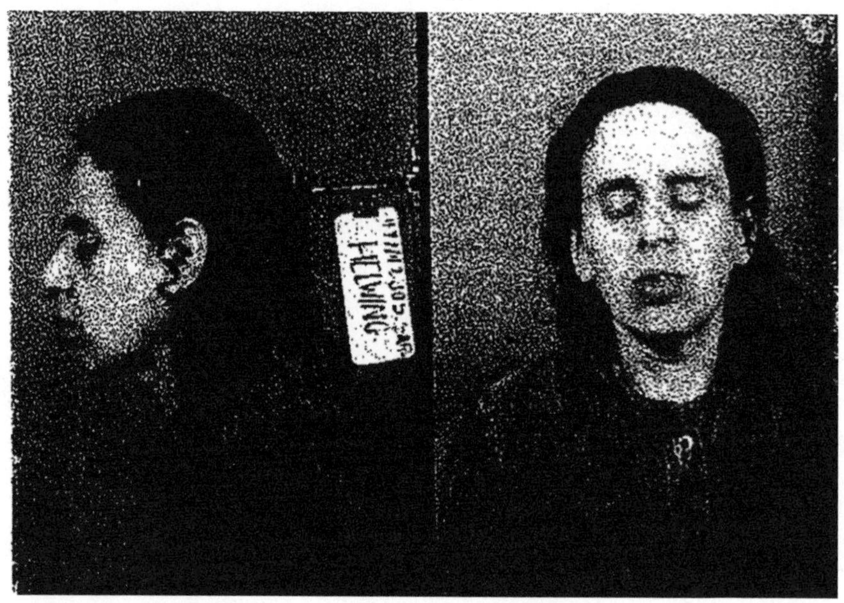

Photographs from the medical record of my great aunt, 45-year-old Josephine (Pepi) Helwing, from Am Steinhof, 1942.

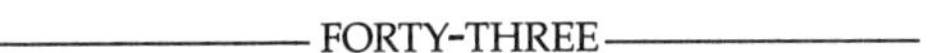

FORTY-THREE

WHEN IT HAD finally arrived in my mailbox back in Wayland, the brevity of my father's Aunt Pepi Helwing's medical record shocked me. There were only ten notes documenting her decline—from her admission note after she attempted suicide, dated March 7, 1942, to her death certificate seven weeks later. She was forty-five years old, single, unemployed, Mosaisch—Jewish. Her final weight was seventy-one pounds. The cause of death was written in Latin: *Marasmus e Psychosis*—Severe Malnutrition due to Psychosis. This was not a diagnosis I ever learned in medical school.

There was a set of photographs attached to her file. In profile her head is held up on a post with a label spelling out her last name. Straight on, her mouth is slightly open; her eyes are closed. Her lower lip is swollen, as if she had been struck. I could not tell if the photo was taken when she was dead or alive.

Psychiatrist Victor Frankl wrote Pepi's first evaluation. Frankl survived deportation, concentration camps, and the Death March, and went on to establish a psychiatric institute in Vienna after the war. He wrote a worldwide bestseller, *Man's Search for Meaning: An Introduction to Logotherapy*, describing his particular branch of Existential Psychiatry honed by his experiences during the Holocaust. Although Frankl was head of the female suicide ward at

Am Steinhof in the 1930s, he was no longer allowed to work there after the Anschluss. He could only recommend admission from the Rothschild Hospital, the Jewish hospital that would be closed down a few months after Pepi's death and his own deportation.

Frankl's approach to life reminds me so much of my father's, and of so many I interviewed who survived and went on to flourish. They carried on by burying part of the past, erasing other memories, and rewriting the remainder of their stories. It's what we all do—a normal response to suffering so that we can live our lives. But in the setting of overwhelming trauma, I wondered if this adjustment of memory was just another kind of madness.

In Pepi's admission note Frankl states: "The patient has been psychologically disturbed for the last months. She jumped into the Danube Canal and her mother, who is malnourished and half-blind, can no longer care for her at home." The note goes on: "For the last two to three days the patient has refused to eat. She is dysphoric, agitated and voices concerns about cleanliness. She is restless and repetitively strokes the bed linens. She admits she hears voices. She is unkempt and incontinent of urine and feces. She says the whole world is against her. She says she knows the assistant physician: 'He lives in my building ... The Frau Doctor is my cook.'"

Pepi's pulse was described as "rapid and small." Her physical examination was thought to be consistent with "toxicosis." Frankl states that this is a catatonic picture in the setting of an acute psychosis of menopause. I wondered, from this description, if she might have been suffering from hyperthyroidism. The note finishes with: "The patient was normal before this and there is no family history of mental illness ... There is a reactive component to her presentation and there is good hope for recovery." Frankl suggests transfusion with her own blood, heart medication, as well as tube feeding. There is no evidence that any of these recommendations were followed.

On my last visit to Vienna in the spring of 2007, I finally met with Dr. Eberhard Gabriel at an outdoor café in the Inner City. He had retired as the director of Am Steinhof but was still practicing psychiatry. He had just published his book about the history of the institution.

Eberhard shook my hand warmly with both of his. "It's wonderful to meet you finally," he said. I liked him immediately. Over coffee and strudel, we went over Pepi's record together. He told me that although she should have been on a separate ward for Jews, they wouldn't have had the staffing to segregate her in 1942. He confirmed there was nothing in the record to support that she was euthanized, or that she was a subject of medical experiments. He told me there was no evidence that her family ever visited before she died; the trams were closed to Jews and it would have been too far to walk.

I wondered if there was information missing from the record, and why there was such a long delay between her death and her burial by the Jewish Community. But I couldn't bring myself to ask Eberhard; I don't remember what inhibited me. Maybe I thought it was impolite after he'd gone to so much trouble to have the records sent to me. He acknowledged that the Nazi years were a sad chapter in the history of Am Steinhof, but he was clearly proud of the advancements made in the care of patients with mental illness in the years preceding and following the war.

"There is no way to know for sure what happened to Pepi," he said as he flipped through the thin chart. "She arrived starving. She had an ear infection at one point. She might have been hyperthyroid. But my guess is she probably just died of neglect."

"And the photographs? Was she dead or alive?"

"Alive, definitely. That would have been quite routine."

"But her head is on a post," I pointed at the photograph.

Eberhard moved his pastry to one side and considered the pictures. "She was catatonic," he said. "Quite routine."

I'd learned that Viktor Frankl and his wife obtained visas to the United States in 1941, but Frankl didn't want to leave his parents, so he let the visas lapse. His father died at Theresienstadt, his mother was murdered in Auschwitz and his wife in Bergen-Belsen. In his book *Man's Search for Meaning*, Frankl wrote about a vision he

Krankheitsgeschichte Nr. I

Name: HELWING Josefine Sara

Journal-Nr. 471/42 Angekommen am: 7.III.1942.

als: B.Z.

Frauen Abteilung Abgegangen am: 2.5. 1942

als: gestorben um 20. Uhr 15

Verpflegsklasse III Verpflegsdauer: ...... Jahre, ... Monate, ... Tage.

Datum der Geburt: 4.7.1897	Offiz. Diagnose Nr.: 17c
Religion: mos.	
Stand: ledig	
Beruf und Stellung: ohne Erwerb	Klinische Diagnose: [illegible]
Geburtsort: Kolomea, Galizien	
Geburtsland: Galizien	Ätiologie: I. Heredität:
Zuständig nach: ?	
	II. sonstige: Klimax
Letzter Wohnort: 2., Böcklinstrasse 92/12 bei Mutter Sabine Sara H.	
Aufnahmsdokumente: vom B.Z.	Beginn (Dauer) der Erkrankung: Seit Herbst 1941/ psych. verandert,
Parere von Dr.:	

Detail from my father's Aunt Pepi's medical record from Am Steinhof after Vicor Frankl requested immediate hospitalization. Note that all female Jews were given "Sara" as a middle name; all men were given "Israel."

had during the waning days of the war. He'd been separated from his wife. He and other prisoners were being driven along by cruel guards.

> Hiding his mouth behind his upturned collar, the man marching next to me whispered suddenly: "If our wives could see us now! I do hope they are better off in their camps and don't know what is happening to us."
>
> That brought thoughts of my own wife to mind. And as we stumbled on for miles, slipping on icy spots, supporting each other time and again, dragging one another up and onward, nothing was said, but we both knew: each of us was thinking of his wife.

> Occasionally I looked at the sky, where the stars were fading and the pink light of the morning was beginning to spread behind a dark bank of clouds. But my mind clung to my wife's image, imagining it with an uncanny acuteness. I heard her answering me, saw her smile, her frank and encouraging look. Real or not, her look was then more luminous than the sun which was beginning to rise.
>
> A thought transfixed me: for the first time in my life I saw the truth as it is set into song by so many poets, proclaimed as the final wisdom by so many thinkers. The truth—that love is the ultimate and the highest goal to which man can aspire. Then I grasped the meaning of the greatest secret that human poetry and human thought and belief have to impart: The salvation of man is through love and in love.

Victor Frankl knew his wife and his parents were gone when he wrote these words in 1946. Did he really think of his wife as he stumbled along or is that how he chose to remember? Eberhard cleared his throat.

"Do you think survivors rewrite memories to find meaning?" I asked him.

"I think we all do."

"And is it common for survivors to have flashbacks when they get older?"

"Oddly, it's when they get older that it often starts. I don't know if it's time that wears them down, making it harder to compartmentalize memory, or if it's illness, or medications, like the ones your father took for his Parkinson's."

"I often wondered if my father should have had therapy early on, if it would have helped." I stirred my coffee. "Or maybe suppressing so much allowed him to keep going. At the end, when he told me these stories, I didn't know what to do."

"Maybe you didn't need to *do* anything. He chose to tell you these things. Maybe you just needed to listen."

We sat for some time in silence, watching the tourists stroll by.

"Isn't Vienna lovely in spring?" Eberhard asked.

"Yes," I said, stirring my second *café mélange.*

When I spoke again, I had trouble keeping my voice from shaking. "My father used to cringe when I hugged him, like my touch burned him." I took a sip of coffee. "And he never said 'I love you' unless I said it first. People tell me that was generational, but he never once told my brothers he loved them. He never hugged them."

"The reason for that is obvious, don't you think?"

"No."

Eberhard looked at me as if weighing whether to elucidate. "He loved his family. In the end, he lost them. Maybe it felt too dangerous to say it out loud." A child touched the Pestsäule and stepped back to look up. Eberhard waved me away when I reached for the bill. "When will you visit us again?"

"I feel like I'm finished here," I said. "I don't think I will ever return."

Eberhard counted out change. Then we sat together, watching the world pass us by.

Correspondence

Little Susi comes here every day and asks what Uri writes and where Hafner is.

Letter from Elka to Uri.

27. Mai 1942

Bo. **Vermögensverzeichnis**

nachstehender in die Ostgebiete evakuierter Juden:

Name: G r ü n b e r g Leib Isr. Kenn.-Nr. G 070094

geboren am: 3.5.1885 in Kolomea

wohnhaft: 2., Ferdinandstr. 31 /16

Ehefrau: Elka Sara geb. am: 25.11.1889 Kolomea

Kinder: Lia Sara geb. am: 26.1.1926 Wien

Ich erkläre, folgende bewegliche Vermögenswerte, Rechte und Ansprüche zu besitzen:

a) Bargeld RM 47.-- Rente RM. 85.-- Versorgungsamt I

b) Wertpapiere --

c) Sperrkonten und Sparkassenbücher --

d) Versicherungspolizzen --

e) Schmuck --

f) Hausrat und Möbel 2 Betten, 3 Kasten, Küchenmöbel

g) Forderungen (Im In- und Ausland) --

Vor mir unterfertigt:

Unterschrift: Leib Israel Grünberg

Elka Sara Grünberg

On May 27, 1942, Leo and Elka signed a receipt for belongings they were forced to leave behind: Cash 47 marks, Rent 85 marks, 2 beds, 3 boxes, kitchen furniture. Perhaps the document gave them the impression they would be compensated for their losses, although there is no official stamp.

From the archives of the Jewish Community

FORTY-FOUR

For months, then years, I untangled strands of forgotten stories and tugged into view people long dead and only poorly remembered. Then I wrapped myself in the incomplete fabric I had created, like a tattered prayer shawl whose fringe grows finer and finer and then vanishes into our past.

In February 1941, right after Cousin Kurt's foster family agreed to sponsor them, Igo and Berthe Helwing were deported to Opole. They wrote to Menio and Emka that they were cold and starving and infested with lice. They pleaded for money and food.

After only a few months, their letters ceased.

The deportation of Jews from the Opole Ghetto commenced on March 31, 1942, when 1,950 souls were dragged from their crowded hovels and marched by foot to the Naleczow train station and crammed onto cattle cars bound for Belzec. On May 25, 1942, another two thousand were shipped to the gas chambers at Sobibor. The remaining occupants were liquidated on October 24, 1942.

Igo and Berthe were declared dead by the state at the end of the war. Even though my father thought their son Kurt was adopted by his English family, the last government pension check I found through the Holocaust Victims Information and Support Center was signed "Curt Helwing." The envelope, postmarked 2006, was stamped "deceased." As far as I know, he left no heirs.

Gittel and Simel Blaustein were forced from Vienna to Theresienstadt on August 13, 1942. They were accompanied by Rita Barnes's parents, Eisig and Sali Kamil.

Emka Helwing wrote about Simel and Gittel in her memoir:

> Kotek's aunt and uncle, whom we both loved dearly because they were people of unusual quality of heart and character, were the only one [sic] we had definite news of after the war. They were sent to a Czechoslovakian camp and tortured to death.

Gittel died in Theresienstadt on December 15, 1942. The Kamils died there as well. Simel may have died at Theresienstadt, but some records said he was taken on to Auschwitz. Either way, he was never heard from again.

My great-grandmother, Omama Sabine Sarah Brandel Helwing, was the last of my family to depart Vienna. On September 10, 1942, she was deported by passenger train to Theresienstadt and one day later, on September 11, 1942, she was sent east. There is no reason to think she saw Simel and Gittel on her way into the cattle cars. She was murdered at Treblinka on September 29, 1942.

My father's neighbor Abraham Melzer traveled to England to join his older son, Kurt Melzer, in 1939. Hans Melzer, who I imagined skipping arm-in-arm with Susi Harband, sits in a column above his mother, Olga, on page ninety-one of the *Totenbuch Theresienstadt—Deportierte aus Österreich* (The Death Book for those deported from Austria to Theresienstadt.) Hans and his mother were deported from Vienna to Theresienstadt on October 1, 1942. She died there. According to the DÖW, Hans was sent on to Auschwitz on October 2, 1942. He survived another two years, until September 28, 1944. He was only seventeen years old when he was murdered.

In family letters I discovered that my father had a friend named Hafner who was a fellow member of the Tchelet-Levan. He is the Aron who left for a work camp at Ellguth in 1939, went on to Buchenwald and Berlin before he made it to the Zionist farm in Holland. It is

My great-grandmother, Sabine Helwing, c. 1890.

unlikely he escaped to Palestine before the Germans rolled through the Netherlands in 1940. There is no Aron Hafner in the records of the Viennese Jewish Community, but there is an Adolf Hafner, born May 11, 1921. He reappears among thousands on the DÖW website, transported from Holland to an "unspecified camp" where he "perished." An Avi Hafner, born in Vienna in 1920, is listed on a Yad Vashem affidavit filled out in 1949 by a relative of Emka Helwing's. This Hafner was a worker in Holland who was taken to Germany in 1943 or 1944. He did not survive.

Hermann, the half-Jewish boy my father tutored, was imprisoned at Dachau with his father. He survived.

Helen, Sonja, and Borscht, shaved of their last names, cannot be traced.

Aron Menczer, the leader of the Youth Aliyah in Vienna, was deported to Theresienstadt on September 24, 1942. There, he volunteered to be one of the *madrichim* who cared for a group of 1,260 orphans delivered from Bialystok. When the children arrived at Theresienstadt, they were taken to the washroom to be cleansed. They became hysterical, as if they were about to be murdered. When the children were sent east again, Aron Menczer went with them. For a time, rumors circulated that they were all released in Switzerland. But the rumors were unfounded.

On November 7, 1943, they were all murdered in the gas chambers of Birkenau II.

Neighbor Israel Harband can be found in the 1938 Vienna address book. According to the records at the IKG, Israel married Stephanie Cezner in 1930 but their son, Paul Harband, was born eight years earlier, in 1922. Police records confirm what the letters say. Stephanie and Paul Harband left for San Francisco in July 1939.

After his outbursts began, Susi froze in my father's memory as the blond, blue-eyed, irritating, and adorable younger sister of Paul Harband. She writes: "GREETINGS! SUSI!" at the bottom of a letter from Mia to Uri in 1939. My father writes about her in a letter to Uri in the same year:

> Susi came in and I am trying to persuade her to leave. But she absolutely refuses to pay attention to me while she spreads out two teddy bears, a doll and a dog on the table, which leaves me hardly any room to work. Now she starts to babble again but I can't really throw her out.

But if I go back to my father's notes from the 1980s, he questions if Susi is Paul's sister. I found no trace of her in any of the archives in Vienna, or on any of the lists at the DÖW or the USHMM. I stayed up all night, striding the Internet, casting beyond my father's letters and memory. On a business website from California, I located a Joel Harband in an online journal. He responded instantly from Haifa.

"Paul Harband and I shared ancestors," Joel told me. "I never met Paul, but I traced him through the family genealogy," he said. "Paul's father, Israel Harband, and my grandfather were brothers from Tarnapol, in Poland. Israel died in Dachau, or maybe Buchenwald. Paul Harband and his wife lived in San Francisco and had one son, born in 1955. Paul and his wife both died a few years ago. I didn't succeed in tracing the son."

"And Susi Harband?"

"I don't have her listed here. But I can call Israel's nieces in Jerusalem. They survived the camps. They sent what they knew to the archives at Yad Vashem. I'll see if they are willing to talk to you."

Joel Harband called back the next day. "I think you'd better not call the cousins. They were pretty upset. Israel Harband died at Ravensbrook in 1942. It sounded like there was some bad blood between them and Israel's wife."

"Why?"

"They didn't say."

"And Susi?"

"They said there was no Susi."

Transport XXIII

27.5.1942 nach Minsk

383	Grün Elisabeth Sara	1. Neutorg.9	3.2.04
776	Grünbaum Bruche Berta Sara	2. Glockeng. 8	12.7.78
980	Grünbaum Helene Sara	2. Hollandstr. 8	13.8.83
979	Grünbaum Karl Isr.	"	26.9.77
105	Grünberg Elka Sara	2. Ferdinandstr. 31	25.11.89
106	Grünberg Leib Isr.	"	3.5.85
107	Grünberg Mia Sara	"	26.1.26

From the Deportationsliste, May 27, 1942.

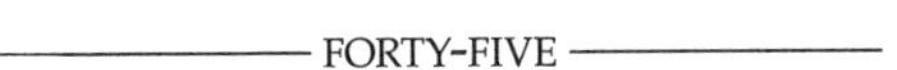

FORTY-FIVE

The Jewish Community provided the names. The women are now all "Sara;" the men are all "Israel." Our Hebrew names have vanished.

Papa sits by the door, dressed in a threadbare suit. Our suitcases surround him; his hat perches on top of the pile. He sips water from a cracked cup. I imagine the smell of hot chocolate from the café on Alserstrasse.

Shouts and the clamor of fists hit the doors, as if the German nation rushes down the hall to roust us out of our beds. Papa sets his cup on a table and stands as the others gasp and stir. The soldiers fall through the door when Papa swings it open.

The face of their leader, the grocer's young son, flushes red when he catches sight of me pulling a ragged blanket around myself.

"It's time," he says.

I pull my coat over two dresses and force my feet into too-tight shoes.

Raimund Nechmac checks the list as our building empties its overfilled rooms. We walk through the streets and join the others selected for deportation today. Mutti leans against Papa; she stumbles on bloated legs. A boy skips along with us, pointing and laughing at the yellow stars staining our chests. It takes two hours to walk to the station.

What is left that we can still carry? A few photographs, some letters, Harry's paperweight?

At the platform we join hundreds, all carrying suitcases or sacs. Their clothes hang loose and inadequate against the chill. The soldiers and their dogs move among us. As we board they check us off. We take our seats and array our bags at our feet.

Salt of my tears, salt on my lips.
A field of green colors and bloom.
Day to night, night to day.
The train, ca clank, ca clank, ca clank
over each rail like a hammer
pounding a stake into the ground.

Over each rail we move.
Over old borders we travel.
To the east, past ghostly shtetls.
To the east, past smoking spirits.
Then, down, down, down, back into the earth.

At the station in Minsk, we climb out to the platform.
A soldier shouts.
Leave your bags!
They will be delivered!
We will feed you when you arrive!
It is a very short drive!
I cannot remember when I ate my last meal.

Correspondence

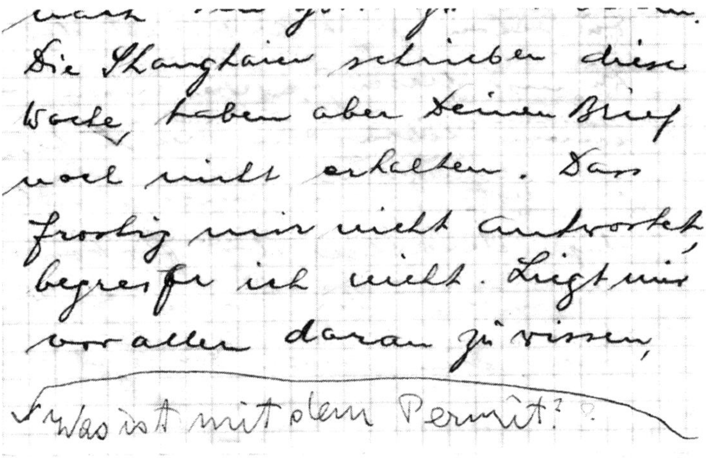
Die Shanghaier schrieben diese
Woche, haben aber Deinen Brief
wohl nicht erhalten. Dass
frostig mir nicht antwortet
begreife ich nicht. Liegt mir
vor allem daran zu wissen,

Was ist mit dem Permit??

Mia adds a note at the end of her parents' letter:
"What's with my permit??"

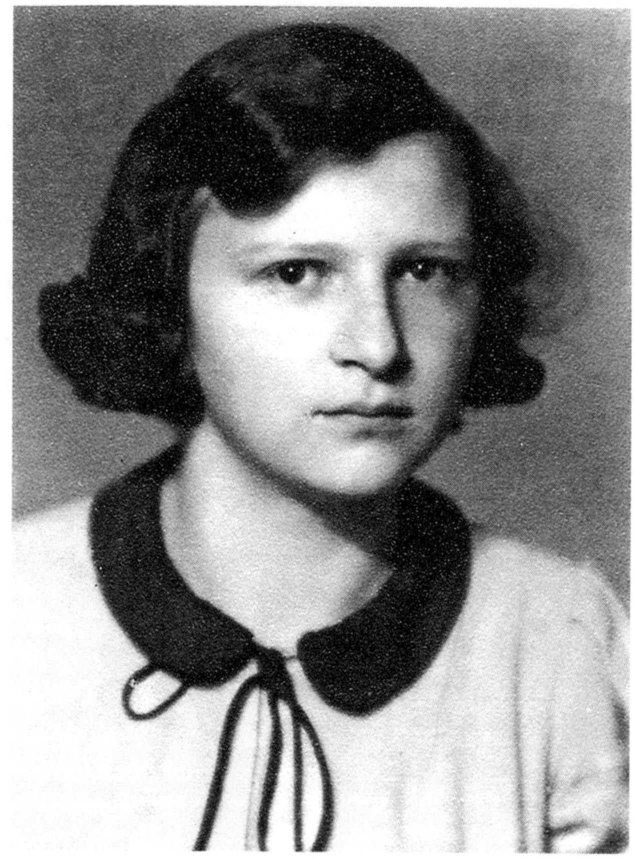

Mia's passport photo, 1939.

FORTY-SIX

I NEVER FOUND the missing letters. But on a visit home between trips to Vienna, I found Mia's 1939 passport photograph wedged into the back of a drawer in my father's office. She didn't look anything like me.

My father had always said that his own father would not let Mia go.

"My father was an optimist."

"At the last moment, he did not let my sister go on the Kindertransport."

"She had a place to Australia, but he did not let her take it."

But in the letters, my grandparents' desperation permeates the spaces between their questions about my father's health and their thirst for news about his day-to-day life. They ask over and over for him to get the permit, the affidavit, the sponsor, the piece of paper that would allow Mia to escape. My father was nineteen when he was arrested by the British. Was there really anything he could have done? I think he went to his grave believing he could have done something that would have altered Mia's and her parents' fates. Their loss tore something out of him and he never recovered.

On my last visit to the DÖW, Elisabeth Klamper and I were back to first names.

"I want to find out if the Germans hold documents with eyewitness reports about Mia's particular transport," I asked. "I mean, how do they know that she was taken in a cattle car to Maly Trostinec and not taken to Auschwitz and gassed?"

"*Ach*, you Americans—you only know about Auschwitz and cattle cars. These people traveled on ordinary trains. They were given assigned seats. They brought suitcases, for God's sake."

Elisabeth rattled her fingers along the computer keyboard. I thought that was it, but then she looked up again. "Do you really think the Nazis started out knowing they were going to murder millions of people? Do you think they organized Jews into a ghetto in Vienna knowing they would ship them out and slaughter them?"

The boys lined up along the wall of the office and watched. I looked back to Elisabeth. She continued. "The Nazis were pragmatists. They took over a country, and they had problems they needed to solve. For one, there was a housing shortage in Vienna. If they crowded two or three Jewish families into one apartment, then the empty apartments could go to a friend or a crony. At first, they just wanted to make the Jews leave. Later, when they took over most of Europe, there were millions more Jews on their hands and nowhere to send them. That was a big problem." Elisabeth took off her glasses and cleaned them on the edge of her shirt.

"They experimented with different things in the East." She put her glasses back on. "Shooting people into pits—they didn't have enough bullets to go around and it actually disturbed some of the officers. So they used the—how do you say that?—they used the 'mental deficients' for experiments—they tried different approaches."

I clutched my notebook and braced my feet against the floor.

"Early in 1941," she continued, "they tried building huts and they herded the deficients and maybe a few Soviet POWs into them and locked them inside. They flew planes over the huts and dropped bombs on them. Body parts flew everywhere. Limbs were hanging from the trees."

Elisabeth rolled around to the boys, who exhaled as one. She swiveled back to me. "Later the Germans were too busy with the war to focus on this problem, and they needed the trains. It wasn't until 1942 that they worked things out. They used their notes from these experiments to plan how to murder large groups of people with the least amount of mess and fuss."

My friend's eyes seemed to grow cold. "They experimented, you see—until they could see what worked best."

She stood up and looked out the window. "Yes, maybe she was gassed, or she could have been shot. When your father's sister arrived in Maly Trostinec, they were still working out the kinks." She extended her hand to me and I took it. We gripped each other for a long time. Her face softened.

"Have a good journey, Lisa. I do wish you the best of luck."

DER MENSCH IN SEINEM DUNKLEN DRANGE
IST SICH DES RECHTEN WEGES WOHL BEWUSST

MAN IN HIS DARK CRAVING
IS WELL AWARE OF THE RIGHT PATH

My father quotes Goethe's *Faust* but leaves out "guten" (good) before "Mensch" (man).

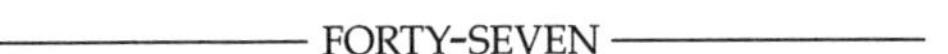

FORTY-SEVEN

THE ORDER COMES. *We look at each other and embrace.* Mutti leaves her small satchel next to Papa's but I don't want to leave anything more behind. As I take up my suitcase, it is yanked from my hands and thrown into a growing pile. Then Papa and I grab Mutti under the arms and we are all pulled in and packed, standing, into the back of an idling truck.

We shudder into motion. Wind whistles as we pick up speed. In the darkness people cry out for their loved ones—Rivkah! Jacob! I lean against Papa and let Mutti lean against me. Light shoots between the canvas flaps on the side of the truck as we pull out of the station. It illuminates a face, a neck, an arm, Papa's blue eyes, Mutti's hair on my shoulder. I try to move to ease the ache in my back. Mutti whispers, "I have to go." I tell her, "Go ahead" and feel the warmth of her urine as it runs over my shoes.

The truck pulls over and stops. For a few moments there is quiet, but then the moaning begins again as the space grows hot. Soldiers shout, "*Schnell! Schnell!*" They draw aside the canvas, and I stumble toward the bright light, almost falling. People stream past me and pool beside the road. Looking over their heads my vision is accosted by the view, a wide green field of wildflowers: lupine, daisies, and buttercups. The sky is clean blue. Close enough to touch gentle hills shine like a painting in one of Omama's art books. The breeze picks up my hair and plays with it. The pale face of a child reflects the sun and an azure butterfly lands on the penumbra of her hair. I turn to take my mother's hand, but she is no longer next to me. Soldiers drag her body onto a waiting cart, already full of the dead.

A blond soldier with a kind face puts a hand up to help me down. "Bitte, Fräulein, come down and join the others." I let my stiff knees bend and feel his hands surround my waist as he lifts me down.

Salt of my tears, salt on my lips, a field of green colors and bloom. Blue sky, white clouds moving. We walk, walk, walk across the field. I kick off my shoes and leave them where they lie. Grass scratches my feet and legs. Light flashes. Salt on my lips. So dry.

His kisses—salty—evaporated. Papa so quiet; we stumble. The sounds of birds, the shovels like bells on the earth tolling the sound of a mourning prayer:

Yishgadal v'yiskadesh. Glorified and sanctified be God's great name throughout the world which he created according to his will. And we say Amen.

A wide field, butterflies, birds, the rustle of the linden trees, the smell of apple blossoms, the breeze.

May he establish His kingdom in your lifetime and during your days and within the life of the entire House of Israel, speedily and soon. Amen.

The clink of shovels, the sighs, the electric crack of gunfire, the soft thud of souls as they hit the ground.

The piles of bodies by the road grow and diminish.

No sound.

The blue of the sky, the white of the clouds, the green of the grass and trees. The silence stops as shepherds bark. The guns crack. The shovels toll.

May His great name be blessed forever and to all eternity.

Papa walks beside me. We don't touch. The light is bright off his copper hair. The light. The bright, bright light. The salt on my lips. No water for tears.

Blessed and praised, glorified and exalted, extolled and honored, adored and lauded be the name of the Holy One. Blessed be He, beyond all the blessings and hymns, praises and consolations and say, Amen.

My head hurts with the beauty. My thoughts are of him as I end.

No more.

The sounds of birds, of shovels, the music of the mourning prayer.

May there be abundant peace from heaven, and life, for us and for all Israel; and say, Amen.

I am frightened and yet I keep moving—from the shadows of the truck to the sun and movement of this place. A stream meanders near us. Its water clatters over stones and reflects sunlight at thousands of angles. I walk into its icy edge. The water is cold as snow. My feet grow numb.

Papa calls me, "Mia." He holds his hand out to me and I follow.

As we approach a dark line of trees the deep voices of soldiers add to the soprano of sighs, the soughing of leaves, the barking of dogs, the whisper of grass against our legs. We pull off our clothes and lay them on a table to be sorted by a woman with needle and thread in her mouth. A boy teeters on a stool and plucks the dentures from Papa's mouth and casts them atop a pile of bloody gold teeth. We pass naked through green shade, through the sounds of birds harvesting rhapsodies in the branches. Here the woods are scarred by an enormous trench. The sweet scent of exhausted flesh rolls over us, as the carts release their contents into the ditch.

The light. The bright, bright light.

Salt on my dry lips.

Tears in your eyes.

The song of the birds, the yipping of shepherds, the music of shovels, the murmurs of the now old men singing the mourning prayer.

He who creates peace in His celestial heights, may He create peace for us and for all Israel; and say, Amen.

I will live on through you and your children. Yet I want to live on this day and not die at the end of this field. We form a line near the edge of the abyss and I feel my voice rising from my chest as I force my eyes down from sky filtered through trees.

Sh'ma Yisrael Adonai Elohaynu Adonai Echad. Hear, Israel, the Lord is our God, the Lord is One.

Bodies on bodies make patterns in the ditch. They are not all quiet. Some still settle. Some still breath. A gray baby crawls to his mother. She lays her head back on her shattered arm and whispers a lullaby. A girl whose ribbons weave through golden braids presses down on restless corpses with blood-stained feet. A boy follows, frosting the bodies with lime.

My mother—dead.

My brothers—gone.

I am afraid, but the world goes on.

I am angry, but you will live on with me within.

I see the ditch. I smell the blossoms and the green grass. I taste the salt of kisses on my lips. I hear the dogs barking, the people moving, the babies crawling, the silent falling.

Papa smiles as his body arches and soars.

You are forgiven for living while we end. You are not forgiven for living while we end. You will end, too.

Why don't you jump?

Salt on my lips.
My eyes are dry.
I take a breath.
I leap.
Baruch, baruch, baruch atah.
Blessed art thou.

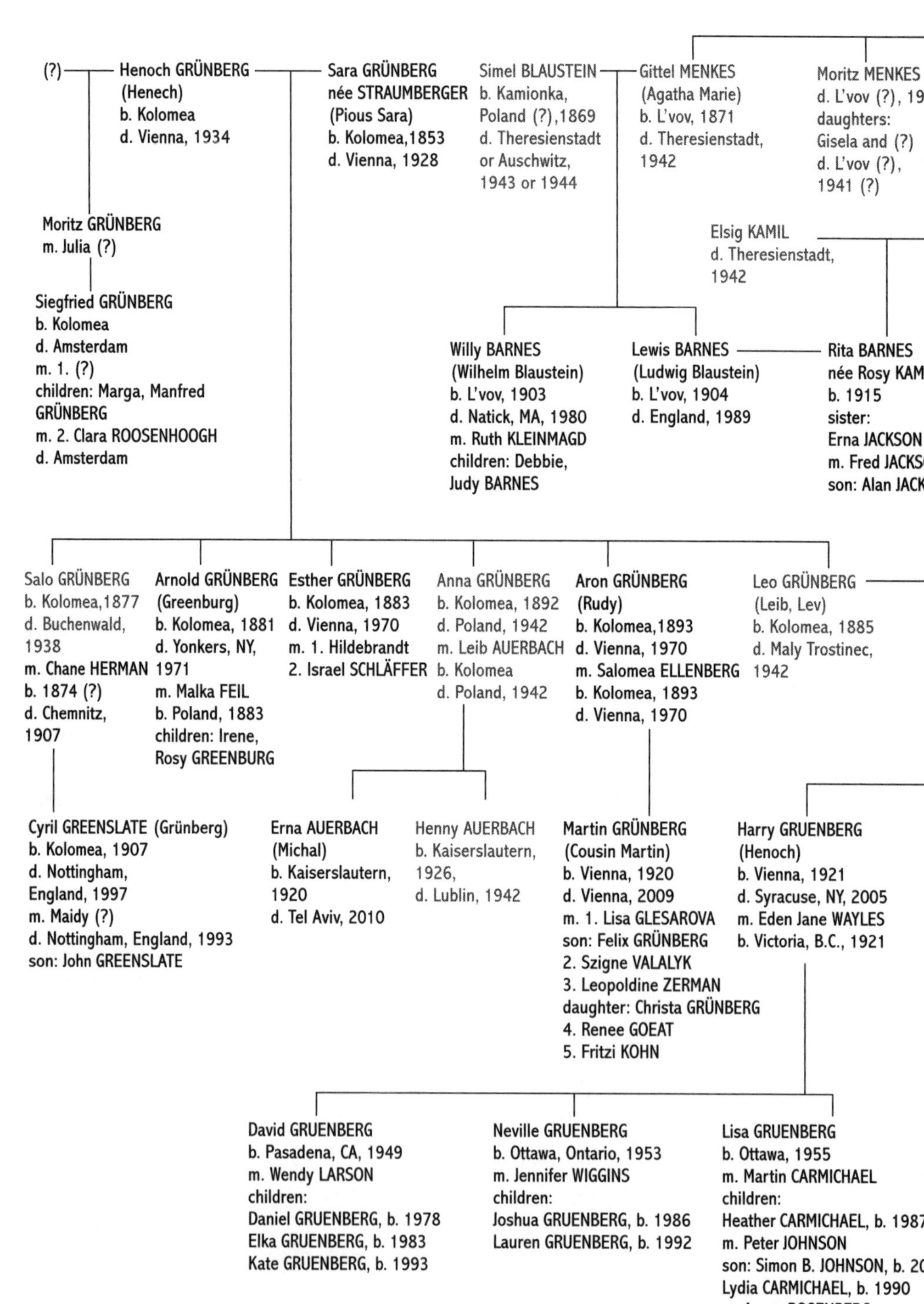

(?)
Henoch GRÜNBERG
(Henech)
b. Kolomea
d. Vienna, 1934
Sara GRÜNBERG
née STRAUMBERGER
(Pious Sara)
b. Kolomea, 1853
d. Vienna, 1928
Simel BLAUSTEIN
b. Kamionka,
Poland (?), 1869
d. Theresienstadt
or Auschwitz,
1943 or 1944
Gittel MENKES
(Agatha Marie)
b. L'vov, 1871
d. Theresienstadt,
1942
Moritz MENKES
d. L'vov (?), 1941
daughters:
Gisela and (?)
d. L'vov (?),
1941 (?)
Moritz GRÜNBERG
m. Julia (?)
Elsig KAMIL
d. Theresienstadt,
1942
Siegfried GRÜNBERG
b. Kolomea
d. Amsterdam
m. 1. (?)
children: Marga, Manfred
GRÜNBERG
m. 2. Clara ROOSENHOOGH
d. Amsterdam
Willy BARNES
(Wilhelm Blaustein)
b. L'vov, 1903
d. Natick, MA, 1980
m. Ruth KLEINMAGD
children: Debbie,
Judy BARNES
Lewis BARNES
(Ludwig Blaustein)
b. L'vov, 1904
d. England, 1989
Rita BARNES
née Rosy KAMIL
b. 1915
sister:
Erna JACKSON
m. Fred JACKSON
son: Alan JACKSON
Salo GRÜNBERG
b. Kolomea, 1877
d. Buchenwald,
1938
m. Chane HERMAN
b. 1874 (?)
d. Chemnitz,
1907
Arnold GRÜNBERG
(Greenburg)
b. Kolomea, 1881
d. Yonkers, NY,
1971
m. Malka FEIL
b. Poland, 1883
children: Irene,
Rosy GREENBURG
Esther GRÜNBERG
b. Kolomea, 1883
d. Vienna, 1970
m. 1. Hildebrandt
2. Israel SCHLÄFFER
Anna GRÜNBERG
b. Kolomea, 1892
d. Poland, 1942
m. Leib AUERBACH
b. Kolomea
d. Poland, 1942
Aron GRÜNBERG
(Rudy)
b. Kolomea, 1893
d. Vienna, 1970
m. Salomea ELLENBERG
b. Kolomea, 1893
d. Vienna, 1970
Leo GRÜNBERG
(Leib, Lev)
b. Kolomea, 1885
d. Maly Trostinec,
1942
Cyril GREENSLATE (Grünberg)
b. Kolomea, 1907
d. Nottingham,
England, 1997
m. Maidy (?)
d. Nottingham, England, 1993
son: John GREENSLATE
Erna AUERBACH
(Michal)
b. Kaiserslautern,
1920
d. Tel Aviv, 2010
Henny AUERBACH
b. Kaiserslautern,
1926,
d. Lublin, 1942
Martin GRÜNBERG
(Cousin Martin)
b. Vienna, 1920
d. Vienna, 2009
m. 1. Lisa GLESAROVA
son: Felix GRÜNBERG
2. Szigne VALALYK
3. Leopoldine ZERMAN
daughter: Christa GRÜNBERG
4. Renee GOEAT
5. Fritzi KOHN
Harry GRUENBERG
(Henoch)
b. Vienna, 1921
d. Syracuse, NY, 2005
m. Eden Jane WAYLES
b. Victoria, B.C., 1921
David GRUENBERG
b. Pasadena, CA, 1949
m. Wendy LARSON
children:
Daniel GRUENBERG, b. 1978
Elka GRUENBERG, b. 1983
Kate GRUENBERG, b. 1993
Neville GRUENBERG
b. Ottawa, Ontario, 1953
m. Jennifer WIGGINS
children:
Joshua GRUENBERG, b. 1986
Lauren GRUENBERG, b. 1992
Lisa GRUENBERG
b. Ottawa, 1955
m. Martin CARMICHAEL
children:
Heather CARMICHAEL, b. 1987
m. Peter JOHNSON
son: Simon B. JOHNSON, b. 201
Lydia CARMICHAEL, b. 1990
m. Aaron ROSENBERG

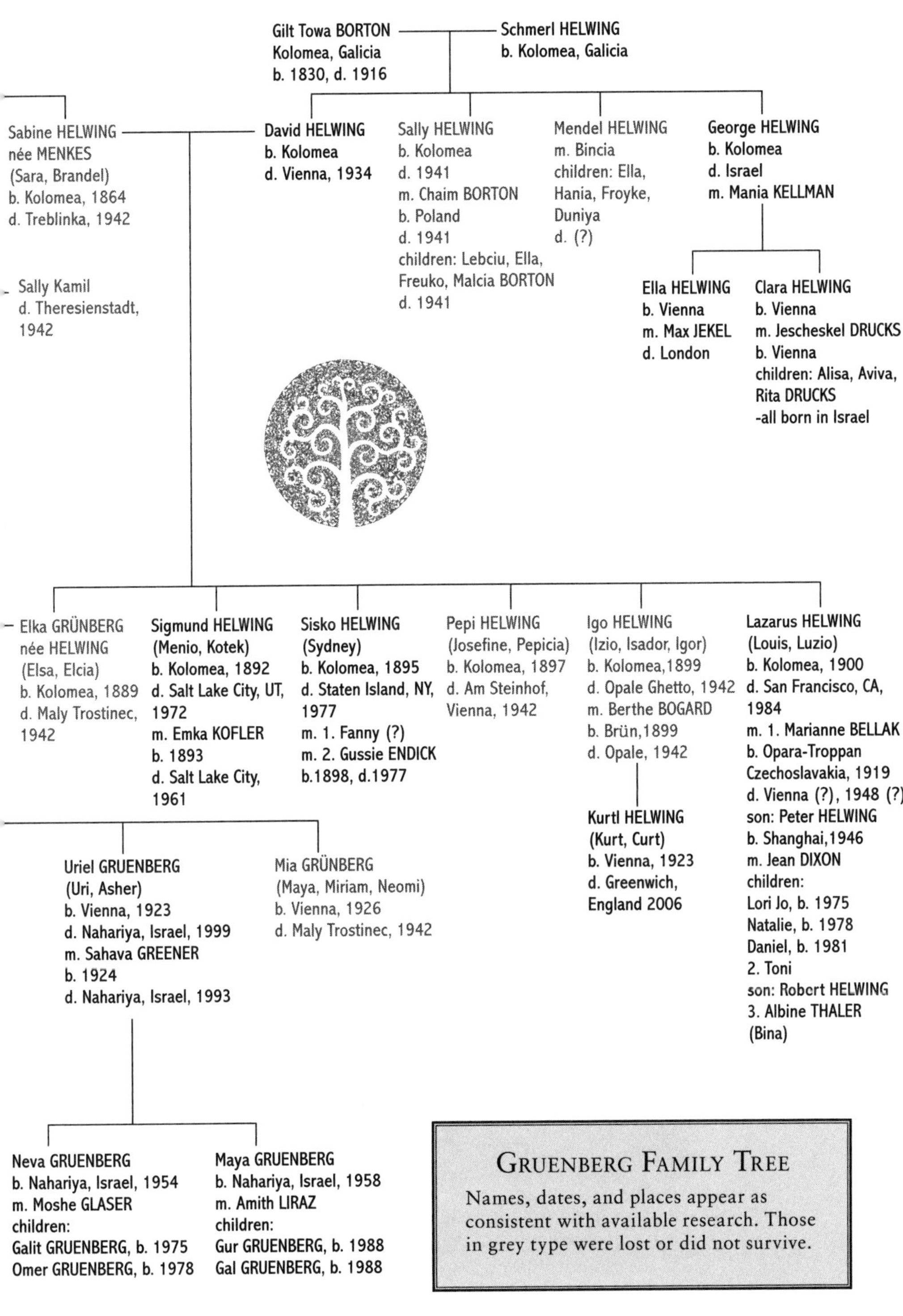
Gilt Towa BORTON
Kolomea, Galicia
b. 1830, d. 1916
Schmerl HELWING
b. Kolomea, Galicia
Sabine HELWING
née MENKES
(Sara, Brandel)
b. Kolomea, 1864
d. Treblinka, 1942
David HELWING
b. Kolomea
d. Vienna, 1934
Sally HELWING
b. Kolomea
d. 1941
m. Chaim BORTON
b. Poland
d. 1941
children: Lebciu, Ella,
Freuko, Malcia BORTON
d. 1941
Mendel HELWING
m. Bincia
children: Ella,
Hania, Froyke,
Duniya
d. (?)
George HELWING
b. Kolomea
d. Israel
m. Mania KELLMAN
Ella HELWING
b. Vienna
m. Max JEKEL
d. London
Clara HELWING
b. Vienna
m. Jescheskel DRUCKS
b. Vienna
children: Alisa, Aviva,
Rita DRUCKS
-all born in Israel
Sally Kamil
d. Theresienstadt,
1942
Elka GRÜNBERG
née HELWING
(Elsa, Elcia)
b. Kolomea, 1889
d. Maly Trostinec,
1942
Sigmund HELWING
(Menio, Kotek)
b. Kolomea, 1892
d. Salt Lake City, UT,
1972
m. Emka KOFLER
b. 1893
d. Salt Lake City,
1961
Sisko HELWING
(Sydney)
b. Kolomea, 1895
d. Staten Island, NY,
1977
m. 1. Fanny (?)
m. 2. Gussie ENDICK
b.1898, d.1977
Pepi HELWING
(Josefine, Pepicia)
b. Kolomea, 1897
d. Am Steinhof,
Vienna, 1942
Igo HELWING
(Izio, Isador, Igor)
b. Kolomea,1899
d. Opale Ghetto, 1942
m. Berthe BOGARD
b. Brün,1899
d. Opale, 1942
Kurtl HELWING
(Kurt, Curt)
b. Vienna, 1923
d. Greenwich,
England 2006
Lazarus HELWING
(Louis, Luzio)
b. Kolomea, 1900
d. San Francisco, CA,
1984
m. 1. Marianne BELLAK
b. Opara-Troppan
Czechoslavakia, 1919
d. Vienna (?), 1948 (?)
son: Peter HELWING
b. Shanghai,1946
m. Jean DIXON
children:
Lori Jo, b. 1975
Natalie, b. 1978
Daniel, b. 1981
2. Toni
son: Robert HELWING
3. Albine THALER
(Bina)
Uriel GRUENBERG
(Uri, Asher)
b. Vienna, 1923
d. Nahariya, Israel, 1999
m. Sahava GREENER
b. 1924
d. Nahariya, Israel, 1993
Mia GRÜNBERG
(Maya, Miriam, Neomi)
b. Vienna, 1926
d. Maly Trostinec, 1942
Neva GRUENBERG
b. Nahariya, Israel, 1954
m. Moshe GLASER
children:
Galit GRUENBERG, b. 1975
Omer GRUENBERG, b. 1978
Maya GRUENBERG
b. Nahariya, Israel, 1958
m. Amith LIRAZ
children:
Gur GRUENBERG, b. 1988
Gal GRUENBERG, b. 1988

GRUENBERG FAMILY TREE

Names, dates, and places appear as consistent with available research. Those in grey type were lost or did not survive.

A Polish poet, Kazimierz Tetmajer said ... that "memory is a cemetery." It sure is true in my case. How else could I write about all these things that happened long ago, without having any notes—just out of random memory? And isn't it a graveyard I am treading on, I that lost almost all of my nearest of kin?—a graveyard unknown to me, probably in the gas chambers where six million perished.

From Emka Helwing's memoir.

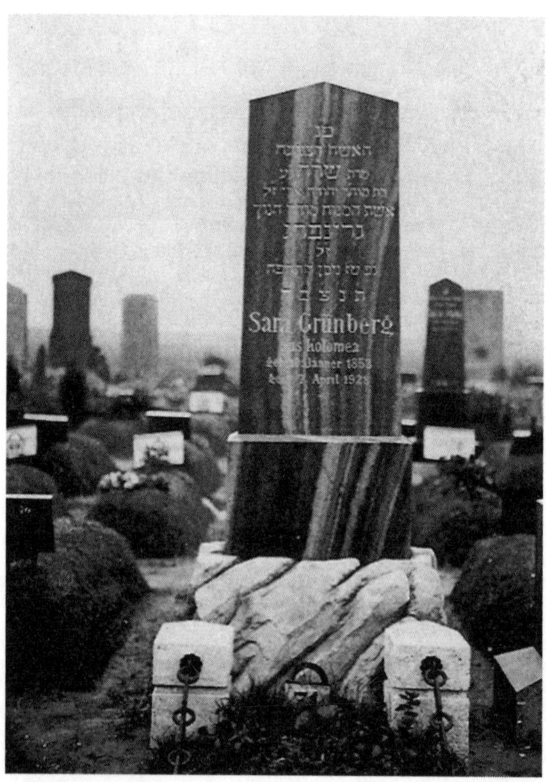

Jahrzeit at my great grandmother Pious Sarah Grünberg's grave, Zentralfriedhof, from Martin Grünberg's album.

FORTY-EIGHT

On my last day in Vienna, I rode Niki's bicycle through the Second District to each of the houses my father's extended family inhabited in the years before their deportations: *Obere Donaustrasse, Bocklingstrasse, Hermanstrasse, Rembrandtstrasse, Ferdinandstrasse.* After I visited Mia's last address, I pedaled into the Prater. Dandelion tufts fell from an azure sky, dusting families picnicking and playing ball. I stopped to gaze up at the slowly circling Riesenrad, and imagined Uri, Mia, and my father looking out from a swinging car—out over their city and the Vienna Woods beyond.

On May 27, 1942, Mia took her last walk through the streets of her city. She boarded a train at Aspang Station with the 988 souls chosen to make the journey that day. A week after the bloodbath outside Maly Trostinec, the Nazis replaced the vehicles that shuttled Jews from the train station in Minsk. The new trucks were rigged so that the exhaust turned inward to poison their cargo. By the time the convoy arrived at the killing fields, the passengers would already be dead.

According to Soviet documents, the Nazis returned to the killing fields at Maly Trostinec in the waning days of the war. In a feral effort, they dug up mass graves and exhumed thousands of bodies. They piled them high and tried to ignite them, but they were damp and burned poorly. The Germans buried the charred remains, but with the next rain, the dirt and ash fell in around the corpses. When the Russians rolled through on their way to Vienna, the bodies made patterns that looked like a frieze of people fleeing across the earth.

Before the war, 180,000 Jews lived in Austria. After the Anschluss, thousands fled and hundreds committed suicide. By 1945, 65,000 Austrian Jews had been slaughtered.

Like the tchelet weaving through a prayer shawl, this tale of my family is a faint blue strand running through an ocean of white. As my father once said: Take the biggest number you can think of; you can still always add one more.

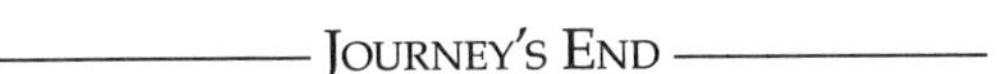 Journey's End

I PERCH ON a picnic table on the empty beach at Squam. Quiet water steams like an ironed sheet in the early morning light. The wind rustles the pine needles and carries their scent to me. I think about all I have learned.

My father discovered the manner of his family's murder long before he died, but he continued to search for how Mia ended up back in Vienna to join their parents on their fateful journey. I will always regret that I began my search too late to bring him that terrible news. This ache I inherited from my father must be a small echo of what he withstood for all his years with us. In turn, his was a shadow of the pain borne by those he left behind.

His final hours come back to me as if they just happened yesterday. He rested on a plastic pillow in a curtained-off corner of the ICU. Thick bandages capped his head and a tube emerging from behind his left ear drained rose-tinged fluid into a bulb clipped to his pocket—a pocket that had once bristled with pencils and ballpoint pens. A hospital band with his name and number cut into his arm. My brothers, my mother, Martin, and I arrayed around him. My childhood friend, Melinda, was right outside the door.

My father's face looked young.

It's him! Beautiful. Like a child fresh from his bath, his covers tucked around him by loving hands.

I wanted to pull the bandages from his ears so I could talk to him.

Open your eyes and be with me.

I put down the side of the bed. I held both his hands in mine.

I lean over and kiss your cheek.

I felt as if I could curl him up in my palms, but the tubes and lines tethered him. When I pulled him to me, he broke apart.

Like old flowers, we crumble.

The pause between each breath stretched out. His fingers and toes and lips turned blue, and then a yellow cast marched across his skin. He took his last breath.

I unfold. I fall away.

It wasn't failure or emptiness that I had sensed below our surface. It was yearning for connection and for the people we have lost. Victor Frankl and my friend Eberhard say we tell stories to make meaning of our lives. I tell mine to find the strength to move forward. After I finished videotaping my father, his nightmares vanished and he never had another flashback. Putting this story on paper, I have found my edges again. But Mia and my father are now within me, and their memories continue, clear in my mind.

I leave the lake and travel back up our road. The old French doors creak open and I tiptoe into the house. Bouquets sit on every table and blossoms tumble down to the floors. I look out our front window down to the lake, gleaming in the valley below me.

There are times on Diamond Ledge when even folding laundry feels like a prayer.

I leave the wide view. The girls turn in their beds. Martin doesn't open his eyes when I walk into the bedroom. He rolls to his side and pats my place. I pull off my clothes and spoon against him and slow my breathing to match his. I squint out the window, trying to bring the deep reds from the perennial border into focus.

I think back to my final telephone conversation with my father, only hours before he slipped into a coma. Marty had just died. Around me, the house bore the remnants of family moving through. The beds upstairs were unmade, dishes were piled in the sink, and

View from Diamond Ledge in summer.

the floors were sticky with bits of food and dirt from the garden. I was sitting at my desk with a mug of strong coffee, almost dozing, feeling the pleasure of an afternoon without the need to comfort anyone. The phone rang. When I picked up the receiver, I knew it was my father.

"Hi, Dad," I said into the silence. While I waited for him to respond, I pulled out my questions. We spoke for close to an hour that day. I scrawled his answers into the margins of my notebook with purple ink.

"What ever happened to your neighbors?" I asked.

I think they all made it out," my father answered.

"Even Paul and Susi?"

"Yes, even them."

Those were the last questions I asked him that day. I didn't want to tire him out, and I figured we could finish up another time.

"No worries," he said. "None of this bothers me anymore."

"How are you feeling since the accident?" I asked.

"I don't think I'll drive any more."

I wrote that down. "No more driving!" underlining it three times.

I wanted him to ask me how I was doing. And out of the blue, my father asked. "Well, how are you doing with all this with Marty?" I started to cry. "You know, I remember something about Marty from when we first met him in New York," my father said. "Tell Martin this story, will you? I hope it will comfort him."

"OK."

"Marty invited me to dinner one night, just on my own. He was late, so I waited for him in the lobby of his apartment building." My father knew that Marty had flexible ideas about time, but after a few hours, he got up to go back to where my mother and I were staying. "But, just then, Marty burst through the doors with two bags of groceries. He didn't apologize for being late, just said his meeting ran over—or maybe he missed the bus. It doesn't really matter." My father cleared his throat, the way he always did. "Marty uncorked a bottle of red wine and cooked a marvelous meal for me. He asked me about my life and my childhood, and then he told me about himself."

Something about my father's telling of that story felt like a gift I had already received. Then it dawned on me. I had heard it before. Marty had tried to tell me about it while we waited for the doctors to come in to diagnose one more complicated infection. His speech was garbled with fever. At the time I hadn't made an effort to hear what he was saying.

The Southern cadence of Marty's voice comes back to me now. "It was a wonderful meal. I love your father's quiet fortitude—his sense of humor."

And I see my young father standing in front of me, and hear his thick accent saying his last words to me. "Don't worry about asking about the past. You know, despite everything, I had a wonderful childhood. I was loved—when you come down to it, that's the only thing that really matters."

And I remember now, what came next.

"I love you, Lisa."

"I love you too, Dad."

Then we both hung up.

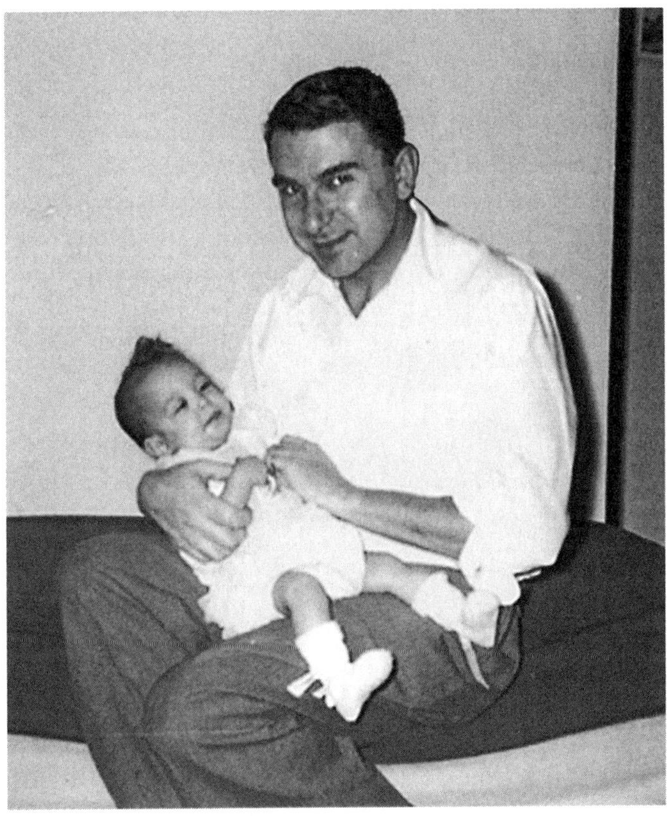

My father and me, 1955.

My parents, 2002.

Afterword

I translated dozens of letters, visited more than twenty archives, and spent hours in libraries and on the internet to research this book. I've only taken you on some of my journeys.

I supplemented Mia's story from documents and books about the time, particularly *Exile and Destruction, The Fate of Austrian Jews, 1938–1945* by Gertrude Schneider and *A Nazi Officer's Wife* by Edith Breer Hahn. The idea for the snow scene came from Wolf Gruner's *Jewish Forced Labor under the Nazis, Economic Needs and Racial Aims, 1938-1944*. He details the use of old people and children to clear snow in Vienna in the late winter of 1942. Mia's death scene is reconstructed from *Holocaust by Bullets*, by Father Patrick Desbois, *Das Vernichtungslager Trostenez, Augenzeugenberichte und Dokumente* by Paul Kohl, translations from Soviet war news from microfiche found at the archives at the United States Holocaust Memorial Museum, and information on the DÖW website. However, Mia's poem intermixed with prayer emerged from my subconscious before I read any of these. It was a result of a meditation on the word "salt" during a writing workshop at Lesley University.

Details of Aron Menczer's life were drawn from Elisabeth Klamper's book, *We'll Meet Again in Palestine: Aron Menczer's Fight to Save Jewish Children in Nazi Vienna*, and from *Trotz Allem ... Aron Menczer* published by Böhlau Verlag. Elka and Leo

Grünberg, Rudy Grünberg, Sabine, Pepi, Igo, Berthe and Kurt Helwing, Simel and Gittel Blaustein, the Melzers, the Harbands, Susi, Paul, Borscht, Hafner, Sonja and Helen are based on letters, and my father's writing and stories. My mother, brothers, husband, daughters, Uri and Sahava Gruenberg, Melinda Johnson, Martin and Fritzi Grünberg, Rita and Ludwig Barnes, the Jacksons, Dr. Elisabeth Klamper, Martin Vogel, Christa Prokisch, Dr. Eberhard Gabriel, Dr. Hans Hartenstein, Marty Carmichael, Ditta Lowry, Niki Macke, Karin Bachman, Sonja Grabowsky, Ursula, and Daniel O'Connor and the cities of Syracuse and Vienna are drawn as I saw and remember them. I recreated conversations from notes, memory, and audio and video recordings.

In one of the later letters to Uri, letters my father never translated, Mia writes: "With Susi Scharfstein's departure on the 25th I got from her a suitcase, so only my departure is missing." Was this the Susi my father remembered? There are several letters that mention neighbors or friends, the Scharfsteins, who traveled to Hamburg, then Lisbon and on to the free port of Cuba in early 1939. A letter in July says the Scharfsteins were "among those allowed to disembark at Havana," which means they could have been on the ill-fated St. Louis, many of whose passengers were sent back to Europe. But there is no Susi Scharfstein listed on the St. Louis manifest. I still search for her.

My mother turned 98 this year. She still beats me at Scrabble. In the process of writing this book, I realized how much I inherited from her as well as my father, including her tenacity and, I hope, her sense of humor and intelligence.

Heather trains to become a surgeon. Lydia graduated with a degree in history, works in the art department of a magazine, and is earning her masters degree in design. Both girls married wonderful men. Martin retired. I went back into clinical medicine, and continue teaching and writing. Niki bought a farm in Kwazulu Natal. He hasn't yet met his future wife.

I cherish each of our numbered days. I try to count them all.

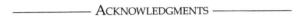

Acknowledgments

This project was supported by many remarkable people and institutions. They include: The DÖW, the City and State Archives of Vienna, the Jewish Museum of Vienna, the Archives of the Jewish Community of Vienna, the Holocaust Victims Information and Support Center, the archives at Magdeburg and Stendal, the University of Utah Library, the Boston and Weston Public Libraries, Allgenerations, and the United States Holocaust Memorial Museum. I particularly want to recognize Dr. Wolf Erich Eckstein of the IKG, Megan Lewis of the USHMM Survivors Registry, Dr. Christa Prokisch of the Jewish Museum of Vienna, and Serena Woolwich of Allgenerations.

Ilana Offenberger was a senior fellow at the USHMM from 2006-2007 and is the author of *The Jews of Nazi Vienna, 1938-1945*, based, in part, on my father's tapes and family letters. Her interest was invaluable.

My father's cousin, Peter Helwing, directed me to the Emma Kohler Helwing collection at the University of Utah and provided Emka and Menio's photographs. Alan Jackson gave me copies of Rita and Ludwig's photographs and surviving documents, as well as her copy of the *Theresienstadt Death Book*. Willy Barnes' daughters, Debbie and Judy, passed on copies of Simel and Gittel Blaustein's letters.

Cyril Grünberg's stepson, John Greenslate, forwarded his memoir about his family. Maya and Neva Grünberg copied their father's letters, offered support in Israel, and their love and friendship.

Survivors Martin Vogel and Ditta Lowry helped recreate wartime Vienna for me. Survivor Werner Buckholtz translated many of the critical letters and documents. I also relied on Nedra Bickham, Miriam Hotzel, Daniel O'Connor, and Christian Uri for translation.

Karin Bachman, Dr. Eberhard Gabriel, Sonya Grabowsky, Martin and Fritzi Grünberg, Hans and Marylou Hartenstein, Nicholas Macke, Daniel and Mary O'Connor, and Dr. David Treadway gave support and guidance.

Evan Sanders scanned the majority of the letters, photographs and documents. Sari Feldman, Bill Kelly, and Laurie Kincer of the Cuyahoga County Public Library offered invaluable insights.

Thanks to readers and friends, including (but not limited to) Sharon Brangman, Karen Braziller, Lea Carmichael, Stacy Carmichael, Hope Coolidge, Dede Cummings, Anne D'Avanas, Helen Doane, Nienke Dosa, Barbara Eisenson, Kathryn Field, Addie Fisk, Ruth Hodges, John and Fran Howe, Jean and Richard Knox, Tatjana Meschede, Joe and Molly Nye, Diana Perez, Lucas Prybil, Chelsea Roden, Diane Savitsky, Joy Silverstien, Becky Sinkler, Wick and Elizabeth Sloane, Laura Hodges Taylor, Rebecca Upham, and Will Viner. I regret that Dru Vaughn, Phyllis's youngest daughter and my dear cousin, passed away before the final draft was completed.

Anne O'Connor carefully edited my first draft. My husband, Martin, the final.

Special thanks to my colleague and friend Sabine Hildebrandt, author of *Anatomy of Murder, Ethical Transgressions and Anatomical Science during the Third Reich*. Her review was used for the synopsis on the dustjacket.

I'd also like to acknowledge Ladette Randolph and the editing team at *Ploughshares* for all their work on *A Beautiful Day*, published in their December 2014 issue. An excerpt was also published in *The Intima, a Journal of Narrative Medicine*.

Steven Cramer nurtured the extraordinary writing program at Lesley University. MFA mentors Tony Eprile and Jane Brox taught me so much. Author, teacher and friend, Rachel Manley, went above and beyond to support my progress as a writer.

Jessamyn Hope gave me the map to find my way into and then back out of the story. Writers Alex Beam, Emily Besh, Sarah Coleman Hartwell, Allan Kozzin, Geoff Kronik, Rose Alexandre-Leach, James Lescesne, Lowry Pei, Tom Piazza, Jim Shepard, Sezen Ünlüönen, and Tim Weed gave me the confidence to finish the final revisions of the manuscript.

My editor Frank Herron, publicist Gail Morgan, and designer Ingrid Mach at TidePool Press put it all together.

Melinda Johnson, my remarkable friend for more than fifty-five years, remains a touchstone for this story and my life.

I thank my husband and daughters, my mother and my brothers, for their love and interest in this book.

Most of all, *My City* would not have been possible without the dedication and expertise of Dr. Elisabeth Klamper at the DÖW in Vienna.

She held the key.